Antichrist
and the FINAL SOLUTION

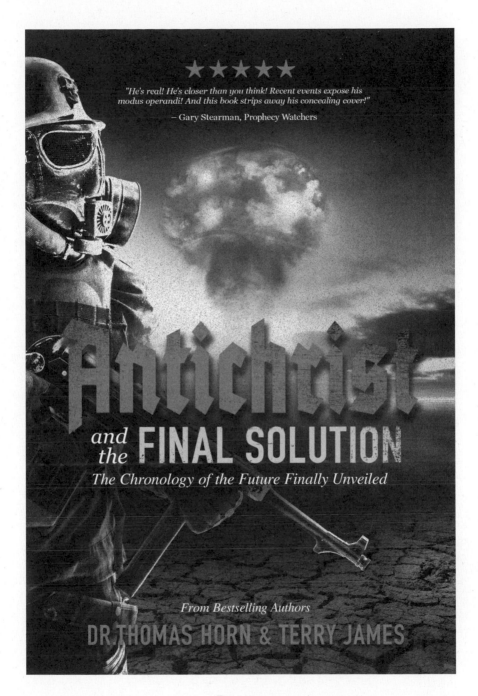

★ ★ ★ ★ ★

"He's real! He's closer than you think! Recent events expose his modus operandi! And this book strips away his concealing cover!"

– Gary Stearman, Prophecy Watchers

Antichrist
and the FINAL SOLUTION
the

The Chronology of the Future Finally Unveiled

From Bestselling Authors

DR. THOMAS HORN & TERRY JAMES

DEFENDER

CRANE, MO

Antichrist and the Final Solution: The Chronology of the Future Finally Unveiled

By Dr. Thomas Horn and Terry James

© Copyright 2020 Thomas Horn

Printed in the United States of America.

Scripture taken from the King James Version of the Bible unless otherwise noted.

Cover design by Jeffrey Mardis.

ISBN: 9781948014342

CONTENTS

1

Hitler and the Final Solution

Those who do not learn from history are doomed to repeat it.
—George Santayana

It is quite remarkable how little those of us who were stationed in Germany during the Nazi time, journalists and diplomats, really knew of what was going on behind the facade of the Third Reich. A totalitarian dictatorship, by its very nature, works in great secrecy and knows how to preserve that secrecy from the prying eyes of outsiders....

Adolf Hitler is probably the last of the great adventurer-conquerors in the tradition of Alexander, Caesar and Napoleon, and the Third Reich the last of the empires which set out on the path taken earlier by France, Rome and Macedonia. The curtain was rung down on that phase of history, at least, by the sudden invention of the hydrogen bomb, of the ballistic missile and of rockets that can be aimed to hit the moon.

In our new age of terrifying, lethal gadgets, which supplanted so swiftly the old one, the great aggressive war, if it should come, will be launched by suicidal little madmen pressing an electronic button. Such a war will not last long and none will ever follow it. There will be no conquerors and no conquests, but only the charred bones of the dead on an uninhabited planet.

—WILLIAM L. SHIER, *THE RISE AND FALL OF THE THIRD REICH*[1]

Fears and anxieties abound. There is an effervescing tumult that sends shivers of foreboding throughout this quaking sphere. Something of a profound sort is building that not even the greatest minds of the geopolitical, socioeconomic, and scientific/medical worlds can explain or cause to go away.

Leadership inadequacies in dealing with trepidation amongst populations around the globe incubate and expand fear. Failure to grasp the nature of all that is going on is at the heart of the world's most terrifying dilemmas.

The source of the sense of impending doom is not the realms of the physical, societal, economic, or medical, but is of a dimension far more virulent. The present fear is spawned by actions inflicted upon humanity by dark wickedness that has been prevalent throughout the history of man.

This volume will look into the malevolent forces that strive against humanity with deadly winds that threaten to destroy not just the life, but the soul, of every man, woman, and child on the planet.

In a global onslaught, earthly victims of the dark forces were struck in early 2020 with shocking surprise by unseen, totally unanticipated evil. The assault came in the form of an enemy of microscopic size. An entity infinitesimally tiny invaded stealthily and swiftly. It destroyed within a matter of weeks the booming economy of the most powerful nation ever to exist upon the planet.

Regardless of arguments over whether the coronavirus was a biological accident in a Chinese laboratory or was deliberately created and then unleashed on America and other nations of the world, its use by the dark powers and principalities in high places, we contend, is incontrovertibly clear. That otherworldly force hasn't ceased its incessant assault against mankind since the beginning of human history. Rather, it has throughout the ages stepped up efforts to infect and corrupt all within the human condition.

The evil that continues to permeate the human sphere has used the most susceptible to corruption among us in accomplishing the intended devastation. This methodology hasn't abated, but has grown and even now is burgeoning in its infectious contagion.

We have only to look back into history to understand that dark-dimensional activity is a longstanding evil within the bloodstream of humankind. Saddam Hussein, for example, is viewed as one of history's most hated, evil despots. Some of the things he and his Iraqi regime perpetrated are legendary in the annals of atrocities inflicted on victims of dictatorship.

He was infamous for killing enemies within his own regime and delivering to the doorsteps of their homes bags full of their family members' body parts. He and his sons were notorious for the rape rooms, wood chippers, and other instrumentalities of torture. And he was one of the most noted dictators because he gassed mass numbers of his own people with deadly nerve agents.

However, Saddam Hussein was a piker when it came to the evilest among our numbers, when compared to despots of the past. On websites with material attempting to categorize the worst of history's dictators, one name that comes up as a prominent candidate for the number-one, most-evil person in all history is the thirteenth-century Mongol leader, Genghis Khan.

One historian writes:

When most people are asked to name the most brutal and murderous leaders in history, they will first mention the names of recent dictators like Hitler and Stalin. Going back further, many people will talk about the Norse raids, the British Empire, Attila the Hun, and so many of the most vicious Roman Emperors. However, going back before any of them came to power, Genghis Khan and the Mongols permanently reshaped an enormous portion of the world, and changed the culture and genetic makeup of the region forever. The khan was a master strategist and his brutal warriors left a path of destruction in their wake....

There are many stories about the legendary brutality of Genghis Khan and his murderous exploits. Most of them tell a similar story of the khan asking enemies to surrender, and then completely annihilating them and their families and friends if they refused. The khan was proud of his murderous rampages and felt that the terror they inspired should be helpful in causing more enemies to join his side without him losing any men. While these campaigns of terror were business as usual for the khan, many people didn't realize that if you made him feel personally insulted, he could be even more brutal and punishing than you could imagine.[2]

Not wishing to get into the graphic details of the malicious atrocities inflicted by this vicious marauder, suffice it to say that the absolute inhumanity to Genghis Khan's victims, as catalogued by the writer of the above and other historians, defies understanding, in consideration of the evil man has inflicted on other of his kind throughout the ages.

We could present here hundreds of accounts of the beastly actions of tyrants and dictators throughout history to prove the "wickedness in high places"[3] that influence and even overtly control the sin-perverted minds of mankind. But there is no greater example of this influence and control than the man with whom we are all too familiar.

This man's name is still front and center in our headlines today, with political adversaries often using it to liken those they're running against as having his characteristics. In this way, they assign the worst possible evil attributes to opponents in order to get votes for themselves.

This man so hated still is featured on television documentaries more than any other person or topic for audiences to explore and examine. His name is even implicit within the title of the book you're reading.

This most reviled name in history—and rightfully so—is, of course, Adolf Hitler, the führer of the infamous Third Reich.

Power to Persuade

You can see it in the stark black-and-white films. The German masses moved and swayed rhythmically, their intensely gazing, tear-glistened eyes transfixed upon him as they adored their führer. Their savior had arrived.

He started unhurriedly, slow to choose his words. He began with almost imperceptible gesticulations of his right hand, which at first was cupped over his left. The words then began to roll from his tongue in escalating volume, the right hand raising with the pointed index finger lifted skyward.

His eyes seemed to project a glowering inner presence. The facial expression transformed from a calm demeanor to a contorted frown that presaged an explosion of sound and fury as the full rage of his growling voice blasted powerfully in a rant that electrified the mass of humanity before him. More and more, as the great, expansive rally hordes gathered following 1936, the rage was directed toward the Jews. But it began building years before in the dark crevices of Adolf Hitler's demented soul.

Hitler became Germany's chancellor in January 1933. Soon thereafter, he brought policies into being that were aimed at isolating German Jews. The policies inflicted persecution on those of the House of Israel. The Nazi Party, which espoused extreme German nationalism and anti-Semitism, perpetrated boycotts against all Jewish businesses. Also, all Jews were commanded to be dismissed from occupying any and all civil posts.

All "non-German" authors' books and writings were ordered to be burned. This was carried out in May 1933 at the Berlin Opera House in a special communal ceremony. German businesses, within two years, were announcing that Jews would no longer be allowed to interact in buying and selling.

In September of 1935, the Nuremberg Laws decreed that Jews were not citizens of Germany. Only Aryans could, from that point forward, have full German citizenship. The laws declared it illegal for Aryans and Jews to marry or have extramarital intercourse. While the persecution against the Jews of Germany were becoming increasingly repressive, harassment didn't become dangerously violent through most of 1938.

On the night of November 9 of that year, however, everything for the Jews changed.

The excuse for the violence sprang from the act of a Jewish teenage boy whose parents the Nazis had exiled to Poland from Hanover, Germany, the town of the boy's birth. Herschel Grynszpan, a seventeen-year-old, ethnically Polish Jew who had been living in France for several years, angered by the treatment of his parents, on November 7, 1938, shot Ernst von Rath, a German diplomat in Paris. Rath died two days later.

Adolf Hitler attended Rath's funeral, and Josef Goebbels, the Nazi minister for public enlightenment and propaganda, used the incident to gin up hatred for all Jews within the Third Reich. On the night of November 9, 1938, rage against the Jews resulted in Jewish businesses, synagogues, and homes being destroyed or greatly damaged. Jewish cemeteries, schools, and hospitals were torched by the frenzy of hate, and more than one hundred Jewish people were killed.

The shattered glass that was everywhere on the streets from the vicious attacks inspired the infamous term *Kristallnacht* ("Crystal Night" or "Night of Broken Glass"). From this point forward, anti-Semitism became the norm in Germany. Goebbels' devilish plan worked, even on the minds of formerly non-anti-Semites. The "Final Solution" that had festered in Hitler's evil thought process had reached its moment of birth.

Following the attacks of the night of November 9 through the next day, the Jewish community was held responsible for a collective fine the equivalent of $4 million in today's money. In addition, more than thirty thousand Jewish men were arrested and sent to the Dachau, Buchenwald, and Sachsenhausen concentration camps in Germany. These camps were specifically constructed to hold Jews, political prisoners, and other perceived enemies of the Nazi state.

Following *Kristallnacht*, the Nazi regime became ever more beastly toward the Jews. By the end of 1938, Jews were forbidden to attend schools and were often severely beaten if found anywhere in public places in Germany. Things got exponentially worse from that point.

Adolf Hitler and the Nazi regime ordered the Final Solution to be put into action during World War II. They proclaimed this was the answer to the "Jewish problem." They began carrying out the systematic murder of as many as six million European Jews. As well, it is estimated that the Nazis murdered as many as four million to six million non-Jews. The genocide, of course, became known as the Holocaust.

As for the teenager, Herschel Grynszpan, whom Goebbels used in the shooting of a German diplomat as a pretext for the genesis of what would become the Final Solution, his fate is yet unknown. He was said by some to have been in a Paris prison before being transferred to Germany. He is believed to have then been executed by the Nazis, according to some accounts. However, other sources say he survived, was married, and raised a family under a different name. This is, obviously, highly unlikely.

The Final Solution

Terror against Jews became the all-consuming drive of Hitler's plan to eradicate the House of Israel from Germany and the planet. Hitler held the Jewish bankers and others of the race responsible for Germany's defeat and humiliation in World War I.

He wrote in his book, *Mein Kampf*, that the Jews were at the heart of most all of the problems in the world—and, particularly, in Germany. They were, he said, a subhuman and inferior race and must be eliminated. This must be done, along with the subjection of all other inferior peoples, so that the Aryan race could dominate Germany and eventually the world.

People of the Aryan race were, he believed, superior human beings—ideally, they were those with blond hair and blue eyes. It is more than paradoxical that Hitler himself and other close henchmen like Goebbels and Heinrich Himmler, head of the SS, looked anything but Aryan. Herman Goering, the head of the German Luftwaffe (air force) and Nazi terror chief Reinhard Heydrich were blond and blue-eyed, but many within the top echelon of the Third Reich looked anything but Nordic.

Hitler's anti-Semitic contagion soon infected all within the top ranks of the Third Reich. The plan to implement the elimination of all Jewry and other "inferior" races percolated and boiled into a froth of hate-filled rhetoric and policies. The Nazis wrapped the horrific plan within a nonthreatening term, one designed to deflect from what the madness really came down to—genocide of a magnitude never seen before in the annals of history.

The name for the plans for genocide became the "Final Solution."

Historians still can't point to the precise beginning of the implementation of the Final Solution. However, it no doubt resulted from a decade of increasingly beastly policies under the directives signed off on by Adolf Hitler. The results were genocidal atrocities that continued to grow alongside Hitler's megalomania that would lead to world war.

The genocide was put into full force after going through stages.

Following the Nazi party's rise to power, Reich-enforced racism eventuated in establishment of anti-Jewish legislation. This included boycotts, "Aryanization," and the genocidal orchestration by the state. The anti-Semitic rage came to a crescendo on the "Night of Broken Glass." The atrocities of the pogrom were brought down full force against the hated Jews. The intention was to see to it that all of Jewry was removed from German society and, eventually, from Europe.

Lebensborn Program

"Aryanization," or "Germanization," was put into effect to see to it that all vestiges of impure racial characteristics were erased from the Reich. Heinrich Himmler ordered that children be taken away from parents to make Germanization work. SS families adopted children stolen from homes throughout territories occupied by Third Reich forces.

Parents never saw their children again in most cases of the kidnappings. Nazification was so brutal and complete that Reich enforcers would ruthlessly murder anyone who didn't conform to the Aryan master race model. Even children who didn't have the physical, Aryan characteristics were subject to removal from occupied territories and placed in camps where most eventually died.

Later, Himmler set up the Nazi Lebensborn program, a breeding scheme to further Aryanize the Third Reich. That program was created and put into force to bring about a super race of Germanized children through breeding, kidnapping, and even murder.

Considering the ghastly evil the Third Reich perpetrated against the Jews in particular, the Lebensborn program has not been as vilified or even scrutinized like other Nazi atrocities. The public in general has paid little attention. This is perhaps because it seems by comparison to the ghettos, gas chambers, and crematoriums to be a sort of an effort to do something positive rather than heinously evil. Nonetheless, the program to bring about a master race violated every principle of humanity as well as morality at its most basic level.

While other Nazi policies aimed at rounding up and murdering people Hitler, Himmler, Goering, Goebbels, and the rest thought of as subhuman in need of extermination, Lebensborn was meant to repopulate society with the very best that genetic manipulation could produce—a nation full of racially pure Aryan children. Therefore, the program seemed almost innocuous.

Himmler, in 1935, started a campaign, through propaganda masterfully orchestrated by Josef Goebbels, to invite any unwed mother who fit the racial profile to give birth inside a Lebensborn home. The effort was to be something that would fly in the face of previous German moral comportment. No longer was having a child out of wedlock to be considered a source of shame. Rather, the Third Reich would celebrate the birth of any Aryan child, regardless of the parents' marital status.

Himmler promised any pregnant woman who met the racial purity qualifications that she would be brought to a Lebensborn facility in a confidential way and offered the very best care. She would be returned home after the birth of her child.

Any girl unable to care for the child would be assisted in finding a suitable Aryan family that would adopt.

The policy's generosity wasn't without its limits. The woman who was to produce a baby for the master race was expected to meet uncompromising standards. She must be racially pure, no matter what her social or other standing might be. Her acceptance and assistance of the Nazi state was strictly based upon genealogy. Only proof of paternity and a racially pure family tree dating back three generations gained her access. The result was an acceptance rate that hovered around 40 percent.

But even the Lebensborn program couldn't meet the Nazis' demands to create the master race in the time frame they wished. So Himmler took the program much further. He ordered the arrangement of secret conjugal visits between willing young women and SS soldiers with Aryan traits. The aim was to create more babies for the Nazi party—with no offer of marriage on the table.

The Nazis destroyed almost all of the documents on the Lebensborn program as the Allied forces neared victory, leaving an estimated 200,000 victims separated from their families. Some made it home, but others couldn't remember enough of their families to find their way back.

Still others remained convinced their original families didn't want them and believed the retraining; they saw themselves as German citizens, for better or for worse.

The most famous child of the Lebensborn program is Norwegian ABBA singer Anni-Frid Lyngstad, who was fathered by a German sergeant. Her widowed mother escaped after the war and took her daughter to Sweden, where the government accepted several hundred refugee children and saved them from persecution.

Many parents chose not to tell their children about their heritage and the Lebensborn program, inventing better stories and fictional fathers for their young ones to believe in.

And some are still in the dark about their heritage to this day, unaware of the part that Adolf Hitler and Heinrich Himmler would have had them play in their quest to build a master race that would rule for a thousand years—the ultimate goal of Lebensborn.[4]

The beginning of World War II brought on unrestrained institution of the Final Solution—the demonically inspired plan to murder every person of the Jewish race the Nazis could locate and eliminate.

While the matter of racial purity was being dealt with, the Final Solution was in full rage. Ghettos were established in occupied areas. The Jewish people of Poland were the first and most notable to suffer being sealed up in these brutally controlled inner-city areas. Not only Polish citizens, but western European Jews as well, were deported to the ghettos.

The Nazi forces began killing Jews in massive numbers during the German invasion of the Soviet Union in 1941. Mobile killing squads (*Einsatzgruppen*) began massacring entire Jewish communities.

At first, the killing was accomplished through shooting or gassing in makeshift ways using mobile vans. Soon, however, those assigned the task of murder were suffering psychological ill effects. Thus, this method was considered inconvenient and inadequate for eliminating the massive numbers Hitler, Himmler, and the rest desired in order to carry out the Final Solution.

Hitler himself, having observed the protests of much of the German population over growing brutalization by the Nazi Party, never again put his personal signature to any document authorizing such heinous activity. He wanted to appear to have nothing to do with the mass murdering to come.

The Nazis began the systematic deportation of Jews to accomplish greater killing capacity after the Wannsee Conference in January 1942.

The term "Final Solution of the Jewish Question" was a euphemism used by Nazi Germany's leaders. It referred to the mass murder of Europe's Jews. It brought an end to policies aimed at encouraging or forcing Jews to leave the German Reich and other parts of Europe. Those policies were replaced by systematic annihilation.

Key Facts

1. It is unclear when exactly Hitler decided to murder Europe's Jews. The decision was probably made sometime in 1941, with the invasion of the Soviet Union.

2. On January 20, 1942, Reinhard Heydrich, the chief of Germany's Security Police, held a secret meeting known as the Wannsee Conference. Leading police and civilian officials discussed the continuing implementation of the "Final Solution."

3. The Nazi leaders envisioned killing 11 million Jews as part of the "Final Solution." They succeeded in murdering 6 million.[5]

Jews were moved from all over Europe to various extermination camps established in territory formerly belonging to Poland. Names like Chelmno, Belzec, Sobibor, Treblinka, Auschwitz-Birkenau, and Majdanek were to become the infamous death camps of the Third Reich. These were killing centers designed to carry out genocide. It is estimated that about three million Jews were gassed in extermination camps.

The Final Solution, in the ultimate accounting, resulted, as stated above, in the deaths of about six million Jews—two-thirds of European Jewry. The ghastly evil was accomplished through gassings, shootings, random acts of terror and violence, disease, and starvation.

Nazi brutality proved beyond any shadow of doubt that the evil prevalent in the times of Genghis Khan continued to rage into the twentieth century. With firearms available, the murderous Third Reich killing machine was many times more lethal to humanity than the primitive weapons wielded by Khan's butchers.

And even the guns and bullets could not satisfy the bloodlust. Heydrich, Himmler, and their master, Adolf Hitler, determined that the process of murdering Jews and other undesirables by shooting them was inadequate to their ambitious plan for the Final Solution. The method evolved from herding a few victims into the wooded areas, forcing them to kneel, then shooting them in the back of their heads. But even this wasn't taking care of their intended purpose quickly enough. So, Nazi troops would have workforce prisoners from death camps dig long trenches. They also had the victims, themselves, dig their own trench graves. The doomed people would be told to turn and face the deep ditches, then were shot in the back of the head. They fell dead into the ditches.

This still wasn't efficient enough for the murderous upper echelon of the Nazi regime. So, next, they contrived what was known as "sardine packing." Victims would be forced to prostrate themselves face down in the trenches. They would then be shot. Then another group would be forced to lie atop the first layer of corpses. They, too, were shot. This went on until the trench was filled. Dozers then moved gigantic mounds of earth back into the mass grave and the horrific deed was complete.

However, this method was soon seen as inefficient as well. It cost too much in terms of ammunition. Plus, in many cases, the soldiers charged with the ghastly executions suffered from psychological breakdowns. Even the chief architect of the evil, Heinrich Himmler, upon witnessing one of the executions, became so ill when a bit of brain matter splashed on him that he had to be carried out from the site in an almost-passed-out state.

This "inefficiency" brought to the fore an even more dreadful process of carrying out the Final Solution. "Killing centers," as they were known, were placed throughout occupied Europe to carry out the assembly-line murder of Jews and other "undesirables." Prisoners who weren't immediately chosen for being put to death were forced into the grisly task of helping with the executions and their aftermath. They had to clean up after the blood-letting and dispose of bodies, knowing their own numbers were soon to come up for extinction. They were worked until the lack of nourishment and endless hours of torturous, physical labor made them no longer useful. They then became fodder for elimination.

Concentration camps were mostly used to house those who were part of the forced labor and for a few, selected, prisoners to be murdered in small groups. The killing centers served exclusively as murder factories. German SS and police murdered nearly 2.7 million Jews in the killing centers either by asphyxiation with poison gas or by shooting.

While Third Reich authorities overseeing the death camps often lived in luxuriously appointed homes surrounding the centers, their victims were killed by people manning trucks, in which the exhaust pipes had been reconfigured to pump carbon monoxide gas into sealed, paneled spaces behind the cabs of the vehicles. So the genocidal methodology continued to evolve toward meeting the führer's goals. The bodies were driven into a nearby forest, where mass graves had been dug.

Still, the rate of the extermination of the Jews was not sufficient to satisfy the goals demanded by those charged to implement the Final

Solution. The next method developed was to become known as "Operation Reinhard," named after Reinhard Heydrich, one of the most feared of all the Nazi overlords. This became thought of as the deadliest phase of the Holocaust. Extermination camps became the center of the murderous campaign. Two million or more Jews and others marked for elimination were sent to the camps that were constructed in various locations. Belzec, Sobibór, and Treblinka housed specially built facilities for the gassing of those sent by train cattle cars filled so tightly with humanity that some suffocated before reaching the killing chambers.

At the Majdanek concentration camp, meanwhile, Zyklon B, a highly lethal gas derived from powerful insecticides, was developed to increase the extermination chambers' killing capacity. This and other gases were used in the gas chambers at Auschwitz II-Birkenau.

In previous killing centers, prisoner laborers had been forced to exhume many of those buried in the trenches and burn the bodies in ovens that also were trenches made useable by train rails, thus to hide their murders. The Nazis now created new, more efficient ways of dealing with corpses: They constructed large crematoriums for the thousands upon thousands of bodies of Jews that were shipped to these edifices of horror.

The prisoners were taken to the killing sites after being reassured they were just being relocated. This was a ploy to spare the Nazis unnecessary problems, as they at first tried not to unleash panic within the ranks of the condemned. They told their victims that the deportations were "resettlement actions."

The deception worked for a time. In the city of Warsaw, thousands lined up to be transported in the "resettlement." Even in the crowded boxcars that caused the deaths of up to 20 percent of those packed in, there still was the hope among those being so treated that the Germans' intentions were genuinely to resettle them in a place they could live.

When the prisoners arrived at their final destination, they were made to leave their luggage after stepping onto the unloading area. They were then marched to the "cleaning area" and instructed to hand over all valuables for safekeeping.

A part of the deception included signs and supposed medical personnel directing the people to disinfectant areas. Once in the appropriate facilities, the prisoners were made to completely undress. They were told they would have showers and that they must hurry, else the water would get cold. The men and boys were shuttled into one area and the women and girls into another. The Jewish victims who resisted out of fear or resentment of such indignities were brutally beaten to speed up them up and complete the genocidal process.

The guards used whips, wooden rods, or rifle butts to force the final move of the victims into the gas chambers. To avoid the sharp blows against their naked flesh, the prisoners would quickly comply. Once in the chambers, they were forced to crowd together until they couldn't move, and then the doors were shut.

While these were being "processed," the old and infirm who had managed to survive the cramped cattle cars were handled in another way. They were herded to a fake infirmary named the Lazarett, which had a large mass grave behind it, and were killed by a bullet in the neck while the rest were being forced into the gas chambers.

With the doors to the chambers sealed, operators dropped Zyklon B or other gas-producing objects into the appropriate places and the toxic gas did its job. The groans, according to later reports at the Nuremberg trials, were horrendous. The noises of agony and dying went on until all sounds stopped.

The chambers were then completely vented of gas so prisoners kept alive in the extermination camps could go in and remove the many bodies of men, women, and children. Testimonies given at the trials reported that the naked bodies in every opening of the death chambers were in a pyramid, with some victims having clawed up the pile of humanity, reaching for a place they could breathe.

Following their genocidal work, the Operation Reinhard camps were dismantled. Auschwitz-Birkenau, however, was kept as a concentration camp for forced laborers after the November 1944 destruction of the gas chambers. Prior to the liberation of the camp by units of the

Soviet Army on January 27, 1945, most of the prisoners had been evacuated by foot or on trains.

The murderous rampage of Adolf Hitler included much more, of course, than just the murder of two-thirds of the world's Jewish people. World War II, which he started with the attack on Poland in 1939, brought death to many millions, the number of which is still debated.

Although the German führer is considered the most hated of all tyrants, there are those who have murdered even more. And their satanic evil can be looked at as even more heinous, if considering numbers of those they murdered.

Soviet Union tyrant Josef Stalin is thought to have been responsible for the murders of as many as forty million people. Chinese dictator Mao tse-Tung is believed to have massacred as many as sixty million.

The thing that makes these perhaps even worse than Adolf Hitler and the Nazis is the fact that the victims of Stalin and Mao consisted mostly of their own people. Stalin's purges and Mao's cultural revolution brutalized their own citizenry in ways that Hitler no doubt would have admired.

Again, it is good to remember the words of wise observers of the human condition and history's way of repeating. "Those who do not know history's mistakes are doomed to repeat them," said Edmund Burke. Lest we think that evil men have changed in their capability to perpetrate horrendous atrocities against their fellow man, we should heed Santayana and Burke's words. If we forget that the thought to inflict evil intentions on others resides within the human, sin-blackened mind, we'll eventually suffer consequences of that forgetfulness.

Absolute control of all of humankind was in the mind of the first rebel, Lucifer. Man has, through that being's seduction, been infected with evil that has the potential to afflict others with brutality exactly like that demonstrated by Hitler, Stalin, Mao, and every other death-dealing tyrant of history. To forget this lesson of the evil that lurks within the human mind and heart is to invite would-be dictators of the future to take our liberties and even our lives.

But mankind—most of us—has either forgotten the admonition of those like Santayana, Burke, and Kissinger, or is simply too busy going about life's daily movement to pay attention.

Throughout the four years since 2016, we have witnessed the hate-filled actions and activities of a cabal of those who have sought to overthrow a duly-elected president. By this ongoing attempted anti-constitutional activity, they exhibit the same dark desire to take away liberty—to control the American electorate. They, it is abundantly clear, won't stop until they have the power they believe they, alone, should have over the rest of us.

All that we have witnessed by this deep-state, globalist-elite attempt at accomplishing the silent *coup d'état* is but a precursor of things to come. One is coming who will make Adolf Hitler and his henchmen look like Cub Scouts. He will make Josef Stalin, Mao tse-Tung, and all tyrants of history seem like choirboys. The result of this one's reign over most of planet earth will be the death of as much as three-fourths of humanity.

Jesus Christ—the greatest of all prophets, because He is God, Him-self—said the following about the time of this wicked person's rule on earth:

> For then shall be great tribulation, such as was not since the beginning of the world to this time, no, nor ever shall be. And except those days should be shortened, there should no flesh be saved: but for the elect's sake those days shall be shortened. (Matthew 24:21–22)

It's terrifying to consider that a time is coming that will be worse than any ever experienced to this point in history. But Jesus says just such a time is scheduled in earth's storm-cloud-obscured future.

There are people right at this moment, while you're reading this, who would enslave you in order to bring about their idea of utopia. And there will be a man who will succeed in doing just that, if you're living during that horrendous time. The Bible calls this man by several names.

"Antichrist" is the one most often used, as in the title of this volume. He'll have his own Final Solution in bringing his satanically controlled regime into being.

He is a "beast," according to God's Word. That is, he will have a *beastly* nature—like Hitler, Stalin, Mao, and the others. But Antichrist will be much, much more powerful—more deadly than they were.

He will have his own version of Hitler's propaganda minister Josef Goebbels. This False Prophet is called the "second beast." He will force everyone to worship the image of Antichrist:

> And he had power to give life unto the image of the beast, that the image of the beast should both speak, and cause that as many as would not worship the image of the beast should be killed. (Revelation 13:15)

We can see, as we look around the geopolitical, socioeconomic, and religious landscape of the hour, the stage being set for the rise of Antichrist. His Final Solution is being prepared even now for all those who inhabit this earthly sphere when he steps upon the stage to rule during the final years of earth's history leading up to Christ's Second Advent.

This book, we prayerfully hope, will convince you that you don't want to be part of Antichrist's Final Solution.

2

The Prophetic Rise of the Fourth Reich

iplomats of the world's governments incessantly proclaim that the quest for peace is their primary mission. War tugs at the ends of the tether of restraint in an unrelenting rage to burst the bonds and destroy all within its devastating power. Peace is among the most elusive of all of mankind's aspirations.

Historians have estimated that the number of wars throughout history exceeds fifteen thousand. But this figure was reported years ago and is likely far short of the true count. The fact is, so many conflicts could be listed as wars that the true number is impossible to ascertain. War at many levels continues to ignite in a never-ending profusion of carnage, bloodshed, and death.

Fear generated by the possibility of one's own death resides at the heart of the term "war." The word is used by politicians and governments to try to unite mass numbers under their governance. Even though the conflict might not be against physical armies from other nations, to dramatically frame a problem that threatens the well-being of those being governed, leaders and officials use "war" to define the severity of the threat.

An example of this in America's past is the Lyndon B. Johnson administration's program to fight against what was built up to be the dire economic circumstances faced by the poor. That administration called the battle against the bad economic circumstances of the welfare class the "War on Poverty." Through this, Johnson declared he would create the "Great Society."

The government was, through this program coming on the heels of the assassination of John F. Kennedy, able to create a warlike campaign against the great enemy, as Johnson and his administration saw it. The true design of all of this, however, was to create bigger government and draw from American taxpayers more revenue to feed the ever-expanding bureaucracy of control. Some $22 trillion later, that mission was certainly accomplished.

The more recent example is the Donald J. Trump administration's "war" on the COVID-19, or coronavirus, pandemic. The president, with the best intentions for America's welfare, and believing the doctors presented him the facts about numbers who might die from the virus, proclaimed in daily "Coronavirus Taskforce briefings" that America and the world were in a war against the unseen enemy. The virus was thought to bring as many as 2.2 million deaths in the US, according to the doctors assigned to update the administration on the pandemic.

This number never materialized or even came close. But, the powers that be caused the most powerful nation on earth and the most booming economy in history to be turned off in less than a couple of months as part of the "war" on the microbe-sized enemy.

As covered earlier, we saw how German Führer Adolf Hitler brought an entire nation and world into all-out war. The mesmerized people willingly followed him, even though they were war-weary from World War I and had suffered the loss of the majority of young, German manhood in the hellish conflict.

War to combat a deadly enemy is a fearful motivator. And it is a mighty tool to force the masses into the channels leadership wants them funneled. Since the advent of the atomic bomb, then of intercontinental ballistic missiles, the terror of war has increased exponentially.

Death by nuclear fire is no more than thirty minutes away, no matter where we live within the continental United States. Nuclear weapons-equipped submarines lurk just off our coasts, their huge, sleek arrows of total destruction targeted by precision satellite and computers to hit American cities programmed for decimation.

With dictators having their fingers on the nuclear buttons and harboring a bloodlust against our nation, it has become understandable how the prophecy might be fulfilled:

> And there shall be signs in the sun, and in the moon, and in the stars; and upon the earth distress of nations, with perplexity; the sea and the waves roaring;
>
> Men's hearts failing them for fear, and for looking after those things which are coming on the earth: for the powers of heaven shall be shaken. (Luke 21:25–26)

Since the invention of the hydrogen bomb, a number of reports over the years have said the world is coming close to the moment these weapons will be unleashed upon humanity. We of the age to remember lived through a time of worry over any-moment nuclear war. We recall the bomb shelters and the instructions when we were children to "duck and cover" in case of a siren warning that an attack was imminent. We were to dive off of our bikes or stop whatever we were doing and hit the ground, placing our heads between our arms and curling up in a fetal position. Or, we should find safety under a park bench or anything else available.

It's ludicrous now to think that we could be protected against a multi-megaton nuclear bomb when entire islands in the South Pacific were completely dissolved in nuclear fire during the Bikini tests. But, such was the fear. It led to what we now consider irrational measures.

There have been several near-misses in tragedies from nuclear weaponry. Off America's East Coast, a hydrogen bomb that was accidentally dropped but never ignited remains buried in the ocean depths. Crashes of other planes carrying nuclear weapons have been reported. In one instance, a huge bomb was found with only one element of several safeguards still intact that prevented its detonation.

Then, we think of the Cuban missile crisis of October 1962. All who were alive then and were old enough to remember recalled vividly the confrontation between the Soviet Union and the United States over nuclear-tipped weapons Soviet Premiere Nikita Khrushchev had secretly placed in Fidel Castro's Cuba just ninety miles off the tip of Florida. President John F. Kennedy confronted the Soviet leader, and the world came to the brink of World War III.

In all of these near-misses, we conclude that it has been God's staying hand that has maintained control.

The prophetic Word of God foretells a time that will be even more fear-filled than back in those late 1950s, in 1962, and even to this day. The Scripture cited earlier tells part of what will make people's hearts fail because of fear in that future time.

Jesus said:

And except those days should be shortened, there should no flesh be saved: but for the elect's sake those days shall be shortened. (Matthew 24:22)

We look around today and see many things that are troubling—some tremendously so. The coronavirus, for example, came out of nowhere and immediately caused the most liberty-loving nation on the planet to throw aside most all liberty and freedom of movement. Lockdown of the nation seemed to have been put into effect with little pushback and with little thought. The fear of death from COVID-19 was so great that the majority of Americans agreed to become like victims of a third-world dictatorship. As stated before, the most prosperous

economy probably ever to exist came to a whimpering close in a matter of weeks. People have been afraid because of the "pandemic" foisted
upon American citizenry.

We might sound a bit skeptical about the things attendant to this
"pandemic." That's because we are, in fact, more than a bit skeptical.

At the very least, the whole matter smacks of contrivance. That is, it
smells of perpetration by those who have for decades—especially for the
four years following the 2016 presidential election—observably desired
to force this nation into a globalist mold.

Such a thing will ultimately eventuate. The efforts of the globalist cabal, consisting of minions, both human and demonic, will bring
about the global consortium of nations that will serve as platform for
the Revelation 13 beast regime. Antichrist will at last have arrived to take
his long-prophesied place of genocidal authority upon this judgment-
bound planet.

Phony Peacemaker

The one who will someday demand that all on earth worship him or face
the guillotine of his Fourth Reich will at first seem a benevolent leader
who is universally loved and adored. His government will not initially be
perceived as a dictatorship deadlier than all preceding despotic regimes.

But the pyroclastic outflow of this man of *false peace* will result in
war. We see the Antichrist coming on the scene, then the explosion of
evil that leads to the deaths of millions, even billions, in the Revelation 6
symbolic description that encapsulates the apocalypse.

God's forewarning of the Tribulation era, or "Daniel's seventieth
week," begins with the coming forth of a rider on a white horse:

And I saw when the Lamb opened one of the seals, and I heard,
as it were the noise of thunder, one of the four beasts saying,
Come and see.

And I saw, and behold a white horse: and he that sat on him had a bow; and a crown was given unto him: and he went forth conquering, and to conquer. (Revelation 6:1–2)

One of professional football's most famous coaches, known for driving his players to exhaustion in practice in order to condition them for the last minutes of their games, said famously: "Fatigue makes cowards of us all." Vince Lombardi, we think, meant that people, when exhausted, most often give in and don't stand courageously to finish their mission. This, we can extrapolate, means that the exhausted will be filled with fears created by their feelings of inability to continue—and they'll give up.

Further, history has shown that people will call on those who show great determination and strength to protect them and take care of their own failed attempts at accomplishing life's hard-to-reach goals. Like in the case of Germany during the late 1920s and the 1930s, troublous times bring out strong-willed personalities. These, because of mankind's fallen nature, are most often of the dictatorial sort. The Nazi regime and the Third Reich were the result of the exhausted Germans' acquiescence to the führer's deceptive promises of return to peace and prosperity.

Adolf Hitler, as we've examined, was post World War I's strong man who took full advantage of the weaknesses caused by the war and the economic depression that followed. The soon-to-come rider on the white steed will be even more deceptive than Hitler and his henchmen. Antichrist will harbor unprecedented hatred for humanity and will exhibit through his deadly actions the exercise of evil powers beyond that possessed by all tyrants of history combined.

There is an even greater force active today than the one behind the man who will emerge as depicted in the first horseman of the apocalypse. This power is, even at this moment, holding back that horseman. Antichrist and all the carnage he will bring with him following his entrance into world history as the greatest "peacemaker" of all time cannot emerge until allowed to do so. We learn of this in the following passage (we've inserted the meanings of relevant words in brackets):

> Let no man deceive you by any means: for that day [Tribulation] shall not come, except there come a falling away [departure] first, and that man of sin [Antichrist] be revealed, the son of perdition;
>
> Who opposeth and exalteth himself above all that is called God, or that is worshipped; so that he as God sitteth in the temple of God, shewing himself that he is God.
>
> Remember ye not, that, when I was yet with you, I told you these things? And now ye know what withholdeth [restrains] that he might be revealed in his time.
>
> For the mystery of iniquity doth already work: only he [God the Holy Spirit] who now letteth [restrains] will let [restrain], until he be taken out of the way.
>
> And then shall that Wicked [Antichrist and his evil] be revealed, whom the Lord shall consume with the spirit of his mouth, and shall destroy with the brightness of his coming. (2 Thessalonians 2:3–8)

Man of Sin Revealed

Antichrist is most frequently referred to as a specific man foretold to be history's last and most terrible dictator; he will rule the world just before the Second Coming of Jesus Christ. The term "antichrist" has two meanings, basically: 1) that which is against Christ; and 2) that which counterfeits and/or takes the place of Christ. The word is mentioned specifically only in the following passages of the Bible (emphasis added):

Little children, it is the last time: and as ye have heard that *antichrist* shall come, even now are there many *antichrists*; whereby we know that it is the last time. (1 John 2:18)

Who is a liar but he that denieth that Jesus is the Christ? He is *antichrist*, that denieth the Father and the Son. (1 John 2:22)

And every spirit that confesseth not that Jesus Christ is come in the flesh is not of God: and this is that [spirit] of *antichrist*, whereof ye have heard that it should come; and even now already is it in the world. (1 John 4:3)

For many deceivers are entered into the world, who confess not that Jesus Christ is come in the flesh. This is a deceiver and an *antichrist*. (2 John 1:7)

The world leader who will be Antichrist is also called other names in Bible prophecy: "the little horn" (Daniel 7:8); "the king of fierce countenance" (Daniel 8:23); "the prince that shall come" (Daniel 9:26); "the king" (Daniel 11:36); "the man of sin" (2 Thessalonians 2:3); "the son of perdition" (2 Thessalonians 2:3); "the beast" (Revelation 13:1–4, 12, 14–15, 17; 19:19–20); and "six hundred threescore and six" (Revelation 13:18).

Prophecy writer/broadcaster Daymond Duck writes the following about the one who is also called "the lawless one":

Most scholars agree that John's usage of the word [Antichrist] implies two different meanings: 1) against the Christ, and 2) instead of the Christ. Both meanings fit the final führer. The antichrist will be against the Christ; that is, he will be an enemy of the Christ, and he will try to replace the Christ; that is, he will be a false Christ.

Daniel revealed the final führer's opposition to the Christ when he said the antichrist will "stand up against the Prince of princes" (Daniel 8:25). And Paul revealed the evil one's effort to replace the Christ when he said the antichrist will sit in the Temple as God "shewing himself that he is God" (2 Thessalonians 2:3, 4). Many people have opposed Christ, but other than Satan, there has never been a more sinister or worthy opponent on the face of planet earth.[6]

Many false christs have arisen, and some have been noteworthy imposters, but there has never been a greater or more evil deceiver than this one.

What We Don't Know About the Antichrist

We later address in this chapter, in a question-and-answer format, much more about this, earth's last dictator. Meanwhile, here is food for thought.

Four things we *don't* know about the Antichrist are the subject of much speculation. The first is his nationality. It isn't hard to find writers who teach that he will be a Syrian. The Bible doesn't say he will come from that ancient nation, but some conclude this through reasoning that usually goes like this: "Antiochus Epiphanes was a type of the antichrist and he was a Syrian. Therefore, the antichrist will be a Syrian."

Although it's permissible to conjecture in these matters to some extent, the problem with this kind of thinking is that it overlooks individuals of other nationalities who were also a type of the Antichrist. Nebuchadnezzar was a type of the Antichrist, and he was a Chaldean. So why not say the Antichrist will be a Chaldean? Adolf Hitler was a type of the Antichrist, and he was a German. So why not say the Antichrist will be a German? The same can be said for Pharaoh, an Egyptian. We could go on and on, but the point is that maintaining an adamant position doesn't settle the issue.

The second thing we don't know about the Antichrist is whether he will be a Jew or a Gentile (a non-Jewish person). Some say he'll be a Jew, because the Bible says "neither shall he regard the God of his fathers" (Daniel 11:37). Others say he will be a Gentile because this verse has been incorrectly translated and it should read, "He will show no regard for the gods of his fathers" (Daniel 11:37, NIV). If the correct translation is "God," he will come from a monotheistic religion (probably Jewish); if the correct translation is "gods," he will come from a polytheistic religion (probably Gentile).

Then there are those who reason that "the antichrist will be Jewish because the Jews will accept him as their Messiah and they would never accept a Gentile." Or, "The antichrist will be Jewish because he will be a counterfeit of Christ and He was a Jew." The late Reverend Jerry Falwell, whose theology was almost always very sound, got in trouble on this one. He believed the Antichrist will be a Jew—and he might have been right, but the fact is, whether the Antichrist will be a Jew or a Gentile is not revealed in the Bible. Those who think he will be a Jew are definitely in the minority. Incidentally, one of the complaints against Reverend Falwell was that he was anti-Semitic for thinking like this. On the contrary, Falwell was one of Israel's strongest supporters and did much to help the Jewish people.

The third thing we don't know about the Antichrist is his name. We know "his number is six hundred threescore and six," but that's different from his name (Revelation 13:18). Several elaborate systems have been developed in an effort to reveal the name of the Antichrist, but they have all been wrong. Some names these systems have come up with are Adolf Hitler, Benito Mussolini, Henry Kissinger, Ronald Reagan, William "Bill" Clinton, Barack Obama, and several of the popes. These should be seen for what they are—just wild guesses. Furthermore, trying to identify Antichrist is just a waste of time, because he will not be revealed until after the Rapture (2 Thessalonians 2:1–12). As Dr. Ed Hindson concisely stated:

Only after the rapture of the church will the identity of the antichrist be revealed. In other words, you don't want to know who he is. If you ever do figure out who he is, you have been left behind! This is absolutely true. Nothing is more futile than trying to identify the antichrist before the rapture. Doing so would be an effort to prove the Bible wrong. That has never happened and it is not going to happen now. All anyone does by trying to identify the antichrist before the church is taken out is embarrass himself and bring criticism upon Christians.

In connection with this, let's hasten to add that 666 is the Antichrist's number. It isn't a driver's license number, credit card numbers, Social Security number, or any other numbers associated with us. It will not be several billion different numbers for the several billion different individuals. It is *his* number—one specific number that identifies one specific individual.

The fourth thing we don't know about the Antichrist is whether he is already alive as a person. It seems reasonable that he will have to be a full-grown man when he appears. If the Rapture is as close as we and most prophetic scholars think, it makes sense to assume that he is not only alive, but already grown. The thing to remember is that nobody knows, and all a person can do is speculate.

What the Antichrist Will Be Like

We can better understand what the Antichrist will be like when he appears by observing a few things about the First and Second Coming of Jesus. The first, commonly called His Triumphal Entry into Jerusalem, occurred while Jesus was riding upon a donkey, a symbol of peace (Luke 19:28–38). The Second Coming of Jesus, commonly called the Revelation (the Revelation of Jesus Christ in His power and glory) will take place at the end of the Tribulation period when He returns in righteousness to judge and make war riding upon a white horse, a symbol of conquest (Revelation 19:11–21). The first time, Jesus came peacefully as the Lamb of God; the second time, He will come conquering as the King of kings and Lord of lords (John 1:36; Revelation 19:11–16).

This has relevance to what the Antichrist will be like as he carries out his bloody career. During his rise to power, he will present himself as a man of peace. So we might expect the prophets to depict him riding upon a donkey, a symbol of peace, but that is incorrect. John said:

> And I saw, and behold a white horse: and he that sat on him had a bow; and a crown was given unto him: and he went forth conquering, and to conquer. (Revelation 6:2)

The Antichrist will ride across the pages of history on a white horse, a symbol of conquest. His eloquent promises of peace will not match his horrendous acts of war. This fictitious christ will present himself as a lamb, but he will really be a wolf in sheep's clothing. When asked about the sign of His coming and the end of the age, Jesus answered:

> Take heed that no man deceive you. For many shall come in my name, saying, I am Christ; and shall deceive many. (Matthew 24:4, 5)

The list of people who have done this is long, but the ultimate false christ will be the Antichrist. Multitudes will think they have met the Messiah, but he will really be the man of sin.

The bow was a weapon of war and a symbol of military power in John's day. The Antichrist will appear with a bow in his hand, but he will have no arrows. This is like carrying a gun without bullets. The Antichrist will have weapons of war, but he will act like he is unarmed. Daniel said, "by peace shall [he] destroy many" (Daniel 8:25).

A crown is worn by people who earn or inherit the right to wear one, but the Antichrist will not earn or inherit the right to wear his crown. It will be a gift from the wicked power brokers of the world. What a terrible mistake! The world's gullible politicians will empower a leader without doing the all-important background check. Some will think they are crowning a godly man, but they'll be elevating a fake with a very dark side. The Bible says this fraud will "ascend out of the bottomless pit" (Revelation 17:8). That is the gruesome, subterranean abode where God is holding the very worst of Satan's demonic spirits. It makes one wonder what kind of background this man will have. Considering his origin, it must be filled with terrible atrocities.

The World When the Antichrist Appears

When addressing this subject, the apostle Paul used the phrase "perilous times" (2 Timothy 3:1). "Perilous times" include war, and one of the signs of the last days that Jesus talked about is "wars and rumors of wars" (Matthew 24:6). While the Antichrist is negotiating peace and consolidating his power, God will release a second horse and rider. John said:

> There went out another horse that was red: and power was given to him that sat thereon to take peace from the earth, and that they should kill one another: and there was given unto him a great sword. (Revelation 6:4)

The second rider will bring war to the earth. God will allow him to do this to show the world that the Antichrist is not the true Prince of Peace, Jesus.

"Perilous times" also include economic disaster. While the Antichrist is boasting about having solutions to the world's problems, God will release a third horse and rider:

> I beheld, and lo a black horse; and he that sat on him had a pair of balances in his hand. And I heard a voice in the midst of the four beasts say, A measure of wheat for a penny, and three

measures of barley for a penny; and see thou hurt not the oil and the wine. (Revelation 6:5, 6)

The third rider will bring economic collapse to the world. God will allow him to do this to show the world that Jesus Christ, not the Antichrist, is the true Bread of Life. Food will be so valuable that it will have to be weighed on scales before it's sold. Money will be so worthless that what a person earns in one day will purchase barely enough food for the survival of one person.

Despite all the terrible consequences of the coronavirus pandemic, financial and otherwise, it seems that America, and perhaps the entire world, has forgotten that a good economy is a blessing of God and not a benefit of having the right kind of politician in office. This moral confusion will be disastrous in the days to come.

"Perilous times" also include starvation and sickness, and two more signs of the last days Jesus talked about are "famine" and "pestilence" (Matthew 24:7). God will release a fourth horse and rider that will fulfill this dire prophecy:

I looked, and behold a pale horse: and his name that sat on him was Death, and Hell followed with him. And power was given unto them over the fourth part of the earth, to kill with sword, and with hunger, and with death, and with the beasts of the earth. (Revelation 6:8)

The Lord of heaven will allow this horse and rider to come on the scene to show the world that Jesus Christ, not the Antichrist, is the Great Physician. One-fourth of the world's population will die as war and economic disaster spread like wildfire, triggering hunger and disease on every continent.

Most conservative Christians believe the "perilous times" Paul prophesied have arrived. Looking around at the ungodly characteristics of mankind, it's difficult to see how the Christian attuned to truth given in 2 Timothy 3 could come to any other conclusion.

Perhaps the top scholar today in the pre-Tribulation, premillennial view of Bible prophecy, Dr. Thomas Ice, writes further about Antichrist and his number-one assistant, the False Prophet.

> While I think it may be possible that the False Prophet (Rev. 13:11–18; 16:13; 19:20; 20:10) could be a Jew (I am not saying that I necessarily think he will be), there does not appear to be any Scriptural grounds to think that the Antichrist will be of the tribe of Dan nor of Jewish descent. It appears that he will be a Gentile and will arise from within the Revived Roman Empire. In the middle of the tribulation he will take his seat in Israel's rebuilt Temple and claim to be God Himself (2 Thess. 2:4). His career will be a short-lived seven-year period for which he will spend eternity in the Lake of Fire upon Christ's return to planet earth (Rev. 19:20; 20:10).[7]

As the Fourth Reich rises, there will arise at the same time a call for "peace and safety" from the troublous times that generate fear among earth's inhabitants. The final führer will emerge from the sea of humanity to take control of world power by force. He ultimately will proclaim himself to be God.

The call for "peace and safety" at a certain moment in the end of days will give this deceptive man the steps leading to his place on the stage of world history. His rise will culminate in the most brutal dictatorship ever to be suffered by the people of this planet. Here is what the apostle Paul prophesied about that time:

> But of the times and the seasons, brethren, ye have no need that I write unto you.
>
> For yourselves know perfectly that the day of the Lord so cometh as a thief in the night.

For when they shall say, Peace and safety; then sudden
destruction cometh upon them, as travail upon a woman with
child; and they shall not escape. (1 Thessalonians 5:1–3)

Left Behind!

Paul said that at a time—one that he could not or would not divulge—
there will come the "day of the Lord." It will come suddenly and without
announcement, like a "thief in the night."

This break-in upon the human conditions of the time, Paul prophesied, will take place when there, as mentioned earlier, will be that great
call by the fearful for "peace and safety." People will be willing to embrace
any leader who seems to offer answers to the desperate times in which
they are embroiled.

The Revelation 6 rider on the white horse will set in motion his
own version of the "Final Solution"—a Fourth Reich that will, when full
blown in its virulence and destruction, overshadow the evil perpetrated
by the Nazis and their Third Reich.

The only saving grace is that whereas the Third Reich lasted twelve
years, the Fourth Reich will last no more than seven. Antichrist's rule of
terror will be ended as promised in the prophecy we looked at previously:

And then shall that Wicked be revealed, whom the Lord shall
consume with the spirit of his mouth, and shall destroy with the
brightness of his coming:
 Even him, whose coming is after the working of Satan with
all power and signs and lying wonders. (2 Thessalonians 2:8–9)

Paul prophesied that when the world is in perilous times and becoming so dangerous that there is a cry for peace and safety, the Day of the
Lord will break into the situation like a thief in the night. This will be

God's judgment beginning to fall on a rebellious, God-opposing generation. Jesus put it this way in the Olivet Discourse:

> Likewise also as it was in the days of Lot; they did eat, they
> drank, they bought, they sold, they planted, they builded;
> But the same day that Lot went out of Sodom it rained fire
> and brimstone from heaven, and destroyed them all.
> Even thus shall it be in the day when the Son of man is
> revealed. (Luke 17:28–30)

God will have had His fill of the evil perpetrated by humanity and
Antichrist's genocidal actions against God's chosen people. Jesus, who
is God, will be revealed to the world, secretly, by completely disrupting
all who live on earth. He will call to Himself all of those who know
Him for salvation through being born again as the Lord said and as
Paul wrote, regarding the gospel of grace (read John 3:3 and Romans
10:9–10).

All others living on the planet at that instant will, within a short
period, begin to suffer a fate many times worse than that of those who
were targeted for Hitler's Final Solution. They will have been left behind
to undergo Antichrist's unadulterated evil straight from the mind of
Satan.

Christians will be instantly and forever in heaven with their Lord.
To the world, it will have been a "thief-in-the-night" break-in, but for
believers, it will be an electrifying moment of jubilant gathering as Christ
fulfills His promise:

> In my Father's house are many mansions: if it were not so, I
> would have told you. I go to prepare a place for you.
> And if I go and prepare a place for you, I will come again,
> and receive you unto myself; that where I am, there ye may be
> also. (John 14:2–3)

The final führer's Final Solution will have begun; the family of God will have been removed, out of harm's way.

There are many questions about this man who will be Antichrist. The following are some of those questions and our answers—based, we believe, on what God's Word says about the first beast of Revelation 13.

Q. Will the Antichrist be a Jew?

A. We don't think the first beast will be a Jew, because he will come out of the sea of Gentile nations, according to Revelation chapter 13. This, against the second beast coming out of the land, indicates he will emerge onto the world scene out of Israel. The second beast will be an "apostate" Jew, in our view of these verses.

Q. Could the Antichrist be a Muslim?

A. No. There are a number of reasons we believe this, but the one that resonates most is based on historical timeline factors. Bible prophecy tells us that the "prince that shall come" is of the people who will destroy the city (Jerusalem) and the sanctuary (the Jewish temple on Mount Moriah). The people who did that were the Romans.

There might have been other ethnic and nation-types of peoples within the ranks of the Roman legion who destroyed Jerusalem and the temple in AD 70, but the overwhelming constituency of that force was from in and around Rome itself. Certainly, Vespasian and his son Titus were born in, and/or lived in areas immediately around, Rome.

Islam didn't come into being until a few centuries later. The eastern leg's capital, Constantinople, likewise. Timeline wise, an eastern Antichrist is out of the question, in our opinion.

Antichrist is referred to as "the Assyrian," of course, in God's Word, so that implies the Middle East. We believe that he might well be of Middle Eastern extraction genetically, but likely born and raised in the area of Europe implied by the "the phrase people that shall come."

Further, the argument that Antichrist will be Muslim because Islam uses beheading as a means of execution, the same method prophesied to be employed by the beast's regime in Revelation 13, is untenable. The Roman Empire of Paul's day used beheading. Paul, himself, died by that method centuries before Islam was invented.

Antichrist will NOT be a Muslim.

Q. Will the Antichrist be killed and resurrected from the dead?

A. No. Christ alone holds the keys to death and hell. Antichrist is Satan's man, and God certainly would not use Satan or anyone to raise anyone from the dead without it being a part of His holy will. Such evil certainly would never be in God's will.

That's not to say the Lord doesn't allow evil to run its course in many cases—but always under His absolute control. So it will be with this false resurrection. The word used to describe this "resurrection" uses language that implies it will be a deception: "I saw one of his heads *as it were* wounded to death" (Revelation 13:3a, emphasis added). This reads as if the point of death is not actually reached, we think.

God will allow people who have rejected His offer of salvation through His Son to come under strong delusion so that they will believe a lie (2 Thessalonians 2). The false resurrection from the dead (healing of the deadly wound) will be part of that lie, which will encompass quite a bit more than most have imagined, we suspect.

Q. Where will the Antichrist's headquarters be located?

A. This question is difficult to answer. He is said to make Rome his seat of power. He is said to make Babylon his headquarters. Yet, Jerusalem and the temple—in the holy of holies—is where he will take up residence and demand worship.

Our thinking is that in the earliest part of his coming to power, Europe (the revived Roman Empire) will be the geographical area where he derives his growth as a politician/leader and his ultimate political power. Babylon—whether the actually rebuilt Babylon or another power center—will be the geographical heart as well as the evil spiritual headquarters while his satanic megalomania grows. Then, the final place he resides is in Jerusalem—which, after all, is called spiritual Babylon by the Lord Himself for allowing evil to reside within its confines.

Q. Is the Antichrist alive today?

A. Based on the geopolitical, socioeconomic, geophysical, and religious exigencies on the scene today, we believe he almost has to be alive now. Israel being front and center, in the bull's eye of the Middle East peace process directed by the "international community" and surrounded on all sides (except the Mediterranean side) by enemies who have blood-vowed to erase them from the earth—as well as being the object of disdain for practically all nations—makes Antichrist's nearness almost guaranteed.

3

Rapture: Escaping Antichrist's Final Solution

This generation is deeply into the rise of what we term the Fourth Reich, in our view of these troubled times as we look through the prism of God's prophetic Word. This emerging "reich"—which means "empire," "realm" or "nation"—will be the bloodiest and most enslaving that has ever afflicted mankind. We believe development of this coming global regime is on the near geopolitical horizon.

At the same time, we believe it's more than obvious that the staying hand of God is at work holding back the rise of that final dictatorship and its führer. Yet the world's last despot and his terror regime will (we believe soon) bring the billions of earth's inhabitants under his genocide-driven evil.

It is therefore profoundly important that those who hold dear all truth in God's Word be "watchmen on the wall." We are exhorted by the Lord Jesus, Himself, to observe the prophetic times: "And what I say unto you I say unto all, Watch" (Mark 13:37).

News at every level—local, national, and international—assaults our senses minute by minute. The messages invading our daily lives,

41

almost always of bad news, make us ask: "What's going to happen next?"

Today's world seems to become more insane with rage and on the verge of something horrifying we can't quite identify. Yet, that impending sense of trepidation somehow is now so familiar that it has almost become the norm. When we hear of even the most bizarre conduct by people these days, we might be shocked for a second or two. Then it's back to business as usual.

Paul warned that "evil men and seducers will become worse and worse, deceiving and being deceived" (2 Timothy 3:13). Jesus forewarned the same end-times things to look for. He told His followers not to be deceived. Many false prophets and deceivers, He said, will show up just before the end of days.

This is just the sort of deception going on today, even in church pulpits and pews. The same can be said for deception and evil seduction at the highest levels of government. This end-times deception and evil have taken place in particular since just before the 2016 presidential election and continue to this day.

Jesus said that it would be at just such a time when He will come back to surprise most everyone:

Therefore be ye also ready: for in such an hour as ye think not the Son of man cometh. (Matthew 24:44)

He also had something to say about the generation alive at the very end of the age:

And as it was in the days of Noe, so shall it be also in the days of the Son of man.

They did eat, they drank, they married wives, they were given in marriage, until the day that Noe entered into the ark, and the flood came, and destroyed them all.

Likewise also as it was in the days of Lot; they did eat, they drank, they bought, they sold, they planted, they builded;

But the same day that Lot went out of Sodom it rained
fire and brimstone from heaven, and destroyed them all. (Luke
17:26–29)

He went on to prophesy that it will be just like it was in Lot's day
when He is next "revealed." That is, it will be like it was during those
ancient times when He catastrophically intervenes in the affairs of
mankind.

The question we're wise to ask is: Could ours be the time of which
Jesus spoke?

The days of Noah and Lot, Jesus said, were times when business
at every level of society was going smoothly, for the most part. People
were getting married, having babies, raising crops, building homes, and
doing every other kind of construction. They were selling and buying
merchandise. They didn't have a clue that their worlds were about to be
disrupted by great cataclysms. While it's true that the booming economy
was recently terribly disrupted—in America, at least—buying, selling,
and other aspects of life survived the COVID-19 pandemic. There is a
building again toward business as usual.

Societies and cultures, at the same ancient time, suffered every form
of crime and perversion, the book of Genesis tells us. Violence, as a matter of fact, filled the whole earth. "Men's hearts [minds] were only on evil
continually" (Genesis 6:5).

Have you watched sitcoms lately? Have you scanned your email
and been deluged with spam and pornography? Have you heard foul
language—with the blasphemous use of God's name often at its core?
Have you been a witness to road rage (or taken part in it)? Have you
seen news reports of the fierceness demonstrated in the destructive riot-
ing and looting of recent days? Have you observed life around you in
general? Do we fit Paul's prediction for the perilous times of the last days
in 2 Timothy 3? Are we, in fact, "lovers of pleasures, more than lovers
of God?"

We can't know the number of people alive on earth at the time of

Noah's Flood or during the time of Sodom and Gomorrah's catastrophic judgments, but it's reasonable to wonder if, percentage wise, there might not be about the same ratio of lost people to saved people as there are in our time.

Noah and seven of his family members were the only people who escaped the Flood. God couldn't find even ten righteous people during the moments just before He removed Lot from the doomed area.

Just like Noah, who preached repentance for 120 years following the time God told him He would destroy the world with water, true preachers and teachers of God's gospel message have for many centuries been preaching and teaching to a rebellious world. God has raised those who have brought His prophetic warnings in more recent decades. But, sadly, God's own people are not listening. In many cases, they aren't even being told by their own pastors and teachers the message that Christ could return at any moment. Christians aren't being informed that there are no signs remaining that must precede His sudden arrival in the air for His saints.

Too many pastors have for a long time preached a message of "feel-goodism," and "do-goodism." Theirs is a social gospel meant to make the people in the pews comfortable. The deeper people are into their comfort zones, the better it makes these preachers feel.

Satan to this point has seen no reason to disrupt such tranquility in the churches. With pastors and their flocks under the "feel-good" and "do-good" sedation, he could perpetually devote more time to planning how to turn the planet into hell on earth. At the heart of his plan is the Fourth Reich.

It seems the devil's plans have been altered. Through what we believe is a move to bring America and the world into a global mindset again, Lucifer is behind the COVID-19 pandemic. Even the churches have been shut down. The pastors of God's flocks are now alert that something of monumental importance is up—at least they should be aware of the strangeness of this hour.

Yet, even in this time of the wickedness carried out by the powers and principalities in high places, God is in full control. His mighty power is available. It is a high-voltage energizer that can infuse Christians with strength for these closing days we face.

The study of Bible prophecy excites students who earnestly desire to learn what God wants them to know. When a child of God looks into the future through His omniscient eyes, that person's worldview separates from the gloomy one of those who see life on earth coming to an end because of global warming, an asteroid impact, or thermonuclear war—or even a worldwide pandemic.

These things, according to vivid descriptions found in Revelation and other prophetic books of the Bible, lurk in the future. The Antichrist regime and his vicious rule during the Tribulation era is coming. Being informed through Bible prophecy gives Christians confidence and comfort that we don't face the gloom and doom of that time, but can anticipate glorious life beyond imagination. We should have no dread of that future, whatever it might hold. The student who is attuned to the prophetic Word is also given the wisdom to understand that all humanistic efforts to create a utopia on earth will fail, just as they always have. Only under the reign of King Jesus will people truly prosper.

It is certain that we are in for some terrible times. But, the world will never end. And, Christians can look forward to a thrilling moment when we will suddenly find ourselves in the marvelous presence of our Lord and Savior, Jesus Christ. This is true whether we die or are raptured in a moment, in the "twinkling of an eye" (1 Corinthians 15:52).

When we die, we are instantly in the presence of Christ. Paul said:

We are confident, [I say], and willing rather to be absent from the body, and to be present with the Lord. (2 Corinthians 5:8)

For whether we live, we live unto the Lord; and whether we die, we die unto the Lord: whether we live therefore, or die, we are the Lord's. (Romans 14:8)

One Thrilling Moment

When the Rapture of the saints occurs, Christians will be with our Lord instantly, and for eternity. Again, Paul tells us what will happen to both the bodies of the dead and of those who are alive when this stunning event takes place:

> Then we which are alive and remain shall be caught up together with them in the clouds, to meet the Lord in the air: and so shall we ever be with the Lord. (1 Thessalonians 4:17)

We'll look closely at all that is associated with this thrilling event and what comes after it in future chapters. But, for now, let's look at what Christians should be doing in anticipation of its any-moment occurrence. Exactly how should we conduct our lives in view of coming face to face with Jesus—whether through death or the Rapture? The great apostle Peter had something profound to say about the matter:

> Seeing then that all these things shall be dissolved, what manner of persons ought ye to be in all holy conversation and godliness,
> Looking for and hasting unto the coming of the day of God, wherein the heavens being on fire shall be dissolved, and the elements shall melt with fervent heat?
> Nevertheless we, according to his promise, look for new heavens and a new earth, wherein dwelleth righteousness.
> Wherefore, beloved, seeing that ye look for such things, be diligent that ye may be found of him in peace, without spot, and blameless. (2 Peter 3:11–14)

Peter, the earliest disciple of Jesus, tells Christians that we should first look for the coming of the Day of the Lord. We briefly examined this time earlier; it will begin with the seven-year era of Tribulation. It will move swiftly into the middle of that era of horror, the last three and a half years of which are known as the time of "Jacob's trouble" (Jeremiah 30:7). It will be the worst time in human history.

Why should Christians be looking for such a horrendous time?

That time will see a series of three terrible manifestations of God's righteous wrath, each of the three including seven judgments, for a total of twenty-one specific judgments. Each judgment that falls upon the incorrigibly wicked and rebellious people of that time will grow progressively more punishing. Things will get so bad that those who are alive will try to hide in the caves and crevices of mountains to get away from God's wrath. They will come to the point that they'll beg the mountains to fall on them.

Why would Peter tell Christians to want these things to hurry up and come?

Actually, he is asking us to consider these things in the most serious terms, to heed God's words on that era of horror. The key part of this passage God wants us to understand is "seeing then that all these things shall be dissolved, what manner of persons ought ye to be in all holy conversation and godliness?" (see 2 Peter 3:10–11). We are to think upon these coming judgments. If we do so with prayerful seriousness, our lives will be changed into lives of godliness.

Concern for the Doomed

We, as God's children, you see, can understand—if we apply ourselves—the things that people of the Tribulation will have to endure because of their rebellion, their sin. We're expected to know (through Bible prophecy) about these things to come.

We aren't expected to know about the coming judgments because God wants us to be afraid of going through them ourselves. We're to understand them out of love for those who will have to go through that time of horrors, if they don't repent and come to a saving knowledge of Christ this side of the Rapture. Knowing about Bible prophecy—future events—will make us more holy and godly in conducting our own lives. It will make us more dedicated witnesses for Christ.

Christians are not appointed to God's wrath, according to 1 Thessalonians 5:9. We're told to comfort each other with that knowledge, according to 1 Thessalonians 5:11. Our future is secure in Jesus. Our concern should be for others who don't know Him in an intimate, saving way.

We're also to be looking for the Day of the Lord, because before it starts, Jesus will come for us and say, "Come up hither" (Revelation 4:1–2). He compared His return, as we've seen, to the break-in of a "thief in the night" (Matthew 24:43). Why on earth would the sinless Creator-God of all the universes refer to Himself this way?

Jesus' return to earth will be in two phases. First will come the Rapture, then, at least seven years later, His glorious appearance will occur. A description of the first phase of Christ's Second Coming is found in Peter's prophecy. It goes on to cover the entire span of time leading to the remaking of the heavens and the earth.

> But the day of the Lord will come as a thief in the night; in the which the heavens shall pass away with a great noise, and the elements shall melt with fervent heat, the earth also and the works that are therein shall be burned up. (2 Peter 3:10)

A thief comes unannounced. He breaks into a tranquil setting such as one's home, and takes something. Jesus was forewarning that He will intervene in the affairs of mankind with a sudden, silent taking-away of something. That something is His saints—all who were saved throughout the Age of Grace.

From Rapture to Recreation of Earth

The entire Day of the Lord then will run its course until the end of Christ's millennial reign, the great white throne judgment, and the remaking of the heavens and the earth. His coming "as a thief in the night" can't be the Second Coming of Christ to set up His rule and reign in Jerusalem at the end of the great war called Armageddon, because every eye will see Him returning at that time.

The King Cometh!

The prophetic Word tells of the second phase of Christ's Second Coming—His return to the earth in power and glory—as follows:

> And I saw heaven opened, and behold a white horse; and he that sat upon him was called Faithful and True, and in righteousness he doth judge and make war.
>
> His eyes were as a flame of fire, and on his head were many crowns; and he had a name written, that no man knew, but he himself.
>
> And he was clothed with a vesture dipped in blood: and his name is called The Word of God.
>
> And the armies which were in heaven followed him upon white horses, clothed in fine linen, white and clean.
>
> And out of his mouth goeth a sharp sword, that with it he should smite the nations: and he shall rule them with a rod of iron: and he treadeth the winepress of the fierceness and wrath of Almighty God.
>
> And he hath on his vesture and on his thigh a name written, KING OF KINGS AND LORD OF LORDS. (Revelation 19:11–16)

Be assured: Absolutely no one will miss that glorious appearance!

At least seven years before that return in the clouds of glory, the Rapture will occur. Jesus, in this "thief-in-the-night" coming, will fulfill his own words:

> Let not your heart be troubled: ye believe in God, believe also in me.
>
> In my Father's house are many mansions: if it were not so, I would have told you. I go to prepare a place for you.
>
> And if I go and prepare a place for you, I will come again, and receive you unto myself; that where I am, there ye may be also. (John 14:1–3)

So, Christians are to be looking toward the Day of the Lord and desiring its soon coming, because Jesus, before that day begins, will come to take us home to heaven to live with Him eternally in magnificent dwelling places He has prepared.

Christians Must Watch

Again, about looking for Him to come for His saints in the Rapture, the Lord instructed all who would be saved during the Church Age: "And what I say unto you I say unto all, Watch" (Mark 13:37). Until that exhilarating moment of Rapture, Christians are to be power-filled sentries!

What, exactly, does this duty entail?

We've seen profound prophetic stage-setting taking place in socio-economic, geopolitical, and religious arenas, as well as in every other category of the human condition. We've watched, as already pointed out, the complete rearrangement of national entities in about a month's time. The coronavirus pandemic has, again, turned all leaderships of sovereign nations toward the supposed need of global guidance and rule. America, the most powerful nation ever to exist economically and militarily, has been forced to lock down its booming economy. More than twenty-six million are out of work in the US as of this writing.

This, we believe, is all in Satan's plans for Antichrist to take power. This pandemic has done what more than four years of deep-state efforts failed to do—bring about a return to globalism, to Babel.

The Gog-Magog coalition is forming just to Israel's north, exactly as in Ezekiel's foretelling. Russia, Iran, Turkey, and all other members of that force destined to attack over the mountains of Israel are now, for the most part, joined together. The Russian leader looks as if he could fulfill the role of that leader of the Gog-Magog military. The current pope is making noises contrary to the Word of God in many instances. He looks as if he could fulfill the role of the False Prophet, the second beast of Revelation 13.

We don't say these will absolutely be the people who will serve in those prophetic positions, just that they exhibit characteristics precisely like those given in the prophecies of Ezekiel 38–39 and Revelation 13. No other generation in history has been privileged to see end-time things developing as clearly as ours. Notice the word "developing." The last-days signals are not prophecy being fulfilled. They consist of issues and events that are *setting the stage for fulfillment* of biblical prophecy.

It is proper to liken these issues and events to a dark, ominous storm that is boiling on the distant horizon. We can see the apocalyptic tempest coming, with jagged flashes of lightning fracturing the black, rolling clouds. But we aren't yet in the storm. We know it's approaching with great swiftness, and it's our job to warn others before it's too late!

Watch God's Radar Screen

Just as a person couldn't issue an accurate tornado warning if he or she couldn't read the radar signals on the monitors of the weather computers, a Christian can't warn of prophetic events without understanding the signals provided in God's Word.

We must study prophecy as well as the other parts of the Bible. We're instructed to "study to shew thyself approved unto God, a workman that needeth not to be ashamed, rightly dividing the word of truth" (2 Timothy 2:15). Note that the apostle Paul didn't tell us to study "part" of God's Word. He simply said to "study…rightly dividing the word of truth." That's a direct order to examine the whole Bible, not just parts of it. This is how God's people are failing today.

We're not only to study the whole Word of God, but we're also to consider our times to determine where we stand on God's prophetic timeline. Jesus scolded the Pharisees along with the Sadducees who, as they always did, sought to trick Him into giving false prophecy so they could legally accuse Him. He answered:

> When it is evening, ye say, It will be fair weather: for the sky is red. And in the morning, It will be foul weather today: for the sky is red and lowring.
>
> O ye hypocrites, ye can discern the face of the sky; but can ye not discern the signs of the times? (Matthew 16:2–3)

If these pious, pompous, self-proclaimed holy men had recognized the signals around them, you see, they would have realized that it was the time of Israel's visitation by the Messiah, Himself! They should have been able to discern the signs of their times, but they couldn't do it.

Many signals today indicate that the Messiah is about to visit the earth once again, this time as King of kings and Lord of lords! We as Christians must be good sentries, filled with the God-given power of prophetic discernment. The only way to serve in this duty is to study the Word and pray for understanding. We must then look at the signals in that Holy Spirit-given ability to comprehend our times.

We'll go into things to come in deeper detail elsewhere in this volume, but a few things for the Christian observer to look for, along with undertaking intensive study and prayer, are the following:

- **The characteristics of end-time mankind**—We've already mentioned some of these. We find a good representation of what mankind will be like at the end of the age, just before Christ's return, in 2 Timothy 3:1–9.
- **The development of the last kingdom of Daniel's dream-vision**—Daniel interpreted Nebuchadnezzar's dream, as told in Daniel 2. Then, the prophet had a night vision himself (Daniel 7). He saw a fifth beast that was strong and terrible. Many believe we see the coming of that final form of world government in our day.
- **The standing of the nation of Israel**—Israel is the most profound signal of all as far as where we stand on God's prophetic timeline. It was born (reborn, actually) on a single day, just as prophesied (see Isaiah 66:8–10). It is back in the land to fulfill its destiny as the head of nations. First, however, Israel will have to endure the most horrific period of persecution there has ever been. We must watch Israel carefully in our hourly news, because that's how we can learn much about how near we are to Christ's return.

Christians should sow the seeds of the gospel while we go through daily life. At the same time, we should continually observe things around us and realize that the coming of Jesus Christ can't be far off. That coming will be one in which millions will vanish from earth in a moment, in the twinkling of an eye!

Seeing all the signals of the nearness of the Lord's shout, "Come up here!" (Revelation 4:1), we should be comforted that we won't face Antichrist or his Fourth Reich.

Jesus exhorted those who believe in Him to:

Watch ye therefore, and pray always, that ye may be accounted worthy to escape all these things that shall come to pass, and to stand before the Son of man. (Luke 21:36)

This often brings up anxieties within the Christian family. The term "worthiness" therefore must be addressed in the matter of God's plan for our escape from the time of Antichrist's Fourth Reich.

On Being Rapture Worthy

More and more, it seems that there are those who believe and teach that Christians might miss the Rapture. This is wrapped up in the thought that Christians who aren't living exemplary lives as believers will miss being taken should they not be fully "repented up" and ready to go. These will be "left behind," as the Tim LaHaye and Jerry Jenkins novel series puts it. First, it's perhaps best to consider what "exemplary life" means in terms of prerequisites for making it to heaven in the Rapture.

Those who insist that one must be living the exemplary life usually frame that as "living a life of holiness" or "living righteously." By this, it is presumed they mean for the most part that one must be doing "good works" rather than living in the "broad way" along which the pedestrian world moves. We, of course, agree that born-again believers in the Lord Jesus Christ should be doing exactly that every day. There's no doubt that God's Word calls us to that model for life.

However, the question is now raised—and it's closely akin to the one brought up in discussions about "losing" one's salvation: At what point does one "lose" salvation? What particular "sin point" is reached that causes the "salvation meter" in heaven to go "TILT," removing the sinner's name from the Lamb's book of life? Or, for our purposes here, at what point does one sin "enough" to be taken off the list of those who hold tickets to heaven, who will be lifted up to be with Jesus Christ in that millisecond known as the "twinkling of an eye" when Jesus calls "Come up hither!" (Revelation 4:1–2)?

Those who believe the names of the redeemed can be removed from the Lamb's book of life, of course, use the following Scripture as one that proves their position:

He that overcometh, the same shall be clothed in white raiment; and I will not blot out his name out of the book of life, but I will confess his name before my Father, and before his angels. (Revelation 3:5)

This is proof, say the "conditional security proponents," that one's name can be removed from the book of life. But, let's have a closer look to examine whether this is true.

Those who hold that believers' names can be erased from the blessed book of life insist that the born-again must "overcome" sin. In their belief dictionary, this means we must stay sin-free—that is, either live above sin or stay continually "repented up" in order to keep our names in the book.

They miss the point entirely as to who actually does the overcoming. It isn't the believer who overcomes all sin, but the Lord Jesus who died to take sin away from those who believe so that we are no longer separated from God the Father in the eternal sense. This is seen, for example, in the following:

For whatsoever is born of God overcometh the world: and this is the victory that overcometh the world, even our faith.

Who is he that overcometh the world, but he that believeth that Jesus is the Son of God? (1 John 5:4–5)

It is simple belief in the Savior who takes away the sins of the world that makes us overcomers. We still sin and come short of the glory of God, but His precious blood shed at Calvary covers all of our sins—past, present, and future. We overcome the world, the flesh, and the devil—all sin in this earthly sphere—exclusively by belief in the only begotten Son of God (John 3:16). Our overcoming is through God's great grace, through faith. We can never overcome by our own power.

When we sin, we break fellowship with our Lord, but we never sever the eternal family relationship. We do the following to take steps toward making right the breach in fellowship that we've caused. First, we must realize and admit that we're not sinless, because repentance cannot truly be made unless we confess that we've sinned. Upon such confession and repentance, we are given a blessed remedy:

> If we say that we have no sin, we deceive ourselves, and the truth is not in us.
>
> If we confess our sins, he is faithful and just to forgive us our sins, and to cleanse us from all unrighteousness. (1 John 1:8–9)

God's Word shows us that our salvation and our ability to overcome are based on what Christ did for us and our faith in Him alone. Going to Christ when He calls, as Paul outlines in 1 Corinthians 15:51–55 and 1 Thessalonians 4:13–18, and given by John in Revelation 4:1–2, is a salvation matter. We know that from the overall gospel message and from the total context of God dealing with His family. Remember when Jesus, as He faced the cross, offered that beautiful prayer to His Father (John 17)? Read it again, and you'll see that it's absolutely clear that born-again believers are forever secure in the Father's hand, based on what Jesus did on the cross.

We know that we are once and forever in God's family because of the words of the One who created all that exists:

> My Father, which gave [them] me, is greater than all; and no [man] is able to pluck [them] out of my Father's hand. (John 10:29)

Paul confirms that the Rapture is a salvation matter as follows:

> For God hath not appointed us to wrath, but to obtain salvation by our Lord Jesus Christ, Who died for us, that, whether we wake or sleep, we should live together with him. Wherefore comfort yourselves together, and edify one another, even as also ye do. (1 Thessalonians 5:9–11)

The Rapture will be Christ keeping us from the hour of temptation, or Tribulation (read Revelation 3:10), the time of God's wrath—to which Paul tells us we are "not appointed." However, there are many who insist that Christians who haven't properly confessed their sins will go through God's wrath (the entire seven years of the Tribulation will be God's judgment and wrath). They use the following verse to make their case:

> Watch ye therefore, and pray always, that ye may be accounted worthy to escape all these things that shall come to pass, and to stand before the Son of man. (Luke 21:36)

The word they state is relevant here is the word "worthy." Does this word not mean that we as born-again believers must be good enough to stand before Jesus in that raptured throng? Doesn't this mean, therefore, that if we fail to live up to God's standards while on this earth, we will (at some point in God's view of what it takes to fall from being Rapture ready) lose our "ticket" in that translation moment, thus not be taken up with Jesus?

Like in examining the issue of salvation, in looking at the term "overcoming," we now consider the word "worthy." What does it mean to be "worthy," as given in this Rapture example? Again, the answer is wrapped up in the same name as before: Jesus. He is the only One "worthy," in God's holy eyes, to be in the heavenly realm.

Remember what Jesus said to a man who addressed Him as "good master"?

> And Jesus said unto him, Why callest thou me good? none is good, save one, that is, God. (Luke 18:18)

Jesus, the second person of the Godhead, wasn't seeking to chastise the man. The Lord was confirming that He is indeed God, the only good, the only righteousness. Righteousness is the only way to heaven—

either through the portal of death or the Rapture. Only through Jesus can we enter the heavenly realm:

> Verily, verily, I say unto thee, Except a man be born again, he cannot see the kingdom of God. (John 3:3)

God's Word says: "As it is written, There is none righteous no not one" (Romans 8:10) and, "For all have sinned and come short of the glory of God" (Romans 8:23). So, Jesus is the only person "worthy" to enter heaven. Only through Him are any of us worthy to stand before Him in that heavenly realm.

On a less magnificent scale, the word "worthy" in this passage means that we should be in a constant mindset of prayerful repentance. We should always want to be found "worthy"—"cleansed of all unrighteousness," as stated in 1 John 1:9—so that we will hear our Lord say to us on that day, "Well done, good and faithful servant" (Matthew 25:23).

Considering these times so near that spectacular moment when Christ calls to His Church, one way we can demonstrate worthiness is by observing issues and events that look to be prophetic signals. We're instructed by our Lord:

> And when these things begin to come to pass, then look up, and lift up your heads; for your redemption draweth nigh. (Luke 21:28)

As stated before, today's Christians who are attuned to Holy Spirit enlightenment see developments that are setting the stage for prophetic fulfillment. These indicators are literally in every direction we look as we scan the prophetic horizon.

Jesus said:

> And when these things begin to come to pass, then look up and lift up your head; for your redemption is drawing near. (Luke 21:28)

Antichrist's Fourth Reich is in an advanced state of development. This geopolitical beast will bring with him a Final Solution even more terrifying than that of the Third Reich's führer.

The Rapture will be the Heavenly Father's removal of His earthly family to their homes with Him in heaven. His Son, Jesus, who died, was buried, and arose to life on the third day to provide salvation for all who believe, will call God's family into the clouds above the planet. All believers alive, as well as those who have died, will accompany their Savior and Lord to the dwelling places He has built for them (John 14:1–3).

> But we do not want you to be uninformed, brethren, about those who are asleep, that you may not grieve, as do the rest who have no hope.
>
> For if we believe that Jesus died and rose again, even so God will bring with Him those who have fallen asleep in Jesus.
>
> For this we say to you by the word of the Lord, that we who are alive, and remain until the coming of the Lord, shall not precede those who have fallen asleep.
>
> For the Lord Himself will descend from heaven with a shout, with the voice of the archangel, and with the trumpet of God; and the dead in Christ shall rise first.
>
> Then we who are alive and remain shall be caught up together with them in the clouds to meet the Lord in the air, and thus we shall always be with the Lord.
>
> Therefore comfort one another with these words. (1 Thessalonians 4:13–18)

4

Man of Sin Takes World Stage

Satan, it is believed, has had a man ready to step in and fulfill the role of Antichrist at many junctures throughout history. Men such as Antiochus Epiphanes, Nero, Hitler, and other tyrants have exhibited traits ascribed to Antichrist in Bible prophecy.

Antiochus, for example, entered the Jewish temple and defiled the altar by sloshing it with swine blood. Antichrist will defile the Jewish temple in a similar way at the midpoint of the Tribulation. Hitler, for another example, persecuted the Jews in the most horrific way to that time in history, murdering some six million of God's chosen people. Antichrist will murder many more of the House of Israel and others than did the German führer.

When the Rapture occurs, vilest man ever to step foot on the earth will take the stage for history's final play. It will be a wicked production. Speculation at its most imaginative can't portray the moments, hours, days, and weeks following the disappearance of many millions of people. Considering the ramifications of the relatively minor crisis the world has recently endured, the coronavirus pandemic, the Rapture will bring crisis magnified many times over.

Besides the emotional devastation caused when losing immediate family members and friends, businesses will undoubtedly instantly fail because of the missing who are needed to carry on commerce and other elements of living. However, the most crushing possibility to consider is that every child below the age of accountability will be removed and taken to be with Christ at that stunning moment.

Children who have died physically and those who will be taken in the Rapture have in common the fact that they were/will be instantly with the Lord. This is because they're seen in God's merciful economy as innocents.

Most importantly, it is an *individual* matter—God dealing one on one, not collectively or corporately, with the salvation issue. Acceptance of Christ is based upon a decision to accept or reject. Those who don't have—and never have had—the ability to accept or reject, because they don't have the mental capacity to understand, cannot accept or reject.

The Bible says those who know to do good and don't do it are sinning. Conversely, the whole body of Scripture presents the case that those who don't know they are lost because of sin are not condemned. But, when maturity that brings understanding comes (and the Holy Spirit draws them, convicting them of sin), they must accept God's offer of reconciliation.

The very character of God, as presented throughout the entire Word of God, is at stake. All in Christ will go at the Rapture. Paul says "all will be changed in a moment, in the twinkling of an eye." What does this mean—"all" who are "in" Christ? It refers to the fact that all who are redeemed by the shed blood of Christ are a part of the Body of Christ—the Church. Children—even though born into sin because of Adam's disobedience—are "in" Christ before they are able to comprehend God's provision for salvation. No one who is "in" Christ will have to face the wrath of God during the coming Tribulation.

One area of Scripture regarding the wrath of God that addresses the position of all in Christ—thus the Rapture—is found here in 2 Thessalonians:

> For God hath not appointed us to wrath, but to obtain salvation by our Lord Jesus Christ,
> Who died for us, that, whether we wake or sleep, we should live together with him. (2 Thessalonians 5:9–10)

During this Age of Grace (also called the Church Age), all who are born and haven't reached the age of understanding (thus accountability)—will go to Christ when they die. This is totally in keeping with God's character—again, as plainly laid out in His holy love letter to mankind.

All the children who have died before they matured enough to make decisions regarding salvation are now with Christ. To God's holy praise, that includes every one of the millions upon millions of babies this evil world system has aborted and continues to murder. This number of innocents includes *every child who has been slain in wars throughout history or who has died due to other causes.*

The Scripture passage that talks about one's name being blotted out of the Lamb's book of life deals with this. The names of all who are born are in that book, we believe. Children who reach the age at which they realize Christ is the way to salvation, but reject God's way (John 14:6) have their names blotted out. They are written back in when salvation does occur in the way God prescribes.

And, we're convinced that not one child born after the Rapture, during that horrendous, seven-year era, will ever reach that age. Thus, all children born following that event will go to be with the Lord—either upon death or during the judgments following the triumphant return of the Lord Jesus. As a matter of fact, read Jesus' words here:

> And woe unto them that are with child, and to them that give suck in those days! (Matthew 24:19)

Jesus is talking here about the Tribulation era. Remember, that is the last seven years of human history before His *Second* Advent. The Lord mentions two age classifications: 1) children who are in the womb, and 2) those who are so young that they are still at their mothers' breast. There is no mention even of toddlers—i.e., those who will have been conceived or born during the Tribulation. Jesus is talking here about halfway through the seven-year period.

All children below the age of being able to make decisions on the salvation matter will go to be with Jesus when He calls (Revelation 4:1). In that stunning instant, the Creator-God of heaven will make a statement of His opinion of abortion and when life begins!

The emotional wrenching among families—particularly, among mothers—that will take place when all children and even those not yet born are instantaneously gone is beyond our ability to imagine. The panic will transcend all horrors of human history.

There will be a call for answers. The fright and alarm will only grow, until the entire world will be in upheaval. Again, we believe the terror that will ensue might be wrapped up in Jesus' description of the time following the Rapture and the time between that stupefying event and the emergence of the man of sin.

> And there shall be signs in the sun, and in the moon, and in the stars; and upon the earth distress of nations, with perplexity; the sea and the waves roaring;
>
> Men's hearts failing them for fear, and for looking after those things which are coming on the earth: for the powers of heaven shall be shaken. (Luke 21:25–26)

At the same time, all the suspicions, mistrust, and hatreds among the nations will grow exponentially. This is because God, who is restraining evil in this fallen sphere, will be removed. We see that truth, again, in the following prophecy by the apostle Paul:

And now ye know what [the force of God the Holy Spirit] withholdeth that he [Antichrist] might be revealed in his [Antichrist's] time.

For the mystery of iniquity doth already work: only he [the Holy Spirit] who now letteth [restrains] will let [restrain], until he [the Holy Spirit] be taken out of the way.

And then shall that wicked [Antichrist and his evil] be revealed, whom the Lord shall consume with the spirit of his mouth, and shall destroy with the brightness of his coming. (2 Thessalonians 2:6–8)

When God's restraining influence is removed from total governance over the evil that permeates earth, the world will again quickly fill with violence and wickedness like it was in the days of Noah. The people of earth will be in full terror mode. Nuclear weaponry will likely be used, at least on a limited basis. This will create even greater panic. There will be a massive outcry for safety—and for peace.

At that time, Satan's man, the man of sin, will gallop forth, riding on the symbolic white steed and promising world peace. Again, here is that prophecy:

And I saw when the Lamb opened one of the seals, and I heard, as it were the noise of thunder, one of the four beasts saying, Come and see.

And I saw, and behold a white horse: and he that sat on him had a bow; and a crown was given unto him: and he went forth conquering, and to conquer. (Revelation 6:1–2)

His vault to power will no doubt be swift and, for the most part, without resistance. The left-behind masses will be willing to place their faith in this great deceiver. Most Jews of the world will embrace this charismatic world leader as one who will bring them peace and security.

Later, some of the House of Israel, maybe most, will claim him as their Messiah. Here is what Jesus foretold in this regard:

> I have come in My Father's name, and you do not receive Me; if another comes in his own name, you will receive him. (John 5:43)

The primary purposes of the Tribulation will be for the judgment of the anti-God rebels of earth and for bringing out of the Jewish people a remnant that will constitute the nation of Israel during the Millennium, Christ's thousand-year reign upon a restored, pristine planet earth.

In the process of bringing forth a third of the Jewish population at that time in order to repopulate earth and be part of Christ's kingdom and King David's Israel, the chosen people will undergo atrocities and martyrdom unparalleled in the persecutions of history. Once the absolute terror of the disappearance of millions around the globe substantially subsides, a completely different mindset will likely develop. Those who detest the thought of a God that governs morality and condemns sinful activity will begin to believe their Utopia can at last be achieved. The about-to-fully-emerge world leader will almost certainly let them have their heady, high-minded way—at least for a time—until he, like Hitler in pre-1933 Germany when he appeared to offer freedom of actions to the German people, becomes totally tyrannical.

The atmosphere of condemnation created by all who look down on their immorality and evil conduct now having disappeared, the hedonistic good times, absent Holy Spirit restraint, will begin in earnest. Satan's man of sin will convince the people that they can have their cake and eat it too, to use a well-worn cliché. He will promise that they can do whatever they wish, free of guilt that they are breaking some god's commandment. Yet, he will at the same time guarantee them complete freedom from fear that the chaos of former times will ever again bedevil their lives. He will convince one and all that he will build—with their cooperation—heaven on earth!

Fear caused by the disappearance of millions around the world will no doubt change to glee now that they have a fresh start. They'll build a world of their own choosing. The party will begin!

Delusions of Grandeur

The world's great one-world thinkers and planners, led more and more by the man who will quickly become known as the greatest of all time, will come up with spectacular ideas to create the New World Order. Part of that grandiose proposal will probably include a peace plan that neither the Jews of Israel nor Israel's blood-vowed enemies will be able to refuse. Included in that plan will most likely be giving Jews permission to build a temple atop Mount Moriah.

Ingredients of the Great Plan

The plan will probably include a complete redistribution of wealth. Possibly, all the properties of those who vanished will be pooled, then divided and distributed within nations and across the world. Everyone will likely have access to computer usage, eventually, so they'll be able to conduct business over the hybrid Internet system that will probably grow at a fantastic rate. The greatest part of this phenomenal system most likely will be the ability of each person to vote on leaders and issues electronically—a true world democracy at last achieved! What the people won't know, however, will be that their voting decisions will be manipulated to show results the grand schemers desire.

Man Creates Wrath from God

Perhaps the most ironic judgment of all will be wrapped up in the fact that people will be allowed to do things their way, basically apart from God's influence. They, themselves, will create their own hell on earth.

But, still, this God-free society will be as much a judgment from the Almighty as those that will occur in the second half of the Tribulation, when God pours His increasingly terrible vengeance upon rebellious earth-dwellers.

It will be a worldwide "earth party" of short duration. At the mid-way point of the Tribulation, the great world leader will prove what, and who, he really is. The man of sin will climb upon that end-times stage for his prophesied rise to unparalleled geopolitical power. He will be a man whose center of origin is in Rome. We know that from the following:

> And after threescore and two weeks shall Messiah be cut off, but not for himself: and the people of the prince that shall come shall destroy the city and the sanctuary; and the end thereof shall be with a flood, and unto the end of the war desolations are determined.
>
> And he shall confirm the covenant with many for one week: and in the midst of the week he shall cause the sacrifice and the oblation to cease, and for the overspreading of abominations he shall make it desolate, even until the consummation, and that determined shall be poured upon the desolate. (Daniel 9:26–27)

Daniel tells us that the "prince that shall come" will originate from the "people who shall destroy the city and the sanctuary." This was done in AD 70, hundreds of years after Daniel issued the prophecy. The Roman military, under General Titus and following the instructions of his father, Roman Emperor Vespasian, laid waste to Jerusalem and completely tore down the Jewish temple atop Moriah.

Antichrist—"the prince that shall come"—therefore, will emerge from the geographical area that comprised the nucleus of Rome. Daniel, here, is describing the evil that this man will commit against Israel and the entire world. Bible prophecy students and scholars agree for the most part that Antichrist will come from a revived Roman Empire. Most believe this to be referring to the European Union as it will evolve and has, in fact, developed to this point in history.

One of the most pronounced scholars, the late Dr. David Breese, framed the emergence of the man of sin and his origins. He gave the things that must eventuate in Europe in order to fulfill the prophecy of Antichrist coming to world power:

The first is that Europe must choose an effective, forceful, charismatic, dynamic leader. In human affairs it is never really possible to put together any great program of unity without that unity being characterized by a person. Leadership means everything in all of the affairs of men. Clever ideas, fine goals, fond ambitions, and lofty hopes are so much empty rhetoric apart from their being embodied in the form of a strong man. Again and again in history, the frustrations of people were vanquished and hope was built within them by the words of a leader. Europe has seen the latest, great example of that in the form of Adolf Hitler and the Third Reich. Pre-Revolutionary France experienced that with the escalation of Napoleon Bonaparte as the emperor. Peter the Great did that for Russia and Alexander for the Grecian Empire of Antiquity. Yes, the key to unity is a charismatic leader. People cannot be beguiled to gather around a strong center unless in the epic center is a person with flashing eyes and visions for the future. He must be the "Man with a Plan."

There's one more characteristic, however, that is imperative in order to produce a vortex of history. That component is what the world calls "ideology." A plan for the future must be characterized by something great to believe, some compelling philosophy, some great truth that draws people up and out of their common, banal circumstances. Passionate unity cannot be created unless the speaker can reach into the vital core of the personality, the spiritual center of everything. Many who otherwise might have been significant leaders, forgetting this, never moved much beyond mediocrity. This quality—charisma perhaps—is found in people only very seldom. It is a one-in-a-thousand, one-in-a-million capability. The ability to press a compelling ideology upon the masses of people is the key to the control of a nation. In that day, the day of the rise of Antichrist, it will be a needed key toward world control. Such a person will emerge out of the European situation. Watch for him.

What could possibly be the trigger mechanism that causes Europe and then the world to turn in admiration and obedience to the Antichrist? There are several possibilities for such a thing in today's world. They certainly would include the following.

1. Global Economic Collapse: The present world economic situation is on the most precarious footing in all of history. Voracious governments have raised the program of taxation to the place where they are now confiscating the wealth of individuals. This is a most shortsighted activity because it will produce depression on the part of people of substance and economic depression in the external world. Economic capability does not grow out of government manipulation. It grows out of individual confidence and individual competence.

2. The Threat of Nuclear War: Nuclear proliferation continues in our time with no assurance that it will come to a halt. Therefore, the possibility of one of the great powers or even a rogue nation of the world producing a nuclear exchange is a very real one.... Russia, savoring the old days, could decide on a fast nuclear conquest somewhere. Israel, facing destruction by a five hundred thousand-man Arab army could begin a nuclear war. The prospect of this is most frightening to the people of earth. Should such a war be threatened, they could be expected to turn to the assuring voice of the great leader who promised peace and safety.

The Man with the Plan

Note that the Scripture says, "For when they shall say, Peace and safety, then sudden destruction cometh upon them, as travail upon a woman with child, and they shall not escape" (1 Thessalonians 5:3). The promise of peace has again and again been the producer of false confidence and the trigger mechanism for war.

The fact is that any kind of percolation—such as a war between small nations—could escalate into a larger conflict and the stated danger of global war. Any one of these developments could cause people and nations to take leave of their senses and opt for global unity. That's when the "Man with a Plan" will appear. We can be sure that the Antichrist will not have to shoot his way into power. Rather, he will be accepted by a grateful people as the proper custodian of the future.[8]

Israel will, upon this false peacemaker's appearance, sign on to the covenant of peace as foretold in Daniel 9: 26. It will be a "covenant with death and hell":

Because ye have said, We have made a covenant with death, and with hell are we at agreement; when the overflowing scourge shall pass through, it shall not come unto us: for we have made lies our refuge, and under falsehood have we hid ourselves....

And your covenant with death shall be disannulled, and your agreement with hell shall not stand; when the overflowing scourge shall pass through, then ye shall be trodden down by it. (Isaiah 28:15, 18)

A leader is coming out of the soon-to-be united Europe who will go "forth conquering, and to conquer" (Revelation 6:2). "There was given unto him a mouth speaking great things" (Revelation 13:5). This mightiest leader ever will come riding the white horse of peacemaking and will confirm the covenant with many for one week. Translation: This leader from a Europe united in a configuration equivalent to the Europe of the Roman Empire days—a revived Roman Empire, a neo-Roman order, of sorts—will make, or confirm, a covenant treaty already constructed, to which Israel will be a major signatory.

The pact will be for seven years, one year equaling one day of the seven-day week indicated in the Scriptures. The "conquering" by the leader at this point is likely to be in the realm of diplomacy. Undoubtedly, he will offer brilliant initiatives, magnified in their allurement by a charismatic, personal charm that convinces Jew and Arab alike to trust him as a friend of all. As the guarantor of the peace not just for that region, but for a global peace upon which can be built a New World Order and a new age of prosperity, he will succeed where others have failed. His promises will be sweet to the ears of a world ravenous for such lies.

And lies they will be.

Globe-trotting exploits by would-be peacemakers have met with fates ranging from abject failure to moderate, though temporary, success. We recall seeing a documentary film of the well-intentioned but fuzzy-thinking Neville Chamberlain holding up the piece of paper Hitler duped him into believing was the megalomaniac's true desire for "peace for our time." Henry Kissinger impressed us mightily with his seeming inexhaustible energy while pursuing an honorable peace in Vietnam. Even his brilliant efforts ultimately faded and failed. Secretary of State James A. Baker III, of the Bush administration, eclipsed even Kissinger's air mileage as he jetted in and out of the capitals of the world in search of a formula that would defuse the time bomb that is the Middle East. He, too, failed to secure the lasting peace for which the world hungers, although temporary, superficial "progress" may be made.

There is, as always, movement in the Arab world to bring great pressure upon their avowed enemy, the much-hated Israel. But now they are more devious. They use diplomatic maneuvering rather than their often-failed military force and/or terrorism. They are aided and abetted by practically every nation on earth represented within the United Nations. All, except for a very few, vote against the Jewish state in practically every instance. Thankfully, the United States is able to block much of the hate-filled attempts against Israel in the UN. These types of tactics are most likely what the world can expect from now until Israel is lulled into a false sense of security. The Scriptures plainly teach that diplomatic deception will make it vulnerable to attack. This prophesied end-time, caution-softening process can be sensed.

Groundwork is being laid to bring about the peace God's Word is against. America's well-meaning diplomacy might be the effort that makes clear the pathway for the final führer to perform his diabolical work when his time comes to step upon the world stage.

From this action by Antichrist, in consort with the rest of the world to make a peace that God considers to come from the bowels of hell, will flow the most horrendous time in human history. Again, Jesus said:

> For then shall be great tribulation, such as was not since the beginning of the world to this time, no, nor ever shall be.
>
> And except those days should be shortened, there should no flesh be saved: but for the elect's sake those days shall be shortened. (Matthew 24:21–22)

Following the Rapture of Christ's saints of the Church Age (all born-again believers who are alive at the time it occurs), prophesied things will start popping quickly. The man of sin will leap upon the prophetic stage of end-times history for his brief reign of evil. Here, sadly, are some of the things those left behind after the Rapture can expect to endure:

- Total chaos will rule for a time.
- Governments will get control through sometimes-harsh methods.
- One world government will come together.
- One world church will form.
- A world leader from Europe will step to the forefront and take charge of the peace process.

- Israeli government and Israel's enemies will sign an agreement that ensures peace and safety.
- Peace will not last, as a coalition of nations led by Russia will invade the Middle East.
- God, Himself, will destroy all but one-sixth of the invader forces.
- Much of the world will be hit by the deadly effects of the invasion. This will possibly include chemical, biological, and nuclear aftereffects.
- The world leader will solidify his power following the Russian-led coalition's destruction.
- Two Old-Testament-type prophets will come on the world scene and preach about Christ while condemning the world's evil.
- Meanwhile, God will put His protection upon 144,000 Jews who have converted to Christianity so that they can begin to preach God's saving message to the people of the Tribulation.
- At the same time, God will allow a strong delusion to come over all who heard the gospel before the Rapture, but, fully understanding the offer of salvation, refused to accept Christ. These people will believe the lies of Antichrist and Satan.
- Antichrist, after months of trying, will finally murder the two Old-Testament-type prophets. But they will come back to life and be taken into heaven while the world watches.
- Antichrist will receive a supposedly deadly head wound.
- He will appear to resurrect from the dead, being now possessed by Satan.
- Antichrist will stand in the temple on Mount Moriah in Jerusalem. He will claim to be God and will demand worship.
- The False Prophet will direct all worship to Antichrist and will erect an image of him.
- Antichrist's regime will institute a computer mark-and-numbers system. It will be both to control the world's

populations and to cause all to worship Antichrist, whose
number in all of this is 666.

- Those who refuse to accept Antichrist's mark will be murdered.
  Beheading will apparently be the regime's chosen method of
  offing these "traitors."
- Antichrist will begin a systematic genocide against the
  Jewish race that will make Hitler's Holocaust look mild by
  comparison.
- He and the False Prophet will also have all the new believers
  they can find rounded up, tortured, then murdered.
- While Antichrist hunts down and murders people by the
  millions, God's judgments will begin to fall directly on the
  rebellious people of planet earth.
- Millions upon millions will die while God's wrath pours out
  in a series of three types of judgments, each consisting of seven
  specific penalties, for a total of twenty-one.
- When all is said and done, more than half, possibly as much as
  two-thirds, of all human life will die of the plagues.
- God will prepare, and the Jewish remnant will flee to, a hiding
  place, probably Petra, the ancient city carved in the rose red-
  colored rocks of the Jordanian wilderness.
- Antichrist and his forces, led by Satan, will pursue the Jewish
  people and try to murder them, but the pursuing forces will be
  swallowed up by the earth.
- While the Jews and many of the Gentiles still alive remain
  safely protected, God's wrath will fall in greater force.
- The sun will go partly dark, while at the same time heating up
  to seven times hotter than normal.
- A great object will fall into the ocean from space. Its impact
  will kill life in the sea and most likely will destroy coastal areas
  with tidal waves.
- Another asteroid or other mass from space will strike the earth
  and poison much of the planet's fresh-water sources.

- Great, unprecedented earthquakes will happen simultaneously all over the earth.
- People will be so frightened that they will have heart attacks, just from the things they see coming.
- A supernatural plague of huge, insect-like creatures will be released from the abyss, and they will sting all who have the mark of the beast. Men and women will try to commit suicide because of their great pain from the stings and bites of these demonic creatures.
- God will then move in the minds of all military forces on earth to gather in the valley of Jezreel, the plains of Esdraelon, near the ancient city of Megiddo. This is Armageddon.
- The "kings of the east," a huge army out of the Orient numbering more than two hundred million troops, will invade to make war with Antichrist and the other world's forces.

Antichrist, the man of sin, must even now be lurking just off camera, awaiting his moment to stand under the spotlight of Bible prophecy. If you know Jesus Christ as your Savior, you won't have to endure this wrath and these judgments. Again, here's how to escape the Antichrist and his Fourth Reich, Final Solution evil:

That if thou shalt confess with thy mouth the Lord Jesus, and shalt believe in thine heart that God hath raised him from the dead, thou shalt be saved.

For with the heart man believeth unto righteousness; and with the mouth confession is made unto salvation. (Romans 10:9–10)

5

Antichrist's Sidekick Rises

German führer Adolf Hitler had his close associate, chief propagandist Josef Goebbels. The Third Reich and the Final Solution flowed as much from the demon-directed mind of Goebbels as from the satanic evil that infected his earthly master's brain and soul. Together they set off on their hellish mission to enslave the world within the Nazi dictatorship.

Thankfully, they failed to accomplish their devilish goals. The ashes of both reside in the dust bin of history better left forgotten in the minds of many. However, the Jews living today whose parents somehow survived the Final Solution to produce them are reminded by the oldest of the surviving Holocaust victims or their immediate offspring.

"Never again!" is the declaration the House of Israel is exhorted to keep in the forefront of their minds. The Holocaust, in which six million or more of their numbers were burned in the furnaces of some of the killing centers among Chelmno, Belzec, Sobibor, Treblinka, Auschwitz-Birkenau, and Majdanek must never be forgotten. To forget will, it is feared, bring about a repeat of the genocide against them.

Sadly, and tragically, this exact fate lurks in the future of the children of Israel, according to Bible prophecy. This time it will be worse than in Hitler's Holocaust. Much, much worse.

The Jewish race will again appear in the crosshairs of a would-be world conqueror. The Jew will be the very object of his main focus of hatred, just as in the case of Hitler and his partner in genocide, Goebbels. That *final* führer will murder so many of God's chosen people that the Lord will secure a remnant of them in a special hiding place prepared especially for them.

Antichrist will be assisted in his demon-possessed rage by an associate even more hate-filled and evil than the dreaded chief propagandist of the Third Reich.

Both "beasts," as they're called in Revelation chapter 13 of the Bible, will at first appear to be the most benevolent and accommodating of all leaders. As a matter of fact, as we've seen already, the great leader will cause all antagonists of the wars raging around the world to sign on to a covenant that will bring all conflict to an end.

He will be almost universally hailed as a champion for world peace.

The assistant—Antichrist's sidekick—will promote in grandiose fashion the great man who will make Goebbels' proclamations of Hitler dim by comparison.

Bible prophecy foretells that the man of sin's peacemaking, using his charm stemming from his perceived glorious persona, will eventuate in his associate, the False Prophet, presenting him as the world's object of worship:

> And I beheld another beast coming up out of the earth; and he had two horns like a lamb, and he spake as a dragon.
>
> And he exerciseth all the power of the first beast before him, and causeth the earth and them which dwell therein to worship the first beast, whose deadly wound was healed. (Revelation 13:11–12)

The first beast, Antichrist, will, John the Revelator tells us, suffer a head wound that is deadly. But, somehow, he will revive to survive the apparent assassination. This great display of supernatural power—appearing to come back to life—no doubt will cause the world to be in awe. Thus there will be a great, swelling desire among the people to obey the second beast's direction to make an image to Antichrist and worship him by worshiping his image.

It isn't known for certain exactly what this means in total, but the brutal regime will see to it that Antichrist's associate, the False Prophet, will be obeyed. The whole world of earth dwellers, as God calls them, will wonder after the first beast, whose deadly wound is healed.

So this combination, Antichrist and his propaganda minister, the False Prophet, will make the world forget about all other dictators of history. Theirs will be far and away more deadly and all-encompassing than the combined regimes of Hitler, Stalin, Mao, and the rest of history's beastly reigns.

Yet those previous tyrants of history provide much prerequisite proof that people are more than capable of bringing down the cruelest of treatment upon fellow men, women, and children. Hitler and Goebbels are the prototype despotic regime to consider when thinking about what earth's last and deadliest tyrannical regime will be like.

As we've looked at before, prophecy observers have assigned, erroneously, a number of men in leadership positions the title of the future Antichrist. All have passed into history. Today, there are some in Europe whom the people prone to set dates and name names think will be the first beast of Revelation 13.

But there is an even stronger candidate today who, many believe, fits the mold of the man who will be Antichrist's sidekick. Pope Francis is that man. We can see, from his many statements that run contrary to what the Bible says on salvation and other issues, how those who set dates and name names could believe him to be the future Antichrist's chief associate.

We don't ascribe to naming anyone to either of those two roles. God's Word says that Antichrist—and, by association, the False Prophet—won't be known until the Rapture has taken place:

> Let no man deceive you by any means: for that day shall not come, except there come a falling away first, and that man of sin be revealed, the son of perdition;
>
> Who opposeth and exalteth himself above all that is called God, or that is worshipped; so that he as God sitteth in the temple of God, shewing himself that he is God. (2 Thessalonians 2:3–4)

We believe this passage foretells that Antichrist, the man of sin, won't be known, or "revealed," until the Rapture, or "falling away" (departure) comes first. The same must be said, then, for the False Prophet, the second beast of Revelation 13. It is the second beast who apparently comes on the scene later than the first. We make that conclusion based on the following:

> And I beheld another beast coming up out of the earth. (Revelation 13:11)

Certainly, he will have much power—the power of Satan, as a matter of fact. He will appear to be like a lamb, we're told, but he will be anything but. He will come speaking like a dragon—telling lies, because Satan, known as the "dragon," is called "the father of lies."

The people left behind after the Rapture will fall for the deceptive words of the False Prophet and Antichrist. They will have so rejected God and His governance that they will believe the great lie these two minions from hell will tell.

God will have given these people over to a "reprobate mind" (Romans 1: 28). God, 2 Thessalonians 2:11 tells us, will send the world of unbelievers "strong delusion that they should believe the lie."

We don't know what that lie will involve, but with the gullibility we see rampant today, even among believers, it isn't difficult to understand how the world will one day fall for the satanic deception of a man who will likely be history's greatest orator.

We can comprehend how mesmerizing Antichrist's oratory powers will be by considering Daniel's prophecy:

And the king shall do according to his will; and he shall exalt himself, and magnify himself above every god, and shall speak marvelous things against the God of gods, and shall prosper till the indignation be accomplished. for that that is determined shall be done. (Daniel 11:36)

Whereas Hitler and Goebbels mesmerized a nation, these future despots will captivate a world with their blasphemous rhetoric. They will be supernaturally endowed with the ability to seduce most of the world's population. Their powers will come from their father, the devil.

Let's look deeper into the second beast, his prophesied rise to power, and his influence on Antichrist's world of eternally lost followers.

His Rise to Power

The False Prophet comes onto the scene at some point after John sees the first beast, Antichrist, come out of the earth. It comes out of the sea of humanity, as John watches the composite animal emerge from his perspective of the vision somewhere high above the Aegean while exiled on Patmos. This animal is basically the same as the one Daniel saw in his vision (read Daniel 7). The beast John sees, like the one Daniel saw, is a merger of all the great world empires. However, it also includes the Antichrist world empire that will reign during the Tribulation period.

The next scene changes to the wicked personage called the second beast. He represents the third member of the infernal trinity. The dragon,

Satan, is a master counterfeiter. He mockingly produces his version of the Trinity (God the Father, God the Son, and God the Holy Spirit). In this evil consortium, Satan counterfeits God, Antichrist counterfeits the Son, and the False Prophet counterfeits the Holy Spirit.

The second beast, the False Prophet, will imitate God the Holy Spirit by mocking and mimicking the third member of the Godhead. Whereas God the Holy Spirit gives honor and glory to God, the Father, the third person of the unholy trinity, the False Prophet, will cause all of humanity to worship Antichrist and Satan.

He is called at first simply the beast that comes out of the earth. Later in Revelation, he is three times called the False Prophet and is closely associated with the first beast and Satan (Revelation 16:13, 19:20, 20:10).

> And I beheld another beast coming up out of the earth; and he had two horns like a lamb, and he spake as a dragon. (Revelation 13:11)

Dr. Henry Morris, one of the top scholars in biblical eschatology, writes:

> John, from his vision-perspective at Patmos sees another beast—the same type as the first—very dangerous and fierce. But this one, rather than coming from the sea, comes from the earth. instead of from the sea like the first beast. Since the first beast is a man, so is the second, but their backgrounds are different. As noted previously, "the sea" probably refers to the Mediterranean, the implication being that the first beast comes from one of the Mediterranean kingdoms. In fact, Daniel 9:27 suggests that he comes from the people of the ancient Roman empire, possibly a direct descendant of the Romans. By the same token, the second beast must come from somewhere in the great land masses

outside the Mediterranean nations, but we apparently have no other clue to his origin.

There has been much speculation as to the identity of this second beast. Since his is later called the false prophet, he apparently first comes to world attention as a miracle-working religious leader, professing to convey supernaturally inspired messages to mankind. His "prophecies," of course, are not from God but from Satan, though it may well be that he will first become known (possibly before the tribulation) as a man supposedly receiving messages from God. He professes to be a true prophet but is in reality a false prophet. Jesus warned of false Christs and false prophets (Matthew 24:24) in the great tribulation, and these two (the Antichrist and the false prophet) are the very prototypes of these two classes of deceivers.

Actually the term "antichrist" occurs only in the epistles of John (1 John 2:18; 4:3; 2 John 7) and is applied to anyone who deceives men by professing to serve God while at the same time denying the supernatural incarnation and the divine/human nature of Christ. However, the concept of "the antichrist" does occur often in both ancient and modern Christian literature, usually referring to the great antichristian world dictator of these last days. The second beast is interpreted by some writes (as Scofield, in his reference Bible) as the Antichrist, but this seems arbitrary. In any case, John calls them the beast and the false prophet here in Revelation and it does seem significant that he, as the author of the only New Testament verses in which the term "antichrist" is used, does not apply it in Revelation to either of these men. He had already, in fact, said that anyone who denied the coming of Jesus Christ in the flesh is "the antichrist" (the definite article is used this way in the 2 John reference).

This second beast is clearly a religious spokesman of some kind and possibly he is the leader of the world religious system as it will culminate in the last days, coming into its ultimate character as the great harlot of Revelation 17.

The modern ecumenical movement, active first among apostate Protestant churches in the first half of the twentieth century, then essentially combining (or at least fellowshipping) with the Catholic and Orthodox churches in the second half of the twentieth century, will eventually amalgamate with all other world religions, especially after the departure of all true churches to be with Christ.

This second beast, or false prophet, will most likely emerge as the patriarch (or pope, or ayatollah, or guru or, more likely, simply "prophet") of this universal religion. He will originally counterfeit the gentle character of Christ ("two horns like a lamb"), but his "inspired" words will be those of Satan, the old dragon. First they will be sweetly deceptive words, soon they will become deadly tyrannical, dragon words.[9]

These two satanically empowered beasts within human personas will join forces at some point, probably before the Tribulation begins. The man who will become Antichrist will likely have solidified power to some extent within the world system. We can safely expect the one who will become the False Prophet to be a notable religious leader. It will be a match made in hell.

And he exerciseth all the power of the first beast before him, and causeth the earth and them which dwell therein to worship the first beast, whose deadly wound was healed. (Revelation 13:12)

Dr. Morris weighs in on this evil duo:

The alliance of religion and state has a long and sad record of despotism and suppression, but the ecclesio-political union of these two human beasts will culminate in the worst period of persecution in the history of the world.

By the time the political power of the first beast is reaching its zenith, the syncretistic religious union of world religions is also being concentrated under control of the second beast. Each leader assists and supports the other, the king enforcing the religious authority of the prophet and the prophet persuading the world's superstitious masses that the king should be worshipped and obeyed as a god.

With his worldwide reputation as a miracle-working prophet already established, he will see that the remarkable pseudo-resurrection of the beast is widely publicized and idolized in every church and temple around the world as the chief argument to persuade people to acknowledge him as divine and deserving of worship. The two will soon become an unprecedented team, working in partnership to establish universal control over all people everywhere.[10]

And he doeth great wonders, so that he maketh fire come down from heaven on the earth in the sight of men. (Revelation 13:13)

His Influence

The second beast will be empowered by Satan to do great wonders and produce great signs that will hold spellbound the deluded people of earth. His reputation as a miracle worker will greatly enhance his power and authority over those under the regime of Antichrist's Fourth Reich.

Among these miracles will be the power to call down fire from the sky. Dr. Morris believed that special understanding and control of atmospheric phenomena by satanic angels will probably be imparted to the False Prophet to enable him to accomplish this and other miracles.

Undoubtedly, this wonder-worker will use his ability to produce fire from heaven. He will likely want to reproduce the miracles involving fire performed by God's two witnesses as given in Revelation.

These men will bring down fire and inflict other judgments of warning on rebellious earth-dwellers. The False Prophet will want to show those under his control that he has power equal to or greater than that wielded by God's men (Revelation 11:5).

Dr. Morris offered that even though the beast had prevailed against Christ's two witnesses and killed them, their resurrection and rapture was known around the world, and people still feared their power. It was important that people everywhere should see (perhaps on television) that the beast and False Prophet had powers similar to those of the witnesses.

The people on earth at this time who have rejected God have become totally susceptible to the deluding influences of demons. The deception is full blown, and the people will wonder in awe of the things they see, thus will go ever deeper into worship of Antichrist.

And deceiveth them that dwell on the earth by the means of those miracles which he had power to do in the sight of the beast; saying to them that dwell on the earth, that they should make an image to the beast, which had the wound by a sword, and did live. (Revelation 13:14)

It is documented that throughout the ages people have been easily seduced by those claiming to produce miracles. It seems that the more people discount and even outright deny or mock the miracles reported in God's Word, the more easily they become seduced by false wonder-workers. Such will be the case during the Tribulation era. People will deny God but grasp the demonic manifestations that delude.

Neither Satan nor his cohorts, the fallen angels, can produce miracles created by their own power. They don't have that power. Only God does. They can, however, manipulate natural matter to produce phenomena that mankind perceives to be miraculous activity.

Miracles must always be tested in relation to their purpose and fidelity to Scripture (Isaiah 8:20). Deluding miracles, the Bible warns, will become more and more manifest as Christ's Second Advent nears.

Morris writes:

> The Lord Jesus Christ warned: "For there shall arise false Christs, and false prophets, and shall shew great signs and wonders; insomuch that, if it were possible, they shall deceive the very elect" (Matthew 24:24). Paul, speaking probably of this same false prophet, says his "coming is after the working of Satan with all power and signs and lying wonders" (2 Thessalonians 2:9). His miracles are lying miracles, in that their purpose is to cause men to "believe the lie" (2 Thessalonians 2:11) that the "man of sin," with his image "sitting in the temple of God" is, as he is claiming, truly God (2 Thessalonians 2:3, 4).[11]

The False Prophet will, through delusion and pseudo miracles, bring about the evilest of all of Satan's plans for humanity. From it will burst forth Antichrist's own Final Solution, one that will make Adolf Hitler's seem mild by comparison. It will eventuate in the harlot religious system prophesied in Revelation chapter 17.

Counterfeit Church

Satan and his henchmen perpetrate the blasphemous counterfeit of the Holy Trinity, as we've just examined. Now the wickedness is taken by these hellish minions to an even more heinous level, when they seek to create the counterfeit of the Church produced by Jesus Christ.

God sees this counterfeit system of religious evil as a woman who is a harlot. The False Prophet will be at the head of this false worship system and will point all within its assemblage to worship Antichrist and Satan, who indwells him at the time the first beast sits in the Temple of God in Jerusalem and declares himself to be God.

"Harlot"—rendered "whore" in the King James Version—denotes a woman who prostitutes herself sexually. In Bible prophecy, the term is applied symbolically to a system of religion that rejects true doctrine from God's Word and gives itself totally to a false system of worship. Just as the true Church is known as the Bride of Christ, the harlot, as depicted in Revelation 17, can be likened to being the mistress of Antichrist. She comes from her father, the devil.

> And there came one of the seven angels which had the seven vials, and talked with me, saying unto me, Come hither; I will shew unto thee the judgment of the great whore that sitteth upon many waters:
>
> With whom the kings of the earth have committed fornication, and the inhabitants of the earth have been made drunk with the wine of her fornication.
>
> So he carried me away in the spirit into the wilderness: and I saw a woman sit upon a scarlet coloured beast, full of names of blasphemy, having seven heads and ten horns. And the woman was arrayed in purple and scarlet colour, and decked with gold and precious stones and pearls, having a golden cup in her hand full of abominations and filthiness of her fornication:
>
> And upon her forehead was a name written, MYSTERY, BABYLON THE GREAT, THE MOTHER OF HARLOTS AND ABOMINATIONS OF THE EARTH.
>
> And I saw the woman drunken with the blood of the saints, and with the blood of the martyrs of Jesus: and when I saw her, I wondered with great admiration. (Revelation 17:1–6)

This harlot church system will, many prophecy students and teachers believe, be made up of an eclectic mix of religions in the time following the Rapture of the true Church. The religious system, called

"Mystery Babylon," will work in concert with the Antichrist regime to enslave the world in every realm of life.

Many believe the ecumenical movement among the religions of the world and the falling-away within Christian church bodies from sound, fundamental doctrines are quickly moving the world toward this prophesied harlot system. Dr. John Walvoord, a scholar and writer considered to have been the dean of prophecy scholars while chancellor of Dallas Theological Seminary, addressed this troubling Bible prophecy for the Tribulation era.

> The great prostitute described in these verses is a portrayal of Apostate Christendom in the end time. When the Rapture occurred, all true believers were caught up to be with the Lord, but left behind were many thousands of those who made some profession of faith in Christ and claimed to be Christians who were not born again. These constituted the apostate Church which will dominate the scene politically and religiously up to the midpoint of that last seven years before the Second Coming.
>
> The apostasy, called adultery and fornication here, of course refers to spiritual unfaithfulness, not to physical adultery. The church, devoid of any redeeming influence, is now completely united with the world, and, as the passage indicates, is working hand in glove with the political powers.
>
> John saw a woman on a scarlet-colored beast with seven heads and ten horns. the beast is obviously the political empire described in 13:1–10. The fact that she is seated on the beast indicates that she is working with the beasts to attain common ends, that is, the subjugation of the entire world to their authority, and that the political power is supporting the apostate church. The woman wears the trappings of ceremonial religion in which purple and scarlet are prominent and which is often enhanced with precious stones. From the title written on her forehead, she is linked with the mystery of Babylon the Great. In

referring to this identification as a mystery, because its ultimate truth is learned only by divine revelation, the influence of Babylon for evil is supported in Scripture from as early as Genesis 11 and continues through the revelation of the destruction of the city in Revelation 18.

Babylon is the title that covers all false religions that claim to be Christian in their content. Babylonian influence clearly crept into the church, and much of its ritual is similar to the Babylonian religious rites.

When Babylon was introduced in Genesis 11, her true character was revealed as rebelling against God and attempting to build a tower in recognition of her worship of heathen deities. Because this was contrary to the Will of God, He confounded the language the people were using at that time so that they could not understand each other; hence, the term "Babel," meaning confusion, applies to the subsequent history of Babylon (cf. Gen. 11:9).

It should be borne in mind that the term "Babylon" applies to Babylonian religion; it also applies to the city of Babylon; and it applies to the empire of Babylon.

Babylon had a long history and rose to considerable prominence in the time of Hammurabi (1726-1686 B.C.)....

In this section, however, the revelation concentrates on the influence of Babylon religiously. Because the religion of Babylon was in the form of a secret religious rite in which they worshipped certain idols, it requires divine revelation to understand completely what they held. The wife of Nimrod, who was the founder of babylon, headed up the mystery religion. which characterized Babylon. She was given the name Semiramis, and according to the adherents' belief, she had a son conceived miraculously whose name was Tammuz. He was portrayed as a savior who fulfills the promise of deliverance given to Eve. This was, of course, a satanic description which permeates pagan religions....

The prophecy concerning Babylon here as well as other allusions to religion in the Book of revelation demonstrate that apostasy will have its final form in the Great tribulation in the worship of the world ruler and Satan.

In the period of the first half of the seven years leading up to the Second Coming of Christ, Babylon combined with Romanism becomes a world religion—Christian in name, but not in content. Those who do come to Christ will be subject to her persecution, and the woman is described as "drunk with the blood of the Saints" (Rev. 17:6). The apostate church has been unsparing in its persecution of those who have a true faith in Christ. Those who come to Christ in the end time will have the double problem of avoiding martyrdom at the hands of the political rulers and at the hands of the apostate church....

One of the outstanding, convincing arguments for worshipping the beast is the fact that he comes back from apparent death to life, as recoded in 13"3. the reference to the Abyss identifies the home of Satan and the demon world. The whole false religion found in Babylon is satanic in its origin and therefore is closely related to the demon world.

The purpose of the alliance between the woman and the beast is that both are seeking world domination. When this is finally achieved, as the end of the chapter indicates, the political power will no longer need the religious power to support it.[12]

The Harlot

The angel showed John the woman decked in gold and purple and with a golden chalice in her hands while riding the scarlet-colored beast. It was much like the one John and Daniel before him saw in their visions. Apparently, she represented all world empires, including the final one—Antichrist's regime.

The angel said the woman was "drunken on the blood of the saints." This is a horrendous picture! This is the Antichrist's—Satan's—Final Solution! It will be carried out under the False Prophet's religious system on behalf of Antichrist, who will no doubt be indwelt by Satan.

Millions upon millions will be martyred for the cause of Christ when the man of sin's power and authority become full blown. The False Prophet will cause all to worship the first beast or be beheaded.

This Final Solution will be designed to get rid of every Jew on the planet and every person who comes to know Christ for salvation during that time of the Fourth Reich. If this generation in which we live is approaching that time, the worst in all of human history, signals of the coming False Prophet and the man of sin are even now pulsing their warnings.

Dave Hunt wrote the following in considering the nearness of that approaching time of unprecedented troubles.

Christ warns us in Matthew 24 not to be deceived by false Christs and false prophets and lying signs and wonders. Paul repeats the warning, but with an added dimension: to beware of being deceived into thinking that the apostasy won't come. It will. It must. Surely Paul would not speak in this manner unless in the last days the popular view would be to reject the idea of apostasy within the church. The grave danger will be that of following false prophets who, with their signs and wonders, will seem to back up their false teaching that revival, not apostasy, is the order of the day. Paul therefore says, "Don't let anyone deceive you with sweet talk about revival: the apostasy must come or the day of the Lord cannot begin."

A False "Signs and Wonders" Movement

That fact becomes clearer when we refer to other passages of Scripture. Christ's statement about false signs and wonders is clarified as we are given further insights into the nature of the apostasy. False signs and wonders will be an integral part of the apostasy. The departure from the truth will be spearheaded by apparent miracle workers and the delusion will be made possible by a prevailing emphasis upon experience over doctrine. Paul says, "For the time will come when they will not endure sound doctrine" (2 Timothy 4:3). And Christ declares:

> Many will say to me in that day, Lord, Lord, have we not prophesied in thy name? and in thy name have cast out devils? and in thy name done many wonderful works? And then will I profess unto them, I never knew you: depart from me, ye that work iniquity. (Matthew 7:22, 23)

These apostates of whom Christ speaks did not lose their salvation, they were never saved ("I never knew you"). Yet they outwardly appeared to be high-profile Christian leaders apparently performing signs and wonders in the name of Christ. They didn't leave the church to become atheists or to join some non-Christian religion. They remained in the church. They even called Jesus Lord—but without really knowing Him. Tragically, they seemed to think that their ability to prophesy and to perform wonders proved that they belonged to Him. Clearly, doctrine is out and experience is in; and the signs and wonders are so impressive that doctrine no longer matters.

Surely these of whom Christ speaks in Matthew 7 must be the same "false Christs and false prophets" to whom He refers in Matthew 24. It is certainly sobering that the signs and wonders these false professors are able to perform are apparently so impressive that even the very elect might be deceived by them were they not given discernment by the Holy Spirit. We can only conclude that something more than mere trickery is involved.[13]

These wonder-workers are backed by the power of Satan, whom they unwittingly serve in the name of the Lord.

Jesus' first warning of things to look for in determining when the end of the age would come must be very important to this generation if we are in the last of the last days of the Church Age (Age of Grace).

> And as he sat upon the mount of Olives, the disciples came unto him privately, saying, Tell us, when shall these things be? and what shall be the sign of thy coming, and of the end of the world?
> And Jesus answered and said unto them, Take heed that no man deceive you. For many shall come in my name, saying, I am Christ; and shall deceive many.... And many false prophets shall rise, and shall deceive many. (Matthew 24:3–5, 11)

With the proliferation of prophetic signs that the end-times stage is being set for fulfillment of Bible prophecy, the False Prophet, along with the man who will be Antichrist, must lurk somewhere in the murky shadows of the immediate future.

6

Israel Signs Hellish Agreement

ntichrist, when he arrives on the world geopolitical scene, will be in the most deceptive disguise ever to obscure truth. One author of this book, Terry James, put it this way:

The first time I saw a television show was around 1950. Our neighbors, an older couple, invited me in each afternoon and allowed me to sit in their living room, with the grandmotherly lady, Omie, serving me home-baked cookies and a "pop" as we called soft drinks in Illinois during those days. It was heaven on earth for those thirty minutes to a boy of eight.

With the "William Tell Overture" thumping in the background, there galloped a huge, white horse, with his rider, who was wearing an equally white hat and a black mask. He was followed closely behind by a pinto horse with a man in fringed buckskin aboard.

That's right. It was Silver and Scout, carrying the Lone Ranger and Tonto, the masked man's ever-present companion.

On every program, the Lone Ranger would ride to the rescue in one situation or another. I remember sitting on pins and needles wondering if he would arrive in time during each episode. He always did, of course.

In the genre of heroic fiction, the protagonist, the "good guy," is frequently depicted as the man in the white hat—at least symbolically. We hear these heroes referred to in general terms as the "man on a white horse." He rides onto the scene with the purpose of righting all wrongs—setting everything as it should be once again.

In those episodes of the *Lone Ranger*, there was always a terrible situation for him to rectify. They were real nail-biters, even with the buffering of cookies and pop to help alleviate the angst.

The world is presently within a problematic time that will soon lead into an even worse time of trouble. As a matter of fact, the greatest of all prophets, the Lord Jesus Christ, said a time will come that will be worse than any other. He said it will be a time of "great tribulation." This is where we get the term "Tribulation," as applied to the seven years immediately preceding the Second Advent of Christ. We have seen so far that this era is also called Daniel's seventieth week; it's the same time frame of those seven years foretold by Jeremiah the prophet as a time of great trouble for God's chosen people, Israel: "Alas! for that day is great, so that none is like it: it is even the time of Jacob's trouble; but he shall be saved out of it" (Jeremiah 30:7).

These seven years of horror will follow the Rapture, and will be initiated with the signing of a covenant of false peace by a man, the "prince that shall come" (Daniel 9:26) who has come to be called Antichrist. The Scripture that speaks most specifically to this coming prince is one with which most students of Bible prophecy are thoroughly familiar:

And I saw when the Lamb opened one of the seals, and I heard, as it were the noise of thunder, one of the four beasts saying, Come and see. And I saw, and behold a white horse: and he that sat on him had a bow; and a crown was given unto him: and he went forth conquering, and to conquer. (Revelation 6:1–2)

We're given the picture of the first of the four horses of the Apocalypse as they carry their riders across the last seven years of human history just before Christ's Second Coming to earth. The first rider on that spectacular white steed is none other than Antichrist. As the prophecy says, he will come forth conquering everything and everyone in his path.

Most scholars and students from the fundamentalist camp who are of the pre-Millennial, Pre-Trib view of Bible prophecy believe the bow in this depiction indicates that this "prince" will come in on a peace platform. He has a bow, but displays no arrows. This is exactly the image the prophet Daniel was given to prophesy: "And through his policy also he shall cause craft to prosper in his hand; and he shall magnify himself in his heart, and by peace shall destroy many" (Daniel 8:25, a, b).

A "crown" is "given" to him, so apparently most of his conquests are like Hitler's were at the very beginning of his aggression. In the Führer's initial demands, he met almost no resistance. It seems the same might be the case when the future tyrant called Antichrist rides onto the scene. He will look like a great peacemaker and one who can reestablish order, which will no doubt have been all but totally destroyed. He will even promise prosperity, as Daniel's prophecy indicates: He will "cause craft to prosper."

However, he "will destroy many" through his conquests, his "peace-making," and his "causing craft to prosper." He will be wearing a mask, for sure, and his motives and intentions will be nothing like those of my childhood hero on his white horse who wore a mask for noble reasons. Antichrist's mask will camouflage for a time the greatest deception ever perpetrated on humanity.

World conditions will make the deception one most everyone will fall for, or will take the bait for, as they say, hook, line, and sinker.[14]

The first atomic explosion brought mankind to the brink of self-destruction. As a matter of fact, the scientists weren't at all certain that when the bomb ignited on that early morning at Alamogordo, New Mexico, the atmosphere itself wouldn't continue to explode in a chain reaction that could not be stopped. True to man's fallen nature and his tendency to destroy everything he touches, the scientists were willing to take the risk.

At the time of the first atomic test, the horrific facts about Hitler's murder of six million Jews were revealed before the eyes of the world. So great was the reaction that even the elite leaders who wanted to achieve one world government through the infant United Nations organization couldn't stop the sympathy for the Jews from producing the rebirth of Israel.

These two monumental events—the birth of the atomic bomb in 1945 and the rebirth of God's chosen nation three years later—set the stage for one of the most dramatic prophecies in the Bible regarding end-time matters.

Filling Up a Cup of Trembling

Again we come to Zechariah's forewarning about Jerusalem and the Middle East region, which God says He will make a "cup of trembling" for the whole world:

Behold, I will make Jerusalem a cup of trembling unto all the people round about, when they shall be in the siege both against Judah and against Jerusalem.

And in that day will I make Jerusalem a burdensome stone for all people: all that burden themselves with it shall be cut in pieces, though all the people of the earth be gathered together against it....

And it shall come to pass in that day, that I will seek to destroy all the nations that come against Jerusalem. (Zechariah 12:1–3, 9)

The cup is filled with an interesting mixture indeed—one of ancient hatreds, nuclear weaponry, and Mideast oil. The Lord didn't fill up this cup of deadly ingredients; fallen mankind did. God simply says He will use man's own sinful mixture to bring this world system to a conclusion so that His Messiah, Jesus Christ, can restore order on this dying, decaying planet.

The cleansing scheduled to take place will see pillars of fire mixed with the blood of the rebels opposed to God. A number of places in the Bible describe warfare that might be nuclear, such as the scene described in Joel 2:2–3, which predicts that on "a day of darkness and gloominess, a day of clouds and of thick darkness…a fire devoureth before them; and behind them a flame burneth."

Even the remaking of the earth at the end of the millennium seems to be thermonuclear. But, this is not surprising. Science has told us for many years about the nature of the atom, which is held together in a way no one really can explain. The electron, neutron, proton, etc., revolve and stick to each other in some mysterious way. Yet, at the same time, the atom gives off great heat and energy.

Jesus, of course, ultimately holds all matter together (see Colossians 1:17). It is Jesus, not the false peacemakers who want to rule the world, who will take the burning fuse from the nuclear nightmare and bring real peace:

The way of peace they know not; and there is no judgment in their goings: they have made them crooked paths: whosoever goeth therein shall not know peace. (Isaiah 59:8)

Satan's Signature

Satan's first attempt to establish world government was stopped when God personally came to earth and stopped it. The Genesis 11 account of the tower-builders of Babel on the plains of Shinar is the story of humanism, mankind's philosophy about who should be in charge. That philosophy puts forward the declaration that man can take care of himself and the planet without any help or interference from God. Actually, humanism declares, according to its champions like German philosopher Friedrich Nietzsche, that "God is dead."

Today there is a movement back to the attitude of the tower builders. Satan's fingerprints are all over present-day attempts to kick the Creator off the planet. We see this in our own nation's recent history.

Prayer and Bible reading in public schools were stopped by Supreme Court decisions in 1963. In 1973, the High Court's decision in the abortion case, *Roe v. Wade*, began the killing of more than sixty-five million babies in their mothers' wombs, at last estimates.

Since those decisions, the US has endured a rise in deadly violence in public schools. Life, in the view of many young people, seems to have been cheapened to the point that murder, rather than playground scuffles, is taking place with more regularity in school hallways and classrooms. Humanism is increasingly ingrained in the thinking of our students. The philosophy is "do what is right in your own eyes," echoing the warning in Proverbs: "The way of a fool is right in his own eyes" (Proverbs 12:15).

The ultimate humanist does what is right in his own eyes; he becomes a law unto himself. Satan's world dictator, Antichrist, will be that ultimate humanist.

The global power brokers are gathering to play God. They think they can force peace upon the rest of us. These internationalist governmental leaders and politicians intend to put an end to war so their New World Order can bring heaven to earth.

The true Christ, of course, is always left out of their plans. The whole world will one day, however, accept a false Christ who promises that elusive thing called peace. Satan will at last have achieved putting his Antichrist in place as absolute ruler of this fallen world. He won't bring peace, but will bring mankind's worst war ever. When the Lord lifts His mighty hand of restraint from the earth, all peace will disappear. God will give the humanists enough rope, and they will hang themselves.

The Dotted Line...

Daniel was given a staggering prophecy for the end of the age:

> And after threescore and two weeks shall Messiah be cut off, but not for himself: and the people of the prince that shall come shall destroy the city and the sanctuary; and the end thereof shall be with a flood, and unto the end of the war desolations are determined.
>
> And he shall confirm the covenant with many for one week: and in the midst of the week he shall cause the sacrifice and the oblation to cease, and for the overspreading of abominations he shall make it desolate, even until the consummation, and that determined shall be poured upon the desolate. (Daniel 9:26–27)

The prophecy indicates a peace process presided over by the devil himself. The satanically possessed human called Antichrist will force the peace "that will destroy many."

Not only will Israel fall for the false peace plan, but the entire world will eagerly accept it. The fear no doubt generated by what happens in the aftermath of the Rapture will be so great that everyone, fearing nuclear devastation, will sign on.

The rider on the second of the horses of Apocalypse (Revelation 6), the red one, most prophecy observers believe, represents war unlike that ever experienced on the planet. It is at this time when nuclear exchanges will likely take place between nations, whereas the atomic genie had previously been kept bottled up by God's staying hand. When the Holy Spirit withdraws as restrainer (2 Thessalonians 2), that hand will be lifted and war will break out on an unprecedented scale.

With the end of civilization on the immediate horizon as a result of the fearful things the leaders of the nations see coming, they will agree to put aside all disagreements—or at least some—for a time. A real cry for peace and safety will indeed be heard around the globe.

The great leader who will become Antichrist will appear to be the savior of the world. His reputation will no doubt begin its most dramatic ascent from the time he seduces all into signing on to the covenant of a peace God says is a contract made "with death and hell" (Isaiah 28:16, 18).

From the point of Israel's agreement to follow the Antichrist and his peace plan, things will heat up—literally, in nuclear fire, no doubt. After war breaks forth with the rider on the red horse, the rider on the black horse will follow, indicating great famine and starvation throughout the earth. Then will come death, with the lost souls of the famine and carnage going into hell because of unbelief. This is prophesied in the symbol of the *chloros,* or greenish-colored, horse and rider, the fourth rider of Revelation 6.

Israel signing onto the covenant made with death and hell will initiate the worst time in all of history. Again, Jesus said it will be so horrendous that if He didn't return to put an end to it, no flesh would survive (Matthew 24:25–26).

So Antichrist will emerge from the revived Roman Empire. Wars will continue until the Tribulation reaches its conclusion. Daniel's 9:27 prophecy stipulates that from the time the temple and Jerusalem are destroyed until the end of human history, there will be no true peace.

The prince to come will make and sign a covenant of security or peace for one week—that is, seven years. After three and a half years of the treaty, however, he will break the agreement, beginning what Jesus called the Great Tribulation and what Jeremiah 30:7 refers to as a time of great trouble, the likes of which no one has ever seen before or will ever see again. This is also called the apocalypse.

The first part of these awesome prophecies has been fulfilled, as we've already seen when, in AD 70, General Titus attacked the rebels in Jerusalem and his troops completely destroyed the temple—just as Jesus had predicted. Many prophecies, however, are yet to be fulfilled. Growing global talk of peace proves that tremendous pressure is building. Not only Mideast war and peace are at issue, but world peace is at stake.

One of the most noted scholars in eschatology, Dr. J. Dwight Pentecost, presented a perspective on the matter of the covenant of Daniel 9: 26 and the turmoil that results from Israel's accepting this false peace agreement:

According to Daniel 9:26–27 the prince of the Roman empire will make a covenant with Israel for a seven year period. This covenant evidently restores Israel to a place among the nations of the world and the integrity of Israel is guaranteed by the Roman powers. This is not only an attempt to settle the long standing dispute among the nations as to Israel's claim to Palestine, but is also a satanic imitation of the fulfillment of the Abrahamic covenant which gave Israel title deed to the land. This action is pictured by John (Rev. 6:2) as a rider going forth to conquer, to whom sovereignty is given by peaceful negotiations. This condition exists for three and one-half years, after which the covenant is broken by the Roman authorities and the period known as the great tribulation (Matt. 24:21) begins. This tribulation on the earth is evidently caused by Satan, who has been cast out of heaven into the earth at the middle of the tribulation period (Rev. 12:9). He goes forth in great wrath (Rev. 12:12) to attack the remnant of Israel and the saints of God (Rev. 12:17). The Satanic activity that moves nations in those days is clearly depicted by John when he says:

"And I saw three unclean spirits like frogs come out of the mouth of the dragon, and out of the mouth of the beast, and out of the mouth of the false prophet. For they are the spirits of devils, working miracles, which go forth unto the kings of the earth and of the whole world, to gather them to the battle of that great day of God Almighty" [Revelation 16:13–14].

This is not to infer that this period is not the period of God's wrath upon sinful men, but it does show that God, to pour out His wrath, permits Satan to execute a program in his wrath against the whole world.

There are a number of theories as to the events in the campaign of Armageddon: (1) Armageddon will be a conflict between the Roman empire and the northern confederacy; (2) it will be a conflict between the Roman empire and the kings of the east, or the Asiatic powers; (3) Armageddon will be a conflict between all nations and God; (4) it will be a conflict between four great world powers; (5) it will be a conflict between the Roman empire, Russia, and the Asiatic powers; (6) it will exclude Russia, but will take place between the Roman, eastern, and northern powers which will exclude Russia, based on the theory that Ezekiel 38 and 39 takes place in the millennium; (7) Russia is the only aggressor at Armageddon, based on the theory that there will be no revived form of the Roman empire. One can see what a wide divergence of opinion there is as to the chronology of events in this campaign.[15]

Israel today stands in the bull's eye of rage. This is true in the case of it being targeted by the Jewish state's perennial antagonists, the Arab and Persian Islamist enemies. It is true in the case of the entire international community, whose constituent nations see Israel as the congestive blockage to regional and world peace while this beleaguered planet wobbles toward a time of unprecedented trouble.

As we've seen, that coming time of unparalleled strife that will bring all nations to Armageddon is termed "the time of Jacob's trouble" by Isaiah: "Alas! for that day is great, so that none is like it: it is even the time of Jacob's trouble" (Jeremiah 30:7a). And, it is Jacob's trouble—the prophesied end-of-days, dastardly treatment of Israel by the nations of earth—that will cause the God of heaven to bring them to Armageddon. This is what the prophet Joel foretells:

> I will also gather all nations, and will bring them down into the valley of Jehoshaphat, and will plead with them there for my people and for my heritage Israel, whom they have scattered among the nations, and parted my land. (Joel 3:2)

Armageddon Beckons

This will be the gathering of the nations of earth predicted in the book of Revelation:

> For they are the spirits of devils, working miracles, which go forth unto the kings of the earth and of the whole world, to gather them to the battle of that great day of God Almighty....
> And he gathered them together into a place called in the Hebrew tongue Armageddon. (Revelation 16:14, 16)

This will be the culmination of mankind dealing treacherously with God's chosen people. The promise the Lord made to Abraham includes severe repercussions for anyone who would curse the progeny of Abraham, Isaac, and Jacob:

And I will bless them that bless thee, and curse him that curseth thee: and in thee shall all families of the earth be blessed. (Genesis 12:3)

History Validates Prophecy

God's declaration is most dramatically validated by looking at twentieth-century history. As we have seen, Adolf Hitler and the Nazi regime made hatred of and genocide against the Jew their focus of the unalloyed evil they spewed. The ashes of the führer and of his Nazi colleagues are scattered in ignominious disgrace across the landscape across the nations that Josef Goebbels and the Nazi propagandists arrogantly boasted would be über allies in the all-powerful homeland for their thousand-year Reich.

Any consideration in research of Germany's history involving the last two years of World War II and the period immediately following must acknowledge that it was as if the very wrath of God was upon the nation. Such documentation includes black-and-white footage of German men and women forced by Allied Commander General Dwight D. Eisenhower to walk by the skeletal remains of thousands of Jewish corpses—thus, Eisenhower stated, so that the German people and the world would never forget the Holocaust. Its aftermath would forever be recorded.

Yet today, even mainstream news journalists are fuzzy-minded in consideration of the genocide that took perhaps six million Jewish lives as well as the lives of other peoples. They show their loss of memory by not jumping full-force down the throats of diabolists like Iranian dictators, who regurgitate the lie that the Holocaust is a fable conjured by the Jews of the world. Rarely is there a repudiation of such blatant falsehoods coming from the would-be destroyers of the Jewish state and the Jewish people.

Tragically, the refusal to educate generations following World War II on the truth about the insane treatment of the House of Israel is leading to a time of even greater atrocities, thus judgment. The God of heaven will react violently—more violently, even, than He reacted to the death-dealing of the Nazi demoniacs.

We've seen the warning before, and it cannot be overemphasized:

> The burden of the word of the LORD for Israel, saith the LORD, which stretcheth forth the heavens, and layeth the foundation of the earth, and formeth the spirit of man within him.
>
> Behold, I will make Jerusalem a cup of trembling unto all the people round about, when they shall be in the siege both against Judah and against Jerusalem.
>
> And in that day will I make Jerusalem a burdensome stone for all people: all that burden themselves with it shall be cut in pieces, though all the people of the earth be gathered together against it.
>
> ...it shall come to pass in that day, that I will seek to destroy all the nations that come against Jerusalem. (Zechariah 12:1–3, 29).

Will America Betray Israel?

Now we come to this question: Will Israel be betrayed by the US?

It is a valid question, because we've witnessed within the past decade a presidential administration dealing treacherously with America's chief ally in the Middle East. Will there come a future president and State Department who will deal treacherously with Israel?

US President Barack Obama's special Middle East envoy, George Mitchell, threatened at one point in 2010 to withhold financial aid to Israel if the Jewish state didn't accept demanded concessions to get the stalled peace process back on track. The Obama administration threatened to withhold aid if Israel didn't comply. It was an act that, in our view, cursed Israel.

America, the nation almost certainly brought into existence to stand with God's chosen people during Israel's rebirth into modernity, has been blessed beyond measure. We must ask whether anti-Israel subterfuge within a US State Department and intelligence agency cabal is at work still to harm the Jewish state. We have—before, during, and after the 2016 presidential election—seen the attempts to overturn a duly-elected president. It isn't beyond reason to wonder if this same cadre of unlawful operatives is leading the way into setting up the worldwide anti-Israel marginalization prophesied by Zechariah.

America's "Christianity"?

Refusal of the former American presidential administration to acknowledge that God has any say one way or the other in the affairs of people, much less any business meddling in the conduct of the American State Department's dealings with Israel and its antagonists, is a foregone conclusion. After all, Mr. Obama himself stated that America is not a Christian nation.

We must say that we agree with this president on that point. The United States was never a "Christian" nation, in the sense that America turned *en masse* to total commitment to following Jesus Christ. That has never happened. However, this country, since its earliest stages of planning by the founding fathers, has had woven into its national documents of inception Judeo-Christian principles for conducting life and government.

Based on that easily provable truth—because all it takes is a quick scan of the founding documents to recognize its biblical influence—it's easy to know that America is a nation under providential watchfulness, to say the very least. God, in starkly plain language, spoke through prophetic omniscience to what will happen when anyone, be it individual or corporate, deals treacherously with His chosen people. Therefore, for anyone—including the president of the United States or any other member of the government of this nation—to ignore what is said in the Bible about interacting with Israel is foolhardiness.[16]

Human Government Oblivious to God's Will

We realize stating that governmental leaders don't recognize God in their governing isn't a profound revelation, because humanistic leadership ignores the Creator of all things. We just wanted to get the fact stated as to the real crux of the problem regarding the lack of lasting peace in the Middle East and around the world. While this administration is a strong supporter of Israel in many ways, it's obvious that the State Department and intelligence agencies' deep-state operatives give God's Word on the matter of Israel no weight whatsoever in considering policy toward the Jewish state. Resisting the president's own plan for dealing fairly with all parties in the peace process, they forge ahead, setting timelines for producing a two-state solution to the "Palestinian problem" as they see it.

When one State Department official was asked in an interview what leverage the US has to get Israel to comply with Arab and international demands, he said, "Under American law, the United States can withhold support on loan guarantees to Israel."

Thankfully, America currently has a president who is perhaps Israel's staunchest of any supporters to this point in our nation's history. Much of Congress, particularly in the US Senate, stands strongly behind the Jewish state. But one day, a covenant of false peace that God considers coming straight from the pit of hell will be forced upon Israel and the other nations of the world. Ramifications will be massive for all who sign on to Antichrist's document of deception.

If America joins the rest of the nations in the gathering against Israel, as prophesied in Zechariah 12:1–3, her betrayal will mean America's doom. All nations who come against the Jewish state, God says, will be cut to pieces. Israel, on the other hand, will remain no matter what, He declares in the strongest possible terminology.

Again:

This is what the Lord says, "He who appoints the sun to shine by day, Who decrees the moon and stars to shine by night, Who stirs up the sea so that its waves roar—the Lord Almighty is His Name;

Only if these ordinances vanish from My sight," declares the Lord, "will the descendants of Israel ever cease to be a nation before Me." (Jeremiah 31:35–36)

7

Rise of Global Government

Satanic rage exploded following the presidential election of 2016 in America. Never in the history of the nation had there been an all-out effort to destroy a presidency. The effort was clear from the very outset—even before the inauguration took place in January 2017.

The United States was clearly on track to having its sovereignty dissolved in order to meld with the burgeoning internationalist blueprint for a changed world order. A new president declared he planned to "drain the swamp" and "make America great again." Draining the swamp meant removing entrenched bureaucrats who wanted the nation to continue down the road toward globalism. Making America great again meant that the new president wanted to bring the country to the full achievement capacity he saw as still within America's people.

We saw the development of the term "deep state," the name given the cabal within the US government and other governments of the world devoted to creating a one-world system of control. Although this term and the considerations behind it are called conspiratorial lunacy and even worse, the evidence that the deep state exists is indelibly etched within the fabric of geopolitics.

America's intelligence agencies—FBI, CIA, NSA, and others—in conjunction with a political party in opposition to the newly elected president, were caught in efforts to falsely accuse him in order to, we charge, achieve a *coup d'état*. The mainstream news—networks and cable outlets that are supposed to report, not create, the news—joined in to try to bring down President Donald J. Trump.

The effort continues to the time of this writing. We remember the "Russian collusion" charges against him. That charge was boiled into an impeachment that had at its base nothing but overtly manifested hatred at its core. It failed in every respect, and the president emerged more popular and stronger than ever, especially with his staunch supporter base.

The coup, although a silent one, continues, and—again, in our opinion—the COVID-19 pandemic has been used to try to accomplish what their lies, false accusations, and other evil machinations couldn't. Still, all the nefarious doings by these internationalist cabalists are not at the heart of the attempt to remove this president and bring globalism back to its state of progress prior to his election. A much more powerful evil festers at the center of the rage, and it's wrapped up in the apostle Paul's words of alert and warning:

> For we wrestle not against flesh and blood, but against principalities, against powers, against the rulers of the darkness of this world, against spiritual wickedness in high places. (Ephesians 6:12)

Dictatorships throughout history have made it their all-consuming purpose to control the masses in their death-dealing grip that tightens at every opportunity. Without exception, tyrants begin regime-building with promises directed at individual citizens, assuring life better than before—usually declaring that prestige and powerful influence will be restored to the homeland. Safety and security will remove all fear from daily life, and peace will prevail under the leadership of the yet-to-be-unveiled tyrant's absolute rule.

Despots vault to their position of power when vigilance against such evil diminishes during times of deepening, seemingly unsolvable, economic hardship.

We look around at the tremendous damage the COVID-19 pandemic has done to the economic situation in America and the world and think how bad things might eventuate as a result. Such devastation is coming that the coronavirus' destruction will look mild by comparison. That which is coming will be a time of hardship, the depths of which humanity has never experienced. We can say this with certainty because Jesus Christ foretold the following about that time:

> For then shall be great tribulation, such as was not since the beginning of the world to this time, no, nor ever shall be. (Matthew 24:21)

Just as the times will be the worst in human history, as we've seen, so a tyrant of unprecedented evil will come forth, wielding the most dictatorial power ever. As mentioned, human government has always sought ever-increasing authority—more and more power that is held by a circle of as few elite oligarchs as possible. These construct ever more restrictive rules and regulations and increasingly draconian methods of keeping their victims under control.

The United States has enjoyed more than two centuries of relative freedom from this kind of government that has afflicted the nations and empires down through history. Still, there has been a growing trend toward such government in America. Humanistic infection has now set in, and this greatest experiment in liberty that has ever been attempted is in the throes of decline.

As mentioned in the "deep state" references, there are forces that desire to bring this once-great republic down so the way will be clear for those who want such change to reshape the entire world in the evil ways they imagine. These forces are constituted by both human and supernatural entities. Again, let's examine Paul's words to understand the threat:

> For we wrestle not against flesh and blood, but against principalities, against powers, against the rulers of the darkness of this world, against spiritual wickedness in high places. (Ephesians 6:12)

Satan's supernatural minions rule the minds of fallen mankind—people of the mindset to establish worldwide control over everyone else. We see this malevolent force at work through never-ceasing attempts by the so-called progressive ideology to change America into a nation far from the principles applied by the founding fathers. Their chief human allies are mainstream media. But their unseen and much more influential allies are the powers and principalities of Ephesians 6:12—spiritual cronies who truly bring the power to make changes in ways contrary to God's.

That supernatural wrestling match has had a profound effect on the nonbelieving world. Those who don't know Jesus Christ as Lord and Savior fall prey to the minions, both human and spiritual, who make up the principalities and powers about which Paul forewarns. The following research makes manifest the deluding influence that's especially on the youth of this generation:

> Current voters may reject the globalist agenda, but according to several surveys, future voters don't. Globally, the Millennials (those born between 1981 and 1996) outnumber both the Baby Boomers and Generation X, and they believe the concept of being a citizen of a single country is outdated. To them, global citizenship is the way of the future. In 2017, Western Union surveyed more than ten thousand millennials from fifteen coun-

tries, including the United States, India, and Russia. What they found provides a glimpse of where we're heading in the years to come. Here are just a few of the results:

- 79% believe limitless movement around the world will empower them.
- 29% believe a single global currency will "foster great global unity."
- 61% believe global institutions like the United Nations are more representative of them versus national (48%) or local governments (44%).

In the 2016 Global Shapers Annual Survey, more than twenty-six thousand Millennials from 181 countries gave their opinions on world issues. Results included:

- 48% of Millennials see climate change as the most serious issue the world faces.
- When it comes to solving global problems, respondents say they trust international organizations (26%) more than they trust themselves (20%).
- 36% of respondents view themselves as global citizens. This is a higher number than those who view themselves as national citizens (22%) or members of a religion (9%).

Many young people see themselves as global citizens first. They think borders should be open. They believe climate change is the world's top problem, and they look to global political institutions for answers. This gives us a glimpse of what the world will look like in the future. Why? Because Millennial opinions will shape the world in the coming decades.

Adolf Hitler once said, "When an opponent declares, 'I will

not come over to your side,' I calmly say, 'Your child belongs to us already. You will pass on. Your descendants, however, now stand in the new camp. In a short time, they will know nothing else but this new community.'"

The globalists don't need to win today's elections because they've already won a generation of children.[17]

Globalism's Siren Song

Powerful humanistic allurements beckon seductively, promising a golden future if all of earth's people will come together as one. Such a glorious world order, long dreamed about and even fervently pursued, seems at last achievable. Those who hold the worldview that national boundaries must fall and sovereignties must diminish because we are all world citizens passionately embrace the earth-shrinking technologies that science continues to produce—the Internet, for example. Yes, the utopian dream at last seems achievable. However, while the sirens of globalism—like the twin sisters who lured unwary sailors to their deaths in Homer's *The Odyssey*—sing their lovely, mesmerizing songs of New World Order, the words pronounced by the Ancient of Days reverberate through the corridors of antiquity and leap at this generation from the pages of God's Holy Word:

Behold, the people are one and they have all one language, and this they begin to do; and now nothing will be restrained from them which they have imagined to do. (Genesis 11:6)

The Creator of all things was not expressing His pride in mankind. He was concerned and saddened because all peoples of that time were united in their determination to build a world to their own specifications. Did this very first globalist effort displease the One who built into people the marvelous ability to do whatever they could imagine?

The Cradle of Globalism

It seems at first glance a supreme paradox: The Creator made people in His own image, gifting us with powerful conceptual abilities, and thus with the ingenuity to build a tower that could ultimately reach into the heavens. Then, just as we began to fulfill our potential, the infallible Creator God manifested His displeasure in the people of that day:

> The whole earth was of one language and of one speech.
> And it came to pass as they journeyed from the east that they found a plain in the land of Shinar, and they dwelt there.
> And they said to one another, Come, let us make bricks and bum them thoroughly.
> And they had brick for stone, and slime had they for mortar.
> And they said, Go to, let us build a city and a tower whose top may reach unto heaven; and let us make us a name, lest we be scattered abroad upon the face of the whole earth.
> And the Lord came down to see the city and the tower, which the children of men built.
> And the Lord said, Behold, the people are one and they have all one language, and this they begin to do; and now nothing will be restrained from them which they have imagined to do.
> Come, let us go down and there confound their language, that they may not understand one another's speech.
> So the Lord scattered them abroad from there upon the face of all the earth, and they left off building the city.
> Therefore is the name of it called Babel, because the Lord did there confound the language of all the earth; and from there did the Lord scatter them abroad upon the face of all the earth. (Genesis 11:1–9)

God Almighty gave the human race a touch of His own genius, but when those people used it in this rebellious way, He confused that genius by disrupting their ability to communicate, thereby putting an end to the globalist project. God's dealings with His creation seemed incongruous: Did He change His mind about having made us in His own image? Did He resent competition in matters involving the creativity this building project might have represented?

Why did He break up the one-world building effort at Babel?

Image of God, Imagination of Man

God puts His mighty finger upon the answer to that question, and His answer at the same time pierces to the heart of the reason He had to destroy by flood the entire antediluvian world, with the exception of Noah, his family, and select animal life.

The cause of why God scattered the Babel builders, thereby ending their venture in globalism, is found even farther back in human history than the era of the Flood. God's Word records about those ancient times and His divine judgment:

> The Lord smelled a sweet savor; and the Lord said in his heart, I will not again curse the ground anymore for man's sake; for the imagination of man's heart is evil from his youth; neither will I again smite anymore every thing living, as I have done. (Genesis 8:21)

The key thought from the mind of God for our purposes here is "the imagination of man's heart is evil from his youth." Let's examine this indictment in the framework of its context.

God declared that He would never again curse the ground as He did following man's rebellion in the Garden of Eden. Neither, He said, would He ever again smite all living things as He did with the worldwide Flood of Noah's day. God placed between these two promises the statement of truth about the fallen state of man, a fact absolutely rejected by today's humanistic social architects. Their denial of this reality is at the core of globalism. So, too, is the demented assertion that man is evolving toward a higher order of being that will ultimately produce heaven on earth—peace, prosperity, and love for all mankind.

Adam and Eve's God-attuned senses must have changed from perfection to imperfection in one cataclysmic moment. What a heart-wrenching scene it must have been when they willfully disobeyed God, choosing instead to yield to the tempter, who told them they would be as God when they ate from the tree of knowledge of good and evil. How devastating that eternity-rending moment must have been when those magnificently beautiful humans discarded the effulgence of God that had shrouded their nakedness. The image of God emanating from within their beings must have begun to dissipate, to change into frightening, darkened countenances. So, too, their minds no doubt became convoluted within their sin-infected thought processes. Both image and imagination in that moment altered into a perpetual state of opposition to the Creator with whom they had previously walked in perfect trust and love along the garden's lush pathways.

Mankind's course has been spiraling downward since that willful decision by the first man to do what was right in his own eyes rather than obey God. The Fall brought a curse upon the earth and death to mankind. Every generation since Adam and Eve were evicted from Eden contributes ample proof that "the heart is deceitful above all things, and desperately wicked" (Jeremiah 17:9).

From the first murder, when Cain slew his brother, Abel, to the slaughter during the more than fifteen thousand wars of recorded history, to the most recent terrorist atrocity or one-on-one killing, fallen man continues through vile actions to testify to the truth of God's indictment: "The imagination of man's heart is evil from his youth" (Genesis 8:21).

Babel Revisited

We make the mystery of the paradox more understandable when we reconsider these fascinating facts. God, who is perfect in all His ways, created humankind perfectly, actually making us in His own image. Once again, we realize that He gifted us with a powerful imagination so that whatever we could imagine, we could eventually do. However, when we began to use that imagination in building a tower that would reach into heaven, God was displeased and stopped the project by confounding the language of the builders, then scattering them abroad. We again consider the question: If a perfect God created a perfect person, why did God act in such a seemingly harsh manner when the creature used God-given talent as recounted in the story of Babel?

The answer, of course, is that God also created us with free moral will. The creature wasn't made a robot, but was made with brilliant conceptual abilities and given freedom of choice—which includes discernment for choosing wisely. But Adam chose to disobey God, so sin entered the world. The human bloodstream became instantly contaminated by the infection. The minds of the people, including their imaginations, became dark in the mystery of iniquity that engulfed them.

The paradox understood, the question is now answerable: What is wrong with people coming together in a united effort to construct a one-world order to achieve peace, prosperity, and love for all mankind? The answer is that we are spiritually separated from the Creator because of original sin. Our thinking is therefore fatally flawed. Nothing good can come from thinking and planning that excludes God.

Had God allowed the globalists of Nimrod's day to continue their tower project, He would have had to ultimately curse the earth again as He did when Adam disobeyed, or He would have had to destroy all living things upon the earth as He did because of the corruption that required cleansing by the great Flood of Noah's day. God wasn't acting harshly at Babel, nor was He acting contrary to His perfect character. Rather, He was displaying unfathomable love by keeping His promises to the tiny fallen creature who deserved judgment and for whom He would one day sacrifice His only begotten Son.

The World-Order Schemers

Children of the tower of Babel builders today carry on the globalist agenda despite the differences in language and geographical separation. They circumvent the barriers through use of technologies designed to serve their one-world purposes.

The obsessive drive toward bringing all men, women, and children into one global configuration arose shortly after the time Jesus Christ walked the earth. It is perhaps indicative of our sordid day that since the time He walked the earth in the flesh, this era has been called "AD," an abbreviation of the Latin *anno domini*, "the year of the Lord," but now we are to acknowledge that we live in the period of human history called the "Common Era," or CE. The revisionists, you see, demand that all vestiges of Jesus Christ be erased—even from our lexicon. There must be many ways for the people of the coming New World Order to come to God, if indeed there is a God.

Jesus Christ, who said He is the "way and the truth and the life" and that "no one comes to the Father" but through Him (John 14:6) simply doesn't fit the globalist mold. Thinkers who formed that mold wanted there to be no doubt that people, through intellect, can do whatever they imagine. They can build a perfect world without input from any deity who might or might not be out there somewhere. This arrogant attitude of self-sufficiency is summed up in the document titled "The Declaration of Interdependence," released by the United Nations' World Affairs Council on January 30, 1976. It reads in part:

Two centuries ago, our forefathers brought forth a new nation; now we must join with others to bring forth a new world order. To establish a new world order...it is essential that mankind free itself from limitations of national prejudice.... We affirm that the economy of all nations is a seamless web, and that no nation can any longer effectively maintain its processes for production and monetary systems without recognizing the necessity of collaborative regulation by international authorities. We call upon all nations to strengthen the United Nations and other institutions of world order.[18]

The zeal for stampeding everyone into a totally controlled global village hasn't subsided. Elitist power brokers continue to fuel the humanist engine that drives the globalist machinery with grandiose declarations and promises of heaven on earth.

As we've seen the deep-state, surreptitious coup attempts to overturn a presidential election, it is prudent and wise to keep one eye on God's prophetic Word and the other on daily, even hourly, news reports. Even now the stage is being set by Satan and his minions, both human and spiritual, for erecting the platform from which will launch the man who will be Antichrist.

Those who are God's children shouldn't look with trepidation upon these foreboding harbingers of the coming Tribulation. However, it's abundantly obvious that developments we've seen in wave after wave of UN intrusions into the lives of Americans should make all of us know that real agendas and activities lie behind our concerns.

All the World as One

Neo-Babel builders construct even their music in a way that clearly demonstrates the luciferian desire to usurp God's throne. John Lennon's universally popular song, "Imagine," could easily be mistaken as portraying the biblically prophesied millennial reign of Jesus Christ. But Lennon, like the other Lenin, preached manmade heaven on earth—an imitative mockery of the true Messiah's coming kingdom. The words and melody of that song are infectious in describing a scenario of people living in a borderless world without heaven, hell, or religion, "living life in peace" as a "brotherhood of man...sharing all the world."

Globalism's siren song is a one-world anthem that the true child of God cannot follow to its murderous, destructive end. The Holy Spirit within us is the tether who binds us to the masthead of truth. With Jesus Christ as the captain of our salvation, we navigate through the treacherous seas of our time.

Still, we must be alert and heed the wake-up call.

Globalist Storm Warning

There seemed to come a calming, refreshing breeze that restored common sense in America with the election of November of 2016. The vicious, destructive winds of socialistic madness had begun to stir early in the twentieth century. They grew to full hurricane strength while being channeled through increasingly liberal legislative and judicial bodies, with powerful assistance from equally liberal media.

The storm raged throughout the nation's culture by the time the 1990s arrived. Occasional executive-branch resistance slowed it only momentarily while it roared against the country's rapidly weakening moral barriers.

Suddenly, just as the great storm seemed to reach its full fury, American voters arose almost as one entity, and the howling leftist assault was brought to a dead calm. Many reasons have been suggested for the loud repudiation of liberal ideology and its influence upon America's governmental policies. Certainly, the electorate's majority voice unmistakably demanded that politicians begin serving the people in a way that benefits the nation rather than continue serving their own parochial interests at taxpayers' expense, as had been the case for decades.

But a sudden pulse of wind disrupted the calm only days after the people's actions in the voting booths brought the tempest to a standstill.

The gust seemed to burst from nowhere, although the clouds of its origin had been seething for many years in the financial stratosphere of the European Common Market.

The new storm front is even now whipping up monstrous economic waves that might very well swamp the nation in their wake. What the socialist engineers of the first part of the hurricane couldn't accomplish with their internal assault, the socialist world economic powers that comprise the backside of the sovereignty-killing storm managed to achieve with little more than a tropical front. When the American voters swept the one-nation-under-godlessness, liberal, utopian schemers out the front door, the ejected ones quickly ran around the side of the house, where they joined with the globalist New World Order-builders, who were being welcomed in the back door with eager smiles and open arms by a lame-duck Congress that was composed in part by rational-thinking patriots who should have detected the ruse.

But there are none so blind as those who will not see. Under the guise of free trade, the one-world parasitic apparatus lit the torch of globalism, then began siphoning strength and resolve from this nation. The globalists-elite now channel America's wealth, along with funds from other geopolitical and economic spheres, into third-world countries at a rate greater than ever before. They constantly strive to solidify power base through material-goods giveaways. They continue to create and consolidate an ever-increasing constituency dependent on the New World Order hierarchy for absolutely everything as those poorest of earth's people move through their miserable lives from cradle to grave. It was done under the need to equalize living standards. The third world was starving, and America's position as superpower, with most of the world's wealth, needed to agree to wealth redistribution.

The one-world schemers would have us believe that all this *noblesse oblige* is being undertaken on behalf of humanity for humanity's own good—egalitarianism at its most glorious peak of achievement!

Mankind in general and Americans in particular fell prey to the sedative effects of globalism's siren song while the eye of the storm passed calmly overhead. The lull allowed, even encouraged, the globalists-elite to start dismantling everything about the apex nation of history to fund their desire to rule the world through so-called social democracy—an ideology that has brought to the lowest rung of nationhood every country in which it has been tried.

Then entered a man who wanted to get America back on track to being the republic the founders had instituted with one of history's greatest documents of human government—the US Constitution. Globalists at every level had a meltdown. Their rage became so intense that they colluded to overthrow the American electorate's right to vote in whom the majority wants through the electoral college process.

God, however, is never fooled or overruled. He raises rulers, and He puts them down. The intervention in the case of the 2016 election was undeniable, in our estimation. God, however, despite the stopgap intervention, has not decided to let mankind continue conducting life in ways egregiously counter to His ways. He put out the storm warning long ago that a time will arrive when an elitist ruling class will combine its power and authority to create a mechanism of control through which it will attempt to enslave every human on the planet.

God's warning stated that the world's authority and power will ultimately be given to one man—the world's last and most terrible despot (read again Daniel 9:27, Revelation 13, and Revelation 17:12, 13).

What Is America's Role?

Those who analyze prophetic matters have long puzzled over why the United States of America isn't mentioned specifically in God's prophetic Word. Certainly there has never been a nation more blessed or more active in the spread of the gospel of Jesus Christ. Small and seemingly insignificant nations and regions like Libya and Ethiopia are recorded in passages of prophecy yet to be fulfilled—but not America.

Could we, with all the strange machinations going on—the evil perpetrated within governments, the religious apostasy developing, the coronavirus pandemic, and all the other things assaulting this generation—be witnessing an accelerated movement into the prophesied Antichrist, global government?

To repeat the thought expressed earlier: With the election of November 2016, there seemed to come a calming, refreshing breeze that promised a return to government that serves the people rather than seeks to rule with mastery. America seemed to have been given a reprieve from the death sentence the woolly-minded had pronounced upon religious (and a growing number of other) liberties. But how deep is the commitment to return to those earlier, saner principles (and thus how realistic the reprieve) remains to be seen.

To those who have studied the Word of God, it's clear that man-made government that refuses to be guided by God's principles of morality will inevitably degenerate and fall to tyranny within its own borders or without. Political parties can't muster the fortitude to either restrain or constrain the oppression and tyranny that incessantly seek to enslave. Government of, by, and for a moral people can ensure those inalienable rights our forefathers fought, bled, and died to secure for us. It is we the people, under God, who must determine to govern wisely. President George Washington said in his Farewell Address, "Reason and experience both forbid us to expect that national morality can prevail in exclusion of religious principle."[19] John Adams, America's second president, said, "Our constitution was made only for a moral and religious people. It is wholly inadequate to the government of any other."[20]

We must begin by governing our own lives in a way that is pleasing to the Creator. There is only one way to please Him, and that is to put ourselves under the lordship of His Blessed Son, Jesus Christ. How wonderful it would be if not just the majority of American people, but a majority of people throughout the entire world, turned to Jesus Christ in humble repentance!

But, tragically, we can be certain that this will not happen. God in His omniscience tells us that "in the last days, perilous times shall come" and that "evil men and seducers will become worse and worse, deceiving and being deceived" (see 2 Timothy 3). The man who will be the world's last and most vicious tyrant is perhaps even now waiting in the shadows just beyond the spotlight's circle. He will take the crown given to him by his New World Order sycophants and use the platform of globalism they have erected to build a monolithic throne upon which he will ultimately sit, claiming to be deity while demanding worship.

Paving the Way for Antichrist

Today, movers and shakers in global politics are paving the way for the world's last dictator, the Antichrist. They do so most likely oblivious to biblical prophecy. But whether wittingly or not, they rush headlong into that dark night of apocalypse.

Thankfully, even though God's judgment upon sin is sure, He is also slow to anger and His mercy is great. It is our opinion that we are currently in a lull God has graciously granted just before the prophesied end-of-time storm that will devastate a wrath-deserving generation. Even so, a brisk wind is already snapping the flag of warning that apocalypse approaches.

God the Holy Spirit earnestly and tenderly beckons all who will heed His call to take shelter within the only harbor where protection from the deadly whirlwind to come can be found. That safe harbor is Jesus Christ. Those who refuse to accept the haven of safety offered by Christ will perish beneath the raging, crashing surge as surely as did the antediluvians during the judgment of Noah's day.

8

Tribulation Temple and the Beast

I t is the most contested land in all the world. Diplomats fear it is the one place on earth that could ignite war that can't be stopped. If conflict ever got started over this piece of real estate, nuclear exchanges could ultimately result and bring about World War III. God, Himself, considers this promontory the most important point on the planet.

All of this was fulfillment of prophecy. Daniel the prophet was told centuries earlier that the city, Jerusalem, and the sanctuary, the Jewish temple, would be completely thrown down, with not even one stone left upon another (Daniel 9:26–27). The Temple Mount remains without a temple of God until this day.

Muslim structures dot the flattened surface, with the Dome of the Rock, the golden-domed structure so familiar to anyone who has seen Jerusalem's skyline—the central feature. Tensions between Jews and Muslims constitute the fuse that makes this landmark the singular most volatile point on earth.

The Jewish temple will, God's Word promises, again dominate the promontory. But the next temple—the third temple—will be the center of the Tribulation.

David, king of Israel, wanted to build a house wherein God could reside. Jehovah, who called David "a man after my own heart," proposed the question of whether He could be contained in such a structure. The answer, obviously, is *no*—of course not.

The Lord did appreciate the thought, though. He told David that he couldn't be the one to build a place where God could reside among people in that fashion. The king had too much blood on his hands from all the wars he had fought to defend Israel and acquire land God had given the chosen people. Instead, God told David that Solomon, the king's son, would build God such a place. The temple that Solomon built had at its heart the Holy of Holies, a fifteen-foot cubed inner sanctum that held the Ark of the Covenant, the elaborately prepared vessel wherein the *Shekinah* glory, the very presence of God, would dwell.

That spot is still somewhere upon the Temple Mount—Mount Moriah, most scholars believe. Religious Jews still are afraid to walk upon the grounds there for fear of accidentally treading on that one spot on earth where God chose to live.

The temple and the holy of holies constituted God's touchstone to humanity—particularly to the Jews. It's the place where Abraham was to offer Isaac before God intervened with the ram caught by its horns in a thicket, providing the sacrifice Abraham made to the God of heaven. Not far from the spot of the holy of holies is Golgotha, where the Son of God—Jesus the Christ, the once-and-for-all sacrifice for all the sins of mankind—hung on the cross. When Christ died, the veil in the temple's holy of holies tore from top to bottom, giving people direct access to God the Father through that sin sacrifice.

Solomon's temple, then, was the first. It was so glorious that it stunned even the queen of Sheba when her eyes fell upon its splendor. Nebuchadnezzar destroyed that temple in 587 BC. The building of the second temple took place following Israel's Babylonian captivity. That structure lasted from 516 BC to AD 70. It became known as Herod's temple, when it was commissioned by the king to be greatly expanded and beautified to the extent that it was considered magnificent by all who looked upon it.

This structure was destroyed by the Roman military (again, in AD 70), when Roman Emperor Vespasian sent his son, General Titus, to put down insurrection in Jerusalem. This fulfilled prophecies of Daniel (Daniel 9:26–27) and Jesus (Matthew 24:1–2).

A third temple will be built at a future time, Bible prophecy says. It is stated to be in place during the last seven years of human history prior to Christ's return. Daniel prophesied that Antichrist, "in the midst of the week...shall cause the sacrifice and the oblation to cease" (Daniel 9:27b). This last tyrant will enter the third temple and desecrate it:

> Who opposeth and exalteth himself above all that is called God,
> or that is worshipped; so that he as God sitteth in the temple of
> God, shewing himself that he is God. (2 Thessalonians 2:4)

The third temple is mentioned in Revelation 11:1–2 where, in a detailed account of unfolding events during the Tribulation, John is told to "measure" the temple. This, apparently, is a symbolic way to assess its spiritual status.

Exactly *when* the third temple will be built is unknown. We're told in Scripture only that it will exist during the Tribulation. Many who study the matter believe the structure must be begun well in advance of the Tribulation. Completing such an edifice, they believe, will take quite a measure of time. Others hold that the Jews are even now contemplating building a tent-like structure like Moses' tabernacle. They believe that worship, with sacrifices reinstituted, could be going on there while the more grandiose temple is constructed around the temporary one.

There are, of course, problems working against beginning construction of the third temple. Dr. David Reagan, one of today's top Bible prophecy experts, has weighed in on some details in this regard:

Currently there are two major obstacles to the reconstruction of the Third Temple. One pertains to its location. The next temple can only be built where the two previous temples stood because the Holy of Holies must be on the exact same spot. But no one knows for sure where the previous temples were located on the Temple Mount. Most scholars believe that they stood where the Dome of the Rock currently stands. That conclusion may be wrong, but there is no way to prove the exact location without conducting archeological excavations on the Temple Mount, something which is currently prohibited by the Muslims. If the Third Temple is to be built where the Dome of the Rock now stands, then that Muslim structure must first of all be removed either by man or God. It could, of course be burned to the ground by a saboteur, or it could be destroyed by an earthquake.

The second obstacle is the attitude of the Jewish people and their leaders. Currently, there is no desire among them to build a Third Temple. The average Israeli is very secular. He knows that any attempt to build a Third Temple would result in immediate war with the Muslims. Only a handful of ultra-Orthodox Jews have a passion for the Third Temple. They are the ones who have made all the preparations. But they have no popular support. Something will have to happen to create a surge of nationalistic pride that will demand a new Temple. This catalytic event could be the discovery of the Ark of the Covenant.[21]

One thing is sure: If the Bible is to be accepted as God's Word on the matter, the third temple will be built. Jesus Christ, the returning King of kings, will come to the Mount of Olives, the point from which He ascended to heaven following His death, burial, and resurrection. He will return as conquering Lord to put an end to Antichrist's regime.

When Christ's foot touches down on that spot on the Mount of Olives, the mountain will split apart, all the way down and across the Temple Mount. The topography of the entire region—and of the world, for that matter—will be instantaneously changed. There will be a new, greatly elevated mountain, apparently, where the fourth temple—the millennial temple, will be situated. Jesus Christ will reign over the earth for a thousand years. Everyone who is in the millennial kingdom will come to that majestic place to worship at least once a year.

Temple Mount at Center of International Concern

Diplomats of the world in modern times have always poured their greatest efforts into trying to resolve the problems surrounding Israel. The Temple Mount is now, as it has been for many decades, at the center of their concerns. As stated many times, *this is the very spot on the planet that presents the greatest risk for nuclear conflict to ignite.*

Any talk of peace in the Middle East almost always brings thoughts of the Temple Mount and Islam's glistening, golden Dome of the Rock. Many readers will remember the shuttle missions of numerous US administrations' secretaries of state as they were shown getting on the big jets that were headed for the Holy Land. The US State Department had them shuttling back and forth, trying to secure the peace between Israel and its enemy neighbors.

The term "shuttle diplomacy" is most often used when the two primary parties don't formally recognize each other but want to be involved in negotiations in order to disengage opposing armies as well as to promote a lasting truce between the belligerents. The effort continues today. The Trump administration has made a number of moves to secure peace in the region, sending Jared Kushner, President Trump's son-in-law, and others to work through the peace process.

Spectacular moves by the president have also raised controversies. He was instrumental in having the capital of Israel declared to be Jerusalem, not Tel Aviv, in America's view. Also, he moved the American Embassy from Tel Aviv to Jerusalem. Both were powerful changes to show support for the Jewish state.

It is feared by many within the international community that such moves, along with the many seeming uncontrollable elements of inter- actions within the region, will cause the animosities and anger to grow to full-blown war. Such world diplomatic distress is predicted in the Bible (see Zechariah 12:1–3; Luke 21:25).

End-Time Turbulence

Years ago, the whole Middle East was shaken up by the Arab Spring movement, a shake-up begun by supposed Arab factions who wanted to bring democracy to the people who had lived under dictatorships for so long. Arab Spring was an effort, supposedly by and for the Arab people of the Mideast region, to bring down dictatorial regimes and install democracy in their place. It is said to have started on December 17, 2010, with Mohamed Bouazizi's self-immolation in Tunisia. He was a merchant forbidden to conduct business and committed suicide to protest the regime's tyranny.

Tunisian President Zine el-Abidine, Egyptian President Hosni Mubarak, Libyan President Muammar al-Qaddafi, Yemeni President Ali Abdullah Saleh, and later newly installed Egyptian President Mohamed Morsi were ousted as a result of the Arab Spring, with Qaddafi killed when his government was overthrown by foreign military intervention. Syrian president/dictator Bashar Al-Assad's regime as of this writing con- tinues to be under assault by rebel forces that come from that long-ago Arab Spring movement.

Because of all the upheaval, for a time, the Bush administration's Roadmap to Peace initiatives seemed to disappear, and Jerusalem and the Temple Mount appeared to fade in importance. But, the prophet Dan- iel said there would be a "covenant" of peace that "the prince that shall come" will sign at some future point in history (read Daniel 9:26–27).

So, just as always happens, Israel, Jerusalem, and Mount Moriah where the Muslim shrines sit eventually again took stage center as hostilities heated up and the diplomatic missions from the US resumed. All cameras and microphones again were directed at that ancient point of world contention. Pressures from Israel's powerful ally, America, also resumed, and continue even today.

Meanwhile, Iran continues to build its nuclear program, aided by Russia and China. New missile defenses provided by those nations add to the difficulty of a future preemptive strike by the Israelis. The turbulence builds.

At the very heart of all the tumult there comes an increasing call for the Jewish right to worship atop the Temple Mount. Muslims already have the right to worship on this site, which is the third holiest site in Islam (after Mecca and Medina), while it is considered the first holiest in much of Judaism. This discrimination generates increased tension and desire of the religious Jews to be allowed access to their most hallowed place. Further, a growing number is demanding that a third temple be built so animal sacrifice and all the ritual worship of Judaism can resume.

Praying, kneeling, bowing, prostrating, dancing, singing, ripping clothes—any expression of worship such as these actions—is forbidden. Jews visiting the Temple Mount, where the first and second holy temples once stood above and behind the Western Wall in the heart of Jerusalem's Old City, must do none of these things, according to the rules set for them, because the controlling Islamic Waqf, a joint Palestinian-Jordanian religious body, considers Jews visitors, not worshipers.

The Al-Aqsa Mosque and the golden-crowned Dome of the Rock overlooking the city attract daily crowds of Muslim worshipers to the Temple Mount. Jews may only access the mount for four and a half hours per day under Wakf regulations, and, as said, are forbidden from praying there.

Many religious Jews still consider the Western Wall to be the faith's holiest site. But, there is growing demand that is gathering political support for the status quo on the Temple Mount to be changed. Jews must be able to pray upon their ancient site of worship is the demand. The

Israeli police currently prohibit Jews from praying on the mount, fearing an outbreak of violence.

Interest in building a third temple continues to increase. One survey to determine attitudes among religious Jews showed that 43 percent support the construction of one, compared to 20 percent among the ultra-Orthodox and the national ultra-Orthodox, and 31 percent among secular Jews.

The survey showed that among the Israeli Jewish public, 59 percent favor the demand to change the way things presently are on the mount. The survey wanted to know if "the state should enforce an agreement on the mount, similar to one that exists in the Tomb of the Patriarchs in Hebron, which is shared by Jews and Moslems." Just 23 percent answered "no."

The survey's results show a considerable change in attitudes among the religious public in the nation. The direction of thought of the people as a whole is toward building the third temple on Moriah. In fact, many groups today are trying to rev up talk of building a third temple. Some are devoted to reconstructing ancient objects and vessels necessary to carry out rituals of worship once it's built. Training for performing ceremonial acts and services as part of the worship is taking place, and even ritual garbs for the high priest have reportedly been recreated and are being stored for the moment worship in a rebuilt temple is instituted. Preparations for restoring animal sacrifice are also well underway, it is reported.

Others just as devoted to a third temple being rebuilt are involved in political pressures to do just that. They engage in political lobbying and various methods of trying to get the Jewish community to visit the temple site at every opportunity.

Of course, under current circumstances, any effort to remove the Dome of the Rock and the al-Aqsa Mosque would mean that the more than one-billion-strong Muslim world would launch World War III.

At this point, talk of a third temple must remain just that—talk.

However, passion among the Jewish people is building for that prophesied future construction.

Blueprint Blossoming

Rabbi Chaim Richman is the international director of the Temple Institute, an organization based in the Old City devoted to the singular purpose of building the third emple atop Mount Moriah.

"Our goal is to fulfill the commandment of 'They shall make a Temple for me and I will dwell among them,'" says Richman, quoting Exodus 25:8.

Since the destruction of the temple in AD 70 by the Roman legions, rabbis have generally taken the position that rebuilding one should not be undertaken until the Messiah comes. They hold that their religious law on the matter is too unclear. Rabbi Richman and the Temple Mount Institute take a different position. He says there are no Jewish legal barriers against rebuilding a temple, only political ones.

A great concern among those who want the Temple Institute suppressed is that Richman and those within the organization aren't shy about wanting the Dome of the Rock and other shrines of Islam removed from the Temple Mount so construction can begin. The Institute is devoted to laying the groundwork for that purpose. It has put together a blueprint for where the structure will stand. Part of their plans, under the guidance of twenty scholars who study temple law full-time, include what the vessels will look like. Their research and directives have produced replicas of the items of worship used in the ancient temples that were destroyed.

Plexiglass cases at the institute's headquarters in the Old City contain forty such objects, including:

- Silver trumpets to be blown by priests
- A wooden lyre

- Pans with lengthy handles—one for collecting blood from small sacrificial offerings and another for large sacrifices such as the Passover lamb
- Vestments with azure weaves, gold thread, and a breastplate with twelve precious stones to be worn by deputy priests and the high priest displayed on mannequins with beards[22]
- A massive, twelve-spigot sink with electric faucets (modern technology Richman says will be permitted in the third temple)
- A golden, two-hundred-pound, seven-branch menorah in a case overlooking the Western Wall

Very troubling to many who consider these marvelous recreations for worship is the fact that those of the Temple Institute, unlike other museums displaying articles of worship, are intended to be removed as soon as possible and put into use in the third temple.

The world's diplomatic community likely views the goings-on at Richman's organization as creating a future trigger for conflict that could bring all-out war in the Middle East. Many Jews who aren't so religiously minded also worry.

Rabbi Richman's passion—as is obvious from the following interview excerpt—reflects the strong sense of longing for a return to temple worship atop earth's most holy spot from God's perspective:

"All of our outreach here at the Temple Institute is about deepening our feeling of connection—not our feeling of loss, not our feeling of mourning—but our joy with the possibility of our generation being the generation that is leading to the rebuilding of the temple," said Rabbi Chaim Richman, head of the Temple Institute International department in an interview with *Israel National News*.

The Temple Institute website says its short-term goal is to "rekindle the flame" of the temple in people's hearts, and its long-term goal is to rebuild the temple in "our time."

"We consider the rebuilding of the holy temple to be one of the positive commandments. Unfortunately because of the whole long diaspora experience, a lot of ideas crept into our sub-consciousness, and even our consciousness, and there are those that say that the temple is going to come down from heaven, there are those that say that only Mashiach (the Messiah) can build the temple, there are those that say, 'well, the whole idea is just not relevant at all,'" Richman said.

Our position is really just that our lives are like, on hold. The Jewish people are just a skeleton of what they could be. The whole world is really, totally muted and just completely drained of its vibrancy because we don't have the holy temple. And so what we're really trying to emphasize during these days is to rekindle the anticipation and the beauty and the longing for having that closer relationship…when the divine presence returns to the world," he added.[23]

Misplaced Hope

As noble as the desire is to see the coming of their Messiah, as expressed in the Temple Institute's words, the hope is misplaced. Their Messiah came two thousand years ago. He will not again appear to them and be accepted until a terrible time of trouble like never before—the Tribulation—will have run its course. The temple they have plans to begin building will be the one the False Messiah, the first beast of Revelation, will desecrate.

Jesus, the true Jewish Messiah, who was rejected those two millennia ago, told of the moment when this man of sin will come into the third temple and do his evil work:

When ye therefore shall see the abomination of desolation, spo-ken of by Daniel the prophet, stand in the holy place, (whoso readeth, let him understand:)

Then let them which be in Judaea flee into the mountains:

Let him which is on the housetop not come down to take any thing out of his house:

Neither let him which is in the field return back to take his clothes.

And woe unto them that are with child, and to them that give suck in those days!

But pray ye that your flight be not in the winter, neither on the sabbath day:

For then shall be great tribulation, such as was not since the beginning of the world to this time, no, nor ever shall be. (Matthew 24:15–21)

Sadly, the structure the people of the Temple Institute so fervently wish to build will be used to begin Antichrist's reign of genocide upon the Jewish people of that time. They are forewarned by God Himself to flee Jerusalem when they see this evil one sitting in the temple and declaring himself to be God.

No doubt television cameras will be trained on this satanically indwelt minion while he makes his terrifying declaration. The murder of all Jews will begin at that moment, and from his declaration will gush all the terrors of Antichrist's Final Solution. It will make Adolf Hitler's Final Solution seem mild by comparison.

And the beast will have all the tremendously advanced technologies to surveil and track most every human being on earth. There will be no place to escape, except for the supernatural hiding place that will have been especially prepared for Jews and others who trust God for their protection. As mentioned earlier, most believe that hiding place to be Petra, the rose-red city in the Jordanian desert. It is literally carved out of the cliffs and canyons where ancient societies made their homes and commercial center.

Daymond Duck, a noted author and speaker on Bible prophecy, writes:

About 2 percent of the Jews are Messianic Jews and, as far as I know, they understand God's plan. Some of the Jews are religious, but they wrongly think they can go back under the Law (rebuild the Temple, resume the animal sacrifices, etc.) and fulfill God's plan. The remainder of the Jews are secular (not religious) and they have other ideas about what the nation should be doing.

Jerusalem occupies a unique position in two Bible timelines: the beginning and the end of the "times of the Gentiles" (Luke 21:24) and the beginning and the end of the "seventieth week of Daniel" (the Tribulation Period; Dan. 9:24–27).

The "times of the Gentiles" began with the destruction of Jerusalem by Babylon in Old Testament times (Dan. 1:1–2; 2:31–45) and they will end when Gentiles can no longer influence the events in Jerusalem (at the Second Coming of Jesus (Zech. 14:1–4; Luke 21:24).

The "seventieth week of Daniel" (Tribulation Period) will begin when the Antichrist confirms a worthless treaty with Israel and many others for seven years of peace in Jerusalem and the Middle East (Dan. 9:27) and it will end when Jesus comes back to the Mount of Olives in Jerusalem (Zech. 14:1–4).[24]

Following the Rapture of the Church (1 Corinthians 15:51–55; 1 Thessalonians 4:13–18) prophecy fulfillment will quickly begin to take place. The third temple will be a key element of that fulfillment, as the Antichrist will swiftly ascend to power.

Dr. Thomas Ice weighs in on developments from this point forward:

In spite of contemporary turmoil, Israel's Third Temple will one day be rebuilt as Dr. [Randall] Price and I demonstrated in *Ready to Rebuild* from Daniel 9:24–27; Matthew 24:15; 2 Thessalonians 2:4; Revelation 11:1–2; 13:14–15. Few observers of world events ever thought Israel would become a nation again, but it did occur in 1948. Yet, there will be a rebuilt Temple by the middle of the seven-year Tribulation in order to facilitate the fulfillment of Bible prophecy.

I have often taught that the long-awaited permission for the Jews to rebuild their Temple will likely be part of the covenant between Antichrist and Israel that starts the seven-year Tribulation after the Rapture. It appears to me that the Temple will be rebuilt and supervised supernaturally by the two witnesses during the first half of the Tribulation. Since one of the two witnesses will most likely be Elijah, this would mean that the ministry of Elijah should tell us more about the ministry of the two witnesses. Malachi 4:4–5 says, "Behold, I am going to send you Elijah the prophet before the coming of the great and terrible day of the Lord. And he will restore the hearts of the fathers to their children, and the hearts of the children to their fathers, lest I come and smite the land with a curse." Perhaps the ministry of Elijah, where he will help the Jewish people "get right with God," before the return of the Lord will involve their Third Temple, until commandeered by Antichrist.

Regardless of how the Lord works out the details, His plan will be brought to pass. In the meantime, many of the current events now taking place in and around Jerusalem and the Temple Mount are setting the stage for what will be a string of events that will usher in the second coming of Christ. Meanwhile, the Church is looking for the Rapture, when Christ will take us in an instant to be with Himself for all eternity.[25]

9

Israel Invaded!

following the Rapture of the Church, the world situation will forever change for the worse.

Those left behind who are in leadership positions and who
saw Christianity and morality based on biblical precepts to be resistant
to their designs for ruling will no doubt rejoice. Others left behind will
be in panic that is hard to imagine. When that stunning event happens,
the world will explode into chaos. As we've seen, globalism will usurp
national sovereignties and the internationalists will get their deep-state
wishes. The one world they want—the return to Babel mankind has
longed for—will begin its towering rise.

So, too, will the Fourth Reich begin its rise, with an irresistible geopolitical figure emerging with answers to the great fears of the masses.
They will have witnessed millions of people disappearing—including, as
we've said we believe, every child below the age of accountability alive at
the time of Rapture.

Soon thereafter, the red horse of the apocalypse foretold in Revelation 6 will gallop onto the scene. We believe the ignition point of the

war will likely be centered around Mount Moriah—the Temple Mount. All the hatreds within Islam will burst forth at that time.

One primary reason things will go totally out of control is because the Holy Spirit, as restrainer, will remove from His restraining office (as prophesied in 2 Thessalonians 2). People, with all their hatreds and war-making, malicious desires, will rage as never before.

Israel, still possessing thermonuclear weaponry, will possibly use some of its arsenal to launch against those planning to try to destroy the Jewish state. This will be, perhaps, when the ancient city of Damascus will be destroyed in a single day, as the prophet Isaiah declared:

> The burden of Damascus. Behold, Damascus is taken away from being a city, and it shall be a ruinous heap. (Isaiah 17:1)

Today, Syria, whose capital is Damascus, is the incubator of much of the hatred against God's chosen people. Many of the world's most heinous terrorist organizations are given harbor in Damascus while they plot their evil not only against Israel, but against all the world that will not conform to Islam.

Hal Lindsey, author of *The Late, Great, Planet Earth*, writes the following:

> One nation that does not seem to be listed [in the Gog-Magog attack] is Syria. I believe this is the result of actions it is now tak-ing against Israel. Isaiahs prophecy about Damascus in the last days is going to be soon fulfilled.
>
> Twenty-seven hundred years ago, Isaiah warned, An oracle concerning Damascus: See, Damascus will no longer be a city but will become a heap of ruins In that day the glory of Jacob will fade; the fat of his body will waste away. (Isaiah 17:1, 4, NIV)
>
> To establish the time of this event, look at these factors:
>
> First, Damascus is one of the oldest continuously populated cities on earth. It has never been totally destroyed—yet.

Second, it is in a context of events that lead up to the catastrophes that precede the Lord Jesus Second Coming.

Third, it is far enough away from that event that Jacob (Israel) is enduring terrible circumstances.

Fourth, Syria and the tribal name of its forefathers are not mentioned in the Russian-led Muslim Confederacy that launches Armageddon in the middle of the Tribulation.

All of this leads me to believe that Damascus will be destroyed before the Tribulation begins. I believe that Damascus is about to so threaten Israel's existence, by either launching or furnishing bio-chemical weapons or radioactive dirty bombs, that Israel will nuke them. Israel has sworn that it will implement the Samson-Option against any nation that attacks them with any form of weapons of mass destruction. That means a thermonuclear strike. This may soon happen to Syria. This, in turn, will so terrify the world that it will be ripe to embrace the Antichrist when he is unveiled. And that could be very, very soon.[26]

Some prophecy teachers believe the destruction of Damascus will take place before the Rapture. While this is a valid speculation, we are of the opinion that anything so intense as destroying this five-thousand-year-old city—the oldest, longest-surviving city on earth—would've been so convulsing to the world as to take it out of the time Jesus foretold.

The Lord prophesied that things would be going along pretty much as usual when He returns for the Rapture (read Matthew 24:36–42 and Luke 17:26–30.) That time will be just like in the days of Noah and of Lot, prior to the judgments that fell upon those cultures and societies. People will be buying, selling, building, planting, and marrying, etc. It will be business as usual. It might even be business even better than usual.

Jesus said that at the time He is "revealed"—seen by the whole world—judgment will decimate the world of rebels. It will be just like in Lot's day when Lot and his family were removed to Zoar and to safety

(Genesis 19). That very day, judgment fell upon Sodom and Gomorrah and destroyed them all. So, again, we infer that such a cataclysmic action as the (likely) nuclear destruction of that ancient city would take the world out of the time of "business as usual," as Jesus, we believe, indicates.

Then what about the coronavirus and all the things going on economically? Can the Rapture not happen while an economically terrible time such as this disease has wrought is in effect?

Despite what the so-called experts are saying about COVID-19, people in America and around the world are still buying, selling, planting, marrying, and doing all the other things of which Jesus spoke. Things are not as they were months ago, but they haven't changed catastrophically, as they will in the Rapture. And there might yet be a rebound of significant dimension from the effects of the pandemic.

So Damascus will be destroyed—most likely in the gap of time between the Rapture and the confirming of the covenant of Daniel 9: 26-27. Then the red horse of war will run rampant. The rising globalist powers will step in, no doubt, when the nuclear exchanges begin.

From that consortium will come the charismatic geopolitician with a message that can calm the fears of the people of earth—and of the cabal of elitist internationalists from which he emerges.

The one who will be adored by most for calming their fears and for his brilliant plans to bring the world out of chaos will doubtless produce a significant degree of prosperity for a time. As we looked at earlier, Daniel prophesied that he will "cause craft to prosper." This most likely means that he will bring about an economic boom of sorts. It could also mean that his "craftiness"—nefarious activities—will run rampant amongst those who assist him in his governmental impositions.

While his rise to ultimate power continues, there will continue to be great chaos created by the Rapture and the brief nuclear exchanges and conventional military actions at some points around the world. Not all peoples of the world will enjoy the recovery that will likely be taking place within the great leader's sphere of influence.

We believe the Middle East and places to Israel's north will be in economic upheaval as well as in other sorts of turmoil, much as that region is today. One thing that might add to the turmoil is the situation with regard to petroleum. Oil has been the source of economic stability in Russia, Iran, Turkey, and the many Arab nations of regions above and surrounding modern-day Israel.

Recently, in conjunction with the tremendous carnage caused by the coronavirus, the petroleum industry has suffered immensely. Russia and the nations that make up much of the Muslim populations have been hit particularly hard. Even Saudi Arabia, the world's largest producer, has had to make adjustments, often involving hostilities developing in the region.

Gog's Evil Thought

With the Western world recovering from the chaos and even beginning to prosper, perhaps, the oil revenue-dependent nations to Israel's north will still likely be in economic meltdown, with their people in an increasingly out-of-control demeanor. We've already seen from history that the peoples of some of these areas are among the most restless and volatile on the planet.

And this situation—oil and the economic ramifications that flow from its decline as a revenue producer—seems to be at the heart of setting the stage for one of the most profound occurrences next on God's prophetic timeline. To what degree the United States will have been affected by the aftermath of the Rapture is uncertain. That is a whole other matter to explore another time. But, suffice it to say, we believe its power and influence will decline greatly. America will most likely meld with Europe in some way to assure security and economic stability as much as possible. Europe and the Western alliances will be in dynamic rearrangements, and the globalists' long-wished-for desires will be achieved. They will at last garner America's great assets—including its nuclear arsenal—

to add to their blueprint for constructing their one-world order. And the great leader still on the rise in Western Europe will be there to guide and shape all of this at every point of their machinations.

Israel's leaders at this time, in our scenario based on Bible prophecy, will be on edge. America, their greatest ally with the nuclear bludgeon to threaten Israel's enemies set on attacking, will be diminished to become a part of the European alliance. Europe, Israeli leadership will know, has never supported their nation, except as pressured to do so by America's power and influence. They will be in near panic.

They still have their own considerable, formidable nuclear arsenal. They are on hair-trigger edge at this point and will likely use that capability (in fact, they might have already done so in destroying Damascus).

Either way, the newly formed western alliance looks warily at the Mideast situation. It is quite likely that the great leader steps even more forward than he already is and takes personal charge. He, with great, satanic empowerment, uses his charm and persuasive rhetoric to convince Israel that he'll provide even greater promise of protection than did America before the event that caused millions to vanish from the planet. After all, the Euro-centered world power now has all of America and Europe's nuclear and conventional military assets. No one would dare oppose that great power. The leader will promise absolute protection from all of Israel's surrounding enemies. Any attack on that tiny nation, he assures, will bring immediate and total retaliation even more sure than America promised at its most protective.

The only stipulations—or the primary stipulations for their protection—will be that:

1. Israel must give up its own nuclear arsenal to the European consortium to prevent a regional nuclear engagement apart from the European alliance's control.
2. Israel must sign a covenant along with all other nations the alliance will approach. It will be a seven-year guarantee of peace and safety for all who sign.

In return for Israel's agreement to these stipulations, the leader will personally assure that the Jews can rebuild their long-sought-after Temple atop Mount Moriah, and can worship freely as they wish. Israel's leadership, knowing that to say no would put the nation at risk of being totally alone on the world scene, will no doubt readily agree to the great leader's generous offer.

The leadership of Israel's enemies—particularly the Russian leader—watches as Israel agrees to, then gives, all of its military assets to the Western power. He is facing increasing hostility from his economically depressed victims. The dictator begins to think on the tremendous oil and natural gas resources, as well as other economic assets that Israel possesses. We see the possibility of this scenario in the following from the prophet Ezekiel:

> Thus saith the Lord GOD; It shall also come to pass, that at the same time shall things come into thy mind, and thou shalt think an evil thought:
>
> And thou shalt say, I will go up to the land of unwalled villages; I will go to them that are at rest, that dwell safely, all of them dwelling without walls, and having neither bars nor gates,
>
> To take a spoil, and to take a prey; to turn thine hand upon the desolate places that are nowinhabited, and upon the people that are gathered out of the nations, which have gotten cattle and goods, that dwell in the midst of the land. (Ezekiel 38:10–12)

The Russian leader Ezekiel calls Gog begins to gather the forces of those under his nation's banner—those of Iran, Turkey, and a number of nations with Muslim dictatorships who hate Israel and have longed to destroy the Jewish state since its rebirth into modernity in 1948.

Satellite and ground intelligence will no doubt alert the Western alliance that these forces are gathering to attack. Western leaders will almost certainly contact Gog to determine his plans.

The Russian despot will probably give the reason that Israel is stealing gas and petroleum revenue from them and other false accusations. And, maybe Gog will tell the Western leadership that they won't use nuclear weaponry, because Israel has none. But, they will use them if anyone from the West tries to interfere with the assault.

Dr. Jack Van Impe, a top prophecy scholar and teacher for many years, gave the following description of this threat to Israel's north:

> How can anyone be sure that Ezekiel's prophecy has anything to do with modern nations when the words used in his description of this conflict are so unfamiliar to today's Bible reader?
>
> Who is Gog? Where is the land of Magog? Where would one look on a map to find the cities of Meshech and Tubal? To what nations did Ezekiel refer when he wrote of Gomer and Togarmah?
>
> Unless these questions can be answered satisfactorily, there is good reason to question the conclusions being so widely accepted and promoted in our time.

Convincing Evidence

Let us begin at the beginning. A table of nations is given in Genesis 10. At the opening of this important chapter, we are confronted with the key names in Ezekiel's prophecy: "*Now these are the generations of the sons of Noah, Shem, Ham, and Japheth: and unto them were sons born after the flood. The sons of Japheth; Gomer, and Magog, and Madai, and Javan, and Tubal, and Meshech, and Tiras*" (Genesis 10:1, 2).

These key verses describe the repopulating of the earth after the flood. It was the custom in ancient times for the descendants of a man to adopt his name for their tribe. Understanding this, historians and Bible students have been able to trace the movements of some of the tribes and know where their descendants can be found today. Using this system, the editors of the Scofield

Reference Bible have furnished the following information about the names that concern us in the table of nations:

Magog—*"From Magog are descended the ancient Scythians or Tarters, whose descendants predominate in modern Russia."*

Tubal—*"Tubal's descendants peopled the region south of the Black Sea from whence they spread north and south. It is probable that Tobolsk perpetuates the tribal name."*

Meshech—*"Progenitor of a race mentioned in connection with Tubal, Magog, and other northern nations. Broadly speaking, Russia, excluding the conquests of Peter the Great and his successors, is the modern land of Magog, Tubal, and Meshech."*

The Scofield Reference Bible was published in 1909. These notes alone let us know that the identification of Russia as the main aggressor in Ezekiel's end-time battle is not the conclusion of prophetic opportunists. But there is more.

In the orient al tongue, the name of the Caucasus Mountains that run through Russia means "Fort of Gog" or "Gog's last stand." If you were to ask a Russian what he calls the heights of the Caucasus Mountains, he would say, "the Gogh."

The evidence builds.

The word that is translated "chief" in Ezekiel 38:3 is "Rosh" in the Hebrew language. For centuries prophetic scholars have generally agreed that the word "Rosh" is a proper name. Allowing this long-accepted conclusion in the translation of this verse would make it read, *"And say, Thus saith the Lord God; Behold, I am against thee, O Gog, the Rosh prince of Meshech and Tubal."*

But who is Rosh?

"Rosh" was the name of the tribe dwelling in the area of the Volga. And "Rosh" is the word for "Russia" today in some languages of the world. In Belgium and Holland it is "Rus." Here, abbreviated, it's "Russ," and often appears in that form in the headlines of newspapers. An understanding of this truth moved Robert Lowth, Bishop of London two hundred years ago, to write: "Rosh, taken as a proper name in Ezekiel signifies the inhabitants of Scythia from whom the modern Russians derive their modern name. The name 'Russia' dates only from the seventeenth century and was formed from the ancient name 'Russ.'"

It is clear then that Ezekiel was delivering a warning to the Russian prince (leader) of Meshech and Tubal.

We have already seen from Scofield's notes of 1909 that Tubal is the root of the name Tobolsk, but what about Meshech? In his note on Ezekiel 38:2, Scofield continues his work of identification, stating: "That the primary reference is to the northern European powers headed by Russia, all agree.... Gog is the prince, Magog his land, the reference to Meshech and Tubal (Moscow and Tobolsk) is a clear mark of identification."

As has been already shown, Dr. Scofield was by no means the first to come to this conclusion. In 1890, Arno C. Gaebelein wrote a book on Ezekiel. Commenting on chapters 38 and 39, he declared: "This is Russia, Moscow, and Tobolsk."

Another important voice of the past is that of Josephus. In Book I, Chapter VI of his work, this historian who lived almost two thousand years ago stated that the Scythians were called Magogites by the Greeks. Why is that important? The Scythians populated Russia.

It is little wonder then that the weight of prophetic scholarship has gone with the conclusion that Russia is the chief aggressor named by Ezekiel in this end-time war with Israel. The allies of Russia in that fierce conflict will be Persia (Iran and Iraq), Ethiopia, Libya, Gomer (Eastern Germany and Slovakia), and Togarmah (Turkey).

It is interesting that Daniel adds Egypt to the names of nations coming against Israel and the final world dictator, so that the invasion includes attacks from the north and the south, as well as the prospect of trouble from the east (see Dan. 11:40–44).[27]

If this is the scenario that develops—and we fully acknowledge it is all speculative, although based strongly on what the Bible foretells—the Western nations will turn to their up-and-coming great leader. The man of sin knows Bible prophecy. He knows God cannot lie. He knows, from satanically empowered knowledge, how this attack by the Gog-Magog force will end. The great leader just smiles slyly and informs his governmental and military leaders that they will do nothing but observe the action.

This is what the leader that will be Antichrist knows:

Therefore, thou son of man, prophesy against Gog, and say, Thus saith the Lord GOD; Behold, I am against thee, O Gog, the chief prince of Meshech and Tubal:

And I will turn thee back, and leave but the sixth part of thee, and will cause thee to come up from the north parts, and will bring thee upon the mountains of Israel:

And I will smite thy bow out of thy left hand, and will cause thine arrows to fall out of thy right hand. Thou shalt fall upon the mountains of Israel, thou, and all thy bands, and the people that is with thee:

I will give thee unto the ravenous birds of every sort, and to the beasts of the field to be devoured. Thou shalt fall upon the open field: for I have spoken it, saith the Lord GOD. (Ezekiel 39:1–5)

The Western leader's apparent foreknowledge, in holding back these forces to defend Israel, will only further enhance his image. He will almost certainly be praised as one with omniscience and who, somehow, even caused the totally destructive fate to befall the Russians, Iranians, Turks, and all others of the Gog-Magog force—all without losing a single troop of the Western alliance.

His satanic, evil wisdom will do one thing more: clear the way for him to march into Jerusalem unopposed. He will then, at some point, go into and desecrate the third temple. He will declare himself to be God and demand worship.

Antichrist's Final Solution will have begun in earnest!

The religious leader—the second beast, or False Prophet—as we've seen earlier, will point the whole world to the image of Antichrist and will, eventually, cause all who won't worship the image of the beast to be killed. Most will die by beheading, the prophecy states.

Although the leader who will be Antichrist will likely claim that he somehow defended Israel in the Gog-Magog attack, it will be the Lord God of Heaven who will decimate all but one-sixth of the enemy forces who attack His chosen nation.

Current Developments

Developments of recent vintage in the region from which Gog will launch his assault are interesting, to say the least. President Donald Trump announced in 2019 that America would withdraw active military participation in areas hotly contested by Turkey, Syria, and the people known as the Kurds. Contention for the territories involved has been hot and heavy for many years.

Regions directly north of Jerusalem are being stirred to turmoil by the whirlwinds of prophetic destiny. Therefore, it is our responsibility to closely examine all things powerfully affecting that area so concentric to Bible prophecy yet to be fulfilled.

The specific prophecy, of course, involves the one given about the Gog-Magog battle in Ezekiel 38 and 39. We've been watching the scenario develop for some time. Russia (which we believe to be Rosh), Iran (the greatest part of which is almost certainly Persia), and Turkey (which we believe to be a reference to most of what was ancient Togarmah) have been coalescing to Israel's north for quite some time. This alone can be seen as nothing short of astonishing. Now, the whole region directly to Israel's north appears to be lighting up with what looks to be prophetic pyrotechnics.

We have some from the Christian media community declaring what the developments mean. One Christian TV host said: "I am absolutely appalled that the United States is going to betray those Democratic forces in northern Syria, that we possibly are going to allow the Turkish to come in against the Kurds." He offered further: "The President of the United States is in danger of losing the mandate of Heaven if he permits this to happen."[28]

While we can't and don't wish to be able to claim such "word of knowledge" ability to pontificate, we are concerned about, but not necessarily against, the president's decision. We certainly don't believe his decision to withdraw America from the immediate region of hostilities will doom him to loss in a presidential election.

It might just be that the move is by the very hand of God. We can know for sure that America withdrawing in such a manner has in no way slipped up on the Creator; it hasn't escaped His omniscience.

Turkey invading northern Syria to get at rebels of the region is a serious matter. The Kurdish people are in danger. Many among them are Christians, and that is one reason for many concerns among we who pray for our brothers and sisters there. But we should also pray for all who face death and destruction in this or any military incursion. So, we don't view all this lightly.

We do, however, consider these matters from a particularly focused perspective. Things taking place in that part of the world at this late hour in this fleeting Age of Grace must be critically important. In view of all other converging signs we're discerning, any such apparent stage-setting should light up the eschatological radar screens.

We know that America isn't mentioned by name in Ezekiel's Gog-Magog prophecy, just as the nation isn't mentioned by name in any prophecy. Here is what we do know God's Word says about the nations observing that attack from the sidelines—the attackers we believe to be led by Russia, Iran, and Turkey:

Sheba, and Dedan, and the merchants of Tarshish, with all the young lions thereof, shall say unto thee, Art thou come to take a spoil? hast thou gathered thy company to take a prey? to carry away silver and gold, to take away cattle and goods, to take a great spoil? (Ezekiel 38:13)

Our scenario-pondering is wrapped up in the following (again, we claim no "word of knowledge").

With America removed from that region of interminable conflict, the other nations that presently comprise NATO and all other countries of combatant-loaning sorts might not be willing to intervene against the assault. Most consider Israel as the problem in the world. Think about the UN being almost totally against Israel on every issue.

If America isn't there at the time of the Gog-Magog assault, these nations will almost without question not seek to oppose the coalition, led by a powerful Russia.

The removal of America at this time from this theater of future war is most interesting to contemplate. God tells in this prophecy that He, alone, will save His chosen nation. There will be no doubt about who does the rescue.

America's military might won't do so. That's for sure.

10

Temple Defiled in Midst of Week

The Jews' great enemies that have for the years since the nation's birth into modern times threatened to exterminate them will meet their end on the mountains of Israel. God, Himself, will annihilate the Gog-Magog juggernaut as it storms southward. The prophet Ezekiel foretells their fate in no uncertain terms:

Thou shalt fall upon the mountains of Israel, thou, and all thy bands, and the people that is with thee: I will give thee unto the ravenous birds of every sort, and to the beasts of the field to be devoured.

Thou shalt fall upon the open field: for I have spoken it, saith the Lord God.

And I will send a fire on Magog, and among them that dwell carelessly in the isles: and they shall know that I am the Lord.

So will I make my holy name known in the midst of my people Israel; and I will not let them pollute my holy name any more: and the heathen shall know that I am the LORD, the Holy One in Israel.

Behold, it is come, and it is done, saith the Lord GOD; this is the day whereof I have spoken.

And they that dwell in the cities of Israel shall go forth, and shall set on fire and burn the weapons, both the shields and the bucklers, the bows and the arrows, and the handstaves, and the spears, and they shall burn them with fire seven years:

So that they shall take no wood out of the field, neither cut down any out of the forests; for they shall burn the weapons with fire: and they shall spoil those that spoiled them, and rob those that robbed them, saith the Lord GOD.

And it shall come to pass in that day, that I will give unto Gog a place there of graves in Israel, the valley of the passengers on the east of the sea: and it shall stop the noses of the passengers: and there shall they bury Gog and all his multitude: and they shall call it The valley of Hamon-gog.

And seven months shall the house of Israel be burying of them, that they may cleanse the land.

Yea, all the people of the land shall bury them; and it shall be to them a renown the day that I shall be glorified, saith the Lord GOD.

And they shall sever out men of continual employment, passing through the land to bury with the passengers those that remain upon the face of the earth, to cleanse it: after the end of seven months shall they search.

And the passengers that pass through the land, when any seeth a man's bone, then shall he set up a sign by it, till the buriers have buried it in the valley of Hamon-gog. (Ezekiel 39:4–15)

Continuing the scenario of developments as Antichrist strengthens his grip on power, he will see his opportunity to accomplish his master's all-consuming desire. Satan wants to conquer Jerusalem and, in particular, set his earthly throne of authority upon the very spot where the holy of holies and the ark of the covenant sat in ancient times.

The European leader is hailed by his hordes of Western-alliance sycophants as the greatest of all conquerors in history while he and they watch the elimination of all but one-sixth of the forces of the Gog-Magog coalition. He, we can imagine, lifts his head in pride and accepts the adulation of all those under his rule. They believe he has somehow, through supernatural means, seen to the destruction of the Middle East belligerents. He hasn't had to lift a finger, yet their antagonists to their east who might have one day caused their deaths in war were destroyed by an all-consuming power that even their nuclear weaponry couldn't have matched.

The great leader has by this time undoubtedly been adorned by his ten-kings consortium with the mantle of an emperor with godlike powers. He will do nothing to assuage their thinking. He will "magnify himself," as Daniel predicts:

And in the latter time of their kingdom, when the transgressors are come to the full, a king of fierce countenance, and understanding dark sentences, shall stand up.

And his power shall be mighty, but not by his own power: and he shall destroy wonderfully, and shall prosper, and practise, and shall destroy the mighty and the holy people.

And through his policy also he shall cause craft to prosper in his hand; and he shall magnify himself in his heart, and by peace shall destroy many. (Daniel 8:23–25)

This man, more dynamic in magnetic personality and oratory skill than any to ever live will, in fact, come under powers that will make him like a god in the eyes of those who witness his dramatic rise. By this time, he will have been given a supernatural promotion by a religious prelate who, as we have seen, will have propagandist abilities that will far exceed even those of Josef Goebbels. This "holy" man—who some believe might be a pope—will lead the way in attributing to him powers that no other humans have achieved. The second beast—the False Prophet—will himself perform great "miracles" and "wonders" so that they will fool and confound anyone who doesn't have spiritual understanding at that time.

There will be those who have accepted Christ as Savior, and their numbers will grow exponentially. Both the Antichrist and his False Prophet sidekick will hunt down and have murdered all who won't accept the system of tyranny the Fourth Reich will require.

Apparently, the führer of the Fourth Reich won't be loved by everyone. He will supposedly be the victim of an assassination. Prophecy says he'll be injured with a fatal wound (read Revelation 13). This will likely be a matter of the unholy trinity of Satan, Antichrist, and the False Prophet faking a deadly blow to the great leader's head.

Only Christ has the keys to death and life. So this must be a fake death, because there will be a resurrection from the "deadly head wound," and Antichrist will live again in the eyes of all who witness the supposed miracle. People will from that point "wonder after the beast who had the deadly wound and did live" (Revelation 13:3).

The "resurrected" man will then take up the greatest manhunt in all of history. He will try to make everyone within his sphere of authority take a number and mark on their forehead or right hand. If they don't comply, they will likely die, either through beheading or starvation from resisting the 666 system of buying and selling.

Following the Gog-Magog defeat, Antichrist, now probably indwelt by Satan himself, will march in front of his massive Western-alliance forces. They will go to Jerusalem, where Satan will, having been cast out of the heavenly sphere along with his wicked angel cohorts, cause his Antichrist host to do his bidding.

And there was war in heaven: Michael and his angels fought against the dragon; and the dragon fought and his angels, and prevailed not; neither was their place found any more in heaven.

And the great dragon was cast out, that old serpent, called the Devil, and Satan, which deceiveth the whole world: he was cast out into the earth, and his angels were cast out with him.…

Therefore rejoice, ye heavens, and ye that dwell in them. Woe to the inhabiters of the earth and of the sea! for the devil is come down unto you, having great wrath, because he knoweth that he hath but a short time. (Revelation 12:7–9, 12)

Satan's prime directive will be to go into the temple that was constructed shortly after the covenant guaranteeing the Jews security and the right to worship on Mount Moriah. Lucifer's hatred has long burned at the core of his rebellion. The Jewish temple has continued to be in his crosshairs for destruction.

The act of bringing disgrace upon the temple has historical precedence. In 168 BC, Greek king, Antiochus IV Epiphanes, invaded Jerusalem and captured the city. He forced his way into the Jewish temple, erected a statue of the Greek god Zeus, and sacrificed a pig on the altar of incense. This provoked a revolt in Judea as the Jews fought to remove Antiochus' sacrilege from the temple. Such desecration is prophetically scheduled to happen once again during the middle of the Tribulation.

Daniel foretold this moment and Jesus further described this blasphemous act:

And he shall confirm the covenant with many for one week: and in the midst of the week he shall cause the sacrifice and the oblation to cease, and for the overspreading of abominations he shall make it desolate, even until the consummation, and that determined shall be poured upon the desolate. (Daniel 9:27)

Antichrist will go into the temple at the midpoint of Daniel's seventieth week. He will desecrate it by causing the Jews' worship and sacrifices to cease, and by carrying out other blasphemy there. Jesus said further of this horrendous act:

When ye therefore shall see the abomination of desolation, spoken of by Daniel the prophet, stand in the holy place, (whoso readeth, let him understand:)

Then let them which be in Judaea flee into the mountains: Let him which is on the housetop not come down to take any thing out of his house: Neither let him which is in the field return back to take his clothes.

And woe unto them that are with child, and to them that give suck in those days! But pray ye that your flight be not in the winter, neither on the sabbath day:

For then shall be great tribulation, such as was not since the beginning of the world to this time, no, nor ever shall be. (Matthew 24:15–21)

Final Solution

This is the hellish moment Satan and his man of sin have been waiting for. And, yes, we say that correctly, because Antichrist himself is said to arise from the bottomless pit. He has been waiting for this time of incarnation, the prophecy seems to indicate.

It is fair to conjecture whether this beast might be an offspring of a sexual union in the time of Genesis chapter 6 when the "sons of God" came to the "daughters of men," cohabited, and produced offspring. These angelic-human half-breeds are called *nephilim* and are believed by many Bible scholars and students to be the result of the first rebellion in heaven when a third of the angels followed Lucifer in his fall.

The possibility is made stronger by considering two facts the Bible gives about the Antichrist. First, he, like Judas Iscariot, who betrayed Jesus for thirty pieces of silver, is said to be the "son of perdition." Judas was said to have gone "to his own place" upon, apparently, killing himself. Additionally, he is described to have been "lost from the beginning," apparently meaning that he never had a chance to be redeemed by the blood of Christ as have all human beings.

Second, the beast (Antichrist) is summarily thrown in the lake of fire, without standing before the great white throne judgment. Every human will get his or her time in that supreme heavenly court. The Antichrist gets no such turn before that final judgment. Neither, incidentally, will the second beast (False Prophet) be given an appearance before that final court. Both are thrown directly into the lake of fire, as will be the devil and his angels. This makes us think that the Antichrist and False Prophet might indeed be supernatural minions rather than human.

The Final Solution will begin with the full fury of Satan pursuing all of the House of Israel. His whole purpose will be to murder every last son and daughter of Abraham, Isaac, and Jacob. Like Hitler, he will round them up and kill them by the millions. Jesus said:

> And except those days should be shortened, there should no flesh
> be saved: but for the elect's sake those days shall be shortened.
> (Matthew 24:22)

Many Jews and millions of others will die as the result of the genocidal rage. But, God will preserve a third of the Jewish race along with many Gentiles who accept Christ during this holocaust.

Antichrist's Final Solution will fall short, as did Hitler's.

A reference to the Antichrist in the temple is first found in 2 Thessalonians 2:4, the first place in Scripture where we are told specifically that the Antichrist directly sits in the temple declaring that he is God:

> Let no one deceive you by any means; for that day will not come
> unless the falling away comes first, and the man of sin is revealed,
> the son of perdition, who opposes and exalts himself above all
> that is called God or that is worshiped, so that he sits as God in
> the temple of God, showing himself that he is God.

There is no mention of Antichrist desecrating the third temple in the book of Revelation. However, all the wrath and judgment John was given by Christ Himself will begin to come upon the world of rebels from that desecration. Jesus says, again, that it will be the worst time of history, and that if not for God's intervention, no flesh would be saved.

Whereas the confirming of the covenant of Daniel 9:26 sets in motion Daniel's seventieth week, the last seven years of human history that precede Christ's Second Advent (Revelation 19:11), the desecration of the temple sets in motion the time of Jacob's trouble (Jeremiah 30:7). This will be the last half of the Tribulation period. Jesus called this the Great Tribulation. This is when Antichrist's Final Solution gets into full genocide mode. (We'll examine in future chapters the judgments and wrath that flow from this midpoint of Daniel's seventieth week of seven years.)

The "beasts" of the earth—in human terms—have killed millions of people through their satanically driven regimes. These, however, will pale by comparison to the genocide that will take place under Antichrist's beastly reign, especially during the second half of the Tribulation. Here is a look at the number of deaths attributed to some of the previous beasts of history:

> Although dictators and despots have been around since the days of Noah (Nimrod, et al), the twentieth century saw more enslavement, torture and death under "beast" rulers than all the previous centuries combined. People who have accomplished much on this earth in business, sports, agriculture and other endeavors are sometimes inducted into a "Hall of Fame" for outstanding achievement in their chosen field. If recognition was given to the many evil "beast" rulers that have lived on the planet, and they were voted into a "Hall of Shame," some of the top candidates, who have tortured, maimed and killed the most people in the world include:

- MAO ZEDONG, *China* (1949–76), Regime: Communist, Victims: Over 60 million
- JOSEPH STALIN, *Soviet Union* (1929–53), Regime: Communist, Victims: c. 40 million
- ADOLF HITLER, *Germany* (1933–45), Regime: Nazi dictatorship, Victims: c. 30 million
- KING LEOPOLD II, *Belgium* (1886–1908), Regime: Colonial Empire in Congo, Victims: 8 million
- HIDEKI TOJO, *Japan* (1941–45), Regime: Military dictatorship, Victims: 5 million
- ISMAIL E. PASHA, *Ottoman Turkey* (1915–20), Regime: Military dictatorship, Victims: 2 million
- POL POT, *Cambodia* (1975–79), Regime: Communist (Khmer Rouge), Victims: At least 1.7 million
- KIM ILSUNG, *North Korea* (1948–94), Regime: Communist, Victims: At least 1.6 million
- SADDAM HUSSEIN, Iraq (1979–2003), Regime: Ba'ath Party dictatorship, Victims: 600,000
- JOSIP BROZ TITO, *Yugoslavia* (1945–80), Regime: Communist, Victims: 570,000[29]

It's no wonder that Jesus warned all Jews who are in the area to flee for their lives when they see this man claiming to be God while sitting in a throne-like position in the temple. This will be the ultimate act of blasphemy.

The man of sin will have his False Prophet erect an image to him—an object all will be forced to bow down before and worship or be killed. He will speak great, swelling words against the God of gods, the true God of Heaven. He will no doubt sprinkle swine blood to desecrate the inner sanctum of the temple and the altar, as Antiochus did millennia earlier.

Dr. John Walvoord wrote:

The Blasphemous Character of the Beast as World Ruler (Revelation 13:5–6)

13:5–6 And there was given unto him a mouth speaking great things and blasphemies; and power was given unto him to continue forty and two months. And he opened his mouth in blasphemy against God, to blaspheme his name, and his tabernacle, and them that dwell in heaven.

The evil character of the world ruler of that day is shown in his boasting and blasphemy. A similar description of the same character is given in Daniel 7:8, 11, 25. His authority continues for forty-two months, again the familiar three and one-half years of the great tribulation. It is probable that the person who heads the revived Roman Empire comes into power before the beginning of the entire seven-year period of Daniel 9:27, and as such enters into covenant with the Jewish people. His role as world ruler over all nations, however, does not begin until the time of the great tribulation. From that point, he continues forty-two months until the second coming of Christ terminates his reign. It is evident that blasphemy is not an incidental feature of his kingdom but one of its main features, and he is described in verse 6 as blaspheming against God, against the name of God, and against the Tabernacle of God, as well as against them that dwell in heaven. As Satan's mouthpiece he utters the ultimate in unbelief and irreverence in relation to God. If the king of Daniel 11:36–45 is the same individual, as some believe, he does so in total disregard of any god because he magnifies himself above all (Dan. 11:37).

The Universal Dominion of the Beast (13:7)

13:7 And it was given unto him to make war with the saints, and to overcome them: and power was given him over all kindreds, and tongues, and nations.

As is anticipated in Daniel 7:23, where the beast devours "the whole earth," here the worldwide extent of his power is indicated. The expression "it was given to him" refers to the satanic origin of his power. Acting as Satan's tool, the beast is able to wage war against the saints throughout the entire globe and to overcome them. (Cf. Dan. 7:25; 9:27; 12:10; Rev. 7:9–17.) In the will of God, many believers in Christ among both Jews and Gentiles perish as martyrs during this awful time of trial, while others are preserved in spite of all the beast can do. The ultimate in worldwide authority is indicated in verse 7, in that "power was given him over all kindreds, and tongues, and nations." The dream of countless rulers in the past of conquering the entire world is here finally achieved by this last Gentile ruler.

The universal authority of the beast over the entire earth is stated specifically in the latter part of the verse. The word *peoples* should be inserted after the word *kindred* as in the best texts, making the verse read "power was given him over all kindreds, peoples, and tongues, and nations." As the nouns are properly singular, the clause is better rendered "and authority was given to him over every tribe and people and tongue and nation." Such authority was anticipated by Daniel (Dan. 7:23) where it is stated that the fourth beast "shall devour the whole earth, and tread it down, and break it in pieces." The dream of world conquest achieved in part by the Babylonian, Medo-Persian, Macedonian, and Roman empires is now for the first time realized completely and is the satanic counterfeit of Christ's millennial reign permitted by God in this final display of the evil of Satan and wicked humanity.

The time of this universal sway is clearly indicated in verse 5 as being forty-two months, namely the last three and one-half years preceding the return of Christ. This period is otherwise described as the great tribulation. It is apparent, however, that as the period moves on to its end a gigantic world war is under way continuing to the time of the return of Christ. This war is in the form of a rebellion against the universal sway of the beast and comes at the very end of the tribulation time. A universal kingdom and a world war could not coexist, since one is the contradiction of the other.[30]

The man of sin will edict that all who don't believe in him must be hunted down and eliminated. At this time, he will have invaded Jerusalem with an army (Joel 1:6; Daniel 11:31, 9:26). He'll take over Jerusalem and Israel, occupy its territory, and set up headquarters, waging war against Christians and Jews, attempting with all his might to annihilate them (see Daniel 11:33–35, 12:10; Revelation 6:10–11; Jeremiah 50:33; Joel 1:6; Matthew 24:9; Mark 13:9–13). Only a third of the Israelites will survive. Zechariah 13:8 declares:

And it shall come to pass in all the land, says the Lord; two thirds in it shall be cut off and die; but one third shall be left in it.

At the same time, Antichrist and his association of kings will undertake to abolish all religions and their places of worship (Revelation 17). Also at this time, God will judge the great whore (Revelation 17). The Antichrist will not tolerate any religion other than the worship of and devotion to himself and his empire. Daniel 11:37 affirms that the Antichrist regards no man, and thus has no concern for human life or suffering.

The Antichrist will launch an all-out war against all believers in Jesus Christ, and many will be martyred. God permits Antichrist, indwelt by Satan, to prevail and accomplish his aims for a time. But the Lord at the same moment has prepared a hiding place for the Jews, whom Jesus warns to flee once they see that the great leader is really the beast who wants to implement his Final Solution.

We believe the place of refuge to be Petra in the Jordanian desert, as stated in a previous chapter. While Antichrist forces pursue the fleeing Jews, much like Pharaoh's armies pursued the Israelites in the Exodus from Egypt, God will supernaturally intercede.

The Serpent spewed water out of his mouth like a flood after the woman, that he might cause her to be carried away by the flood.

But the Earth helped the woman, and the earth opened up its mouth and swallowed up the flood which the dragon had spewed out of its mouth.

And the dragon was enraged with the woman, and he went to make war with the rest of her offspring, who keep the commandments of God and have the testimony of Jesus Christ. (Revelation 12:15–17)

There seems to be a supernatural opening of the earth that swallows the flood of military attackers. God will prevent Antichrist from inflicting any harm while the Jews and many Tribulation believers in Christ run to the place God has prepared to hide them.

Antichrist, meanwhile, will become more enraged and will increase the slaughter in a holocaust of bloodshed like never before seen in the annals of human history.

11

The Image of the Beast Arrives

In Revelation 13, the most astonishing statement is made regarding the animating of an "image" of Antichrist.

> And [he] deceiveth them that dwell on the earth by the means of those miracles which he had power to do in the sight of the beast; saying to them that dwell on the earth, that they should make an image to the beast, which had the wound by a sword, and did live.
>
> And he had power to give life unto the image of the beast, that the image of the beast should both speak, and cause that as many as would not worship the image of the beast should be killed. (Revelation 13:14–15)

Scholars over the past two thousand years have speculated as to what this curious text implies and in what way an animated object could be brought to "life." Only now does technology exist that is undeniably changing every aspect of human existence and evolving into something indistinguishable from this type of occult magic. Our lives have become so entrenched in technology that most of us are constantly connected to some form of it at all times—computers, iPads, smart phones, Alexa, Siri, security surveillance, and medical devices like pacemakers—and they work around the clock. There is rarely a moment when we are completely disconnected from technology—an idea that would have been absurd only a decade ago.

With this rapid development of transformative technology comes the question of safety. Are some of these emergent technologies demonically inspired, actively leading us down a dark and hellish path towards a dystopian future, as described in the ancient biblical prophetic narrative?

The book of Revelation describes "the beast" and his prophet in great detail, proclaiming that all humans will worship this beast, for his prophet will "perform great signs and deceive the inhabitants of the earth and even order them to set up an image in honor of the beast who was wounded by the sword, yet lived" (Revelation 13:13–14). Widespread acceptance of the beast seems to be largely due to the miracles he will perform, even simulating a resurrection from the dead, revealing his deceptive immortality.

The question is: Will this image of the beast foreseen in the book of Revelation become realized through the emerging transformative technologies of transhumanism, artificial intelligence, the coming *Singularity*, and the speculative theories of the *hive mind*?

Twenty years ago, the idea that one day in the near future, your telephone would navigate you anywhere in the world, scan your thumbprint, allow you to talk to someone face to face anywhere on the planet, handle banking, and provide a "social" life would have been considered science fiction. Society has come a long way in regards to technological innovation in an alarmingly short time. But how fast is too fast? Are we rushing into a technological "relationship" without doing a thorough background check on our rapidly evolving and highly seductive companion? Once humanity delves into this relationship, it can't just break up and abandon the conveniences it's now become completely dependent upon.

The innovations in science, agriculture, medicine, and business certainly make life easier and more convenient for the average person. Many of these advancements are seriously improving the quality of life for the disabled, such as an amputee whose arm is now a fully functioning robotic replacement, or a paraplegic who is given the gift of independence with a self-driving car, wheelchair, or even a robotic exoskeleton. Let's not forget about the personalities we've named Siri and Alexa. These two artificial intelligence (AI) companions accurately suggest music their algorithms predict we will like, answer all our questions, tell us jokes or the weather, and can even buy groceries. In return, they record our conversations and file them away in an online database of information collected about us for an indefinite length of time, while aggregating the nuanced shopping habits and curiosities of every one of their users.

AI is the science and engineering of making "intelligent" machines by simulating cognitive function. It's related to the similar task of using computers to understand human intelligence.[31] Basically, it consists of computers that can make decisions and predictions without the confined interfacing of human programmers. Artificial intelligence has the ability to learn on its own!

AI really became widespread when Google started using an AI neural network as a tool to filter spam out of our email inboxes,[32] which today accounts for 59.56 percent of email traffic worldwide,[33] but it has since vastly evolved beyond that task.

There is no doubt of the beneficial aspects of AI, but it's the dependency we as a society are forming that very possibly make it dangerous in the near future. At what point do we draw the line and say, "It's okay for Siri to tell me where the closest Chinese restaurant is, but it's not okay to record the fact that I like Chinese food and sell that information to companies for advertisement purposes," allowing the subtle and invisible influence of persuasion over us?

In his book, *The Age of Spiritual Machines*, world-renowned transhumanist Ray Kurzweil famously suggests:

Once life takes hold on a planet, we can consider the emergence of technology as inevitable. The ability to expand the reach of one's physical capabilities, not to mention mental technology is clearly useful for survival.[34]

It might be an inevitable future, but according to the concept of "machine learning," it could also be leading us to the destruction of the earth and the near destruction of mankind, as predicted in the Bible. "Machine learning," coined by esteemed computer scientist Arthur Samuel in 1959, is an aspect of computer science in which computers (or machines) "have the ability to learn without being explicitly programmed."[35]

Tech giant Amazon recently became a leader in machine learning with its user-friendly new program "Amazon ML." The website boasts that "Amazon ML reads your input data, computes descriptive statistics on its attributes, and stores the statistics—along with a schema and other information… Next, Amazon ML uses the datasource to train and evaluate an ML model and generate batch predictions."[36] Amazon is basically using algorithms to detect patterns within the data it collects, then uses that information to predict whether individual customers will buy certain products.

Using machine learning for growth and development is a great modern business tool, but there's also a dark side to it that could open demonic doorways, such as the case with Luka, a San Francisco-based software company.

Luka has been using machine-learning technologies to develop some questionable chatbots. (A chatbot is computer software that simulates conversations, like Siri or Alexa.) Luka recently took chatbots to the next level when cofounder Eugenia Kuyda digitally "brought back" her proclaimed soulmate from the dead by using machine-learning software to analyze the deceased person's voice, text messages, and social media conversations in an effort to replicate the person's likeness.[37] Trying to reproduce the dead is teetering on the edge of necromancy, which God commands against:

> There shall not be found among you anyone who…practices witchcraft, or a soothsayer, or one who interprets omens, or a sorcerer, or one who conjures spells, or a medium, or a spiritist, or one who calls up the dead. For all who do these things are an abomination to the Lord. (Deuteronomy 18:10–12)

The Bible warns mankind not to dabble with the dead, yet tech companies like Luka are foolishly trying to open those doors one chatbot at a time. This illustrates the terrifying potential that lies in the hands of these innovations (and their creators) by not only opening the doorways to the dead, but by creating an avenue for them to impersonate anyone on the planet.

There will be a moment in the near future when the student surpasses the teacher—the student being machines and the teacher being humans. The student was never meant to *surpass* the teacher, but rather to *be like* the teacher. Luke 6:40 says, "As the disciple is not above his teacher: but every one when he is perfected shall be as his teacher." So what happens when we are surpassed by those creations we "taught" or programmed?

Does the *physical form* of this artificial intelligence make a difference in whether we accept it in mainstream society? For instance, does the form of an independently intelligent *disk-drive* scare you? How about an independently intelligent *robot* that can make decisions for itself, decisions that could affect or even harm you if it pleases, like Skynet, the maniacal robot network from the classic film *The Terminator*?

Chances are you're more intimidated by the robot, but might not notice the disk-drive from the underground server that is powering the iCloud. This illustrates how easy it may be to influence our acceptance of these artificial intelligences through the physical forms they take on. It's deception through appearance.

Considering that the physical form would solely be a shell containing the machine's mind, so to speak, its only purpose would be to relate to us and perform certain tasks that its "mind" alone couldn't carry out. The idea that this digital mind is a separate entity than the machine or body that contains it isn't a new idea, but a concept that has been discussed by scholars and futurists for centuries.

The term known as "the ghost in the machine" was introduced by Gilbert Ryle in his 1949 critique of René Descartes, a champion of dualism.[38] The idea of dualism is that the human mind is immaterial, existing and working separately from the human brain. As a response to the topic of dualism, renowned philosopher Dave Hunt once said, "I'm not just a lump of protein molecules wired with nerves.... There's a ghost in the machine. We're not just stimulus response mechanisms."[39]

The thought that technology could become aware, or have this "ghost in the machine" becoming more than just *machine,* leads us to the concept famously known as the Singularity. Coined by futurist, transhumanist, and Google engineer Ray Kurzweil, the Singularity is, as he describes:

> ...a future period during which the pace of technological change will be so rapid, its impact so deep, that human life will be irreversibly transformed... this epoch will transform the concepts that we rely on to give meaning to our lives, form the business models to the cycle of human life, including death itself.[40]

So, this concept of "ghost in the machine" illustrates how machines could possibly one day think for themselves, while the Singularity describes a future inevitability of the merging of man and machine.

Futurist and technology innovator Elon Musk warns against this coming merger, stating, "with artificial intelligence, we are summoning the demon."[41] Part of the reason behind Musk's most recent venture into space with his creation, SpaceX, is to try to secure a safety net for *when* artificial intelligence turns on mankind.[42] Having one of the most innovative men in history vehemently warn against AI should be enough to stop it in its tracks, but other tech billionaires disagree. Musk warns that people like Google's CEO, Larry Page, might very well have noble intentions when crafting these technological advancements, but that they might still "produce something evil by accident…a fleet of artificial intelligence-enhanced robots capable of destroying mankind."[43]

Physicist Stephen Hawking also once warned:

Unless we learn how to prepare for, and avoid, the potential risks, AI could be the worst event in the history of our civilization. It brings dangers, like powerful autonomous weapons, or new ways for the few to oppress the many.[44]

Transhumanists generally welcome the possibility of human beings evolving into an enhanced form of humanoid hybrid, but are constantly debating the irreversible ramifications, such as shifts in global power, unparalleled "smart" weapons, and the threat of the total annihilation of mankind and the planet as a whole.

Humans are on the path to becoming hosts for this artificial intelligence-turned-spiritual-creature without fully understanding the irrevocable repercussions of those actions.

Chuck Missler points out:

Scientists are actually connecting their neural network to machinery…. These are people that are incredibly skilled in their technologies, but have absolutely zero understanding of demonology, the realization that opening up a communication channel can be a two way channel and that can create what we call in demonology an *entry*.[45]

We are treading murky waters here and potentially putting mankind in spiritual and physical danger. Scientists will never be able to guarantee the predictability of smart machines or their ability to be obedient and act only in the best interest of humanity. There will always be the danger of becoming a tool, or avatar, for these technological entities.

Father of AI, chief scientist and cofounder of the AI company NNAISENSE, and the director of the Swiss artificial intelligence lab IDSIA, Jürgen Schmidhuber, says "the Singularity is coming in the next 30 years and will have affordable devices to connect to the brain. A device that can compute all human life at once."[46] Many transhumanists predict that the Singularity is coming, like a riptide that is so incredibly powerful that humanity will be unable to resist it.[47]

Once the Singularity has happened and we're all connected to this device, Schmidhuber claims it "can compute all human life at once,"[48] and we will then be ready embrace the concept known by some scholars as the *hive mind*.

The principle behind the hive-mind concept is a collective consciousness, or as the late Jesuit priest and philosopher Pierre Teilhard de Chardin famously predicted, "the manifestation of a kind of super-brain, capable of attaining mastery over some super-sphere [noosphere] in the universe."[49] He saw the merging of mankind and technology as a "necessary first step in the collective evolution of the universe."[50] This thought implies the necessity and favorability of a collective consciousness, hive mind, or noosphere rather than a mere *possibility* to be explored by the technological and scientific communities.

Through the hive mind, "the whole of mankind would be completely connected to everyone else telepathically, and we could all share our thoughts, memories, and even dreams with one another."[51] Imagine a world where your thoughts are involuntarily shared with the whole of humanity. Say goodbye to personal privacy and even to your freedom of thought.

Currently, through the use of social media, we're prompted to volunteer information about ourselves such as personal beliefs, religious affiliations, sexual preference, and political identification. This hoarding of personal information is then indexed and stored in a virtual database that can be used to "predict" advertisements using powerful algorithms.

By searching the account settings in Facebook, one will discover that he or she has already been labeled as "conservative," "super conservative," "liberal," or "super liberal." The ads displayed on Facebook aren't random, but are suggestions based on computer algorithms that an artificial intelligence deems attractive on an individual basis. Best-selling author Frank Peretti says:

> My biggest concern is with the steady encroachment of technology that feeds on the credulity of people that can make them accept and believe things that aren't true, that can make them so amenable to being probed, to being known about, to being followed and tracked that you get use to these things.[52]

This handling of data is already underway on a massive scale and will continue to be used to make collective decisions, such as voting on various policies and leaders. It has already been blamed for the sway in the most recent US presidential election regarding data collected by British political consulting firm, Cambridge Analytica.[53]

Facebook's facial recognition is another one of its AI software that is collecting and storing data on its two billion active users. The most alarming part of this software is its ability to recognize and "tag" a person based on any photo anywhere in the world. This powerful AI software could even be used as a mechanism to track human beings to all corners of the earth at all times.

Considering there are nearly thirty million surveillance cameras in America alone,[54] this idea doesn't seem too far-fetched, but does grossly infringe on our freedom and privacy. English philosopher Jeremy Bentham predicted this scenario in the late eighteenth century. He called this "panopticon" a system that would allow guards to monitor prisoners twenty-four hours a day, without them knowing they were being watched, creating "the sentiment of an invisible omniscience."[55]

Despite these terrifying new possibilities of mass-scaled surveillance and the potential of a collective consciousness, transhumanists continue to support these methods that they claim "would encourage groups to combine their individual knowledge, opinions, and interests in support of the common good, avoiding entrenchment and stagnation."[56] But it could also mean an end to personal thoughts, dreams, and mental privacy as we know it, such as depicted in George Orwell's classic dystopian book *1984*, in which people are controlled by the "thought police" and punished for "thoughtcrimes" committed against the powers that be.[57]

The ramifications of the hive mind (or collective consciousness) on society and on the planet could be devastating not only to freedom of thought, but to mankind as a whole. What happens when a virus is introduced to the hive mind and the entirety of mankind becomes infected or wiped out altogether?

Essentially, this level of corruption could alter our memories, minds, and ability to make decisions based on our own free will. A virus of that caliber could rewrite or reprogram how we think, such as redrafting our memories or even turning us into human robots of sorts, paving the way for a satanic power to take control and lead us down the path to the end times. Chuck Missler said, "There is a super dictator coming, the Bible has warned us about that and he'll be accompanied with a delusion that is gonna be perpetrated on the human race."[58]

This begs the question of who will be running this super mind. Ultimately, it could be a satanic force using this technology to control mankind. What would stop a demonic entity from possessing a smartphone or some other futuristic technological device?

There is speculation that the creatures described in Revelation emerging from the bottomless pit could actually come through a sort of portal through a cyber/spiritual bridge and manifest into the physical realm here on earth using advanced forms of technology. Imagine being able to conjure up a demon through the Internet, like a digital

Quija board or "the Satan app." There is a lot of speculation about what could go wrong, but the only thing for certain is that the Bible warns us strange days are coming. The great deception is truly becoming realized with each passing day.

The Bible warns us "these kings of the earth have one mind, and shall give their power and strength unto the beast" (Revelation 17:13). Is this a warning of the beast's use of the hive mind on the rulers of the world, which John described as "one mind" to reach and control all of mankind as they "give their power and strength unto the beast?" It would be difficult for John to describe the sort of technology on the horizon of today's innovation when writing Revelation more than two thousand years ago. Still, he seems to capture the essence of the hive mind clearly in that one simple statement.

Transhumanist Hugo de Garis, an Australian researcher and professor known for his work in AI, claims his research would enable the creation of "artificial brains" that would quickly surpass human levels of intelligence.[59] Even after spending his career working towards those technological goals, De Garis outlines some shocking predictions about these advances. In his book *Artilect*, De Garis claims, "A major war before the end of the 21st century, resulting in billions of deaths, is almost inevitable."[60] This would basically be a war between man and machine. We saw how well that went in the *Terminator* films.

There could be a point when the hive mind is in effect, artificial intelligence is prevalent, and the Singularity has been reached, a time when man has become a slave to spiritual machines, hopelessly dependent on technology, and completely deceived by the promises that these technologies will improve the entire species, making humans immortal and godlike, much like the first lie promised by Satan in the Garden of Eden.

Many within the transhumanist movement believe the Singularity will inevitably result in postbiological humans. This synthetic hybrid will have the ability to trade in human bodies or even download their genetic makeup and minds into a computer system or server.[61] This gives

Apple's iCloud an eerie new meaning. (Apple probably already knew this was in the near future when they created it.)

Kurzweil predicts and is actively working towards a day when we will be able to bring back the dead, much like the idea behind tech company Luka's chatbot derived from online data about the person they wished to reconnect with. By giving an artificial intelligence as much information as possible about a person through videos, photographs, and possibly even DNA, it will be able to create a replica of that person that is indistinguishable from the original.[62] This leaves an open playing field for Satan to deceive us, possibly by using demonic possession of these avatars created out of the memories of our deceased loved ones. There is even a new "transreligion" called Terasem that is based on this very principle. The company allows its members to create a "mindfile" of information that can later be uploaded into a robot long after they die. The company's motto is "life is purposeful, death is optional, God is technological and love is essential."[63]

Many other technologists today are also actively seeking a hybrid life without death that replicates the omnipotence, omniscience, and immortality of God, uninhibited by the physical constraints mankind once endured. Satan first made this promise in the Garden of Eden and is circling around humanity and making this claim once again: "For God knows that when you eat from it your eyes will be open and you will be like God, knowing good and evil" (Genesis 3:5, NIV).

The idea that man can become immortal and godlike through transhumanism seems like the greatest deception imaginable upon the human race. As discussed in the film *The Last Religion*, once we alter ourselves according to that lie, will we then become beasts ourselves, Nephilim, perhaps even unredeemable in the eyes of God.[64]

The transhumanist agenda, coupled with massive technological advancements, could lead us right into the belly of the beast, the Antichrist system, and completely out of God's grace. Will the hive mind trap our consciousness into a cyber world indefinitely? Will the Singularity bring us to a point of no return in which humans are no longer able to die? Could this merging of man and machine bring about the prophecy made in Revelation 9:6 that says, "In those days shall men seek death and shall not find it; and shall desire to die, and death shall flee from them"?

There is strong speculation that hitting these points of no return and altering our human genetics will be a breaking point and the beginning of what Jesus calls the Great Tribulation: "The Man of Sin will position himself in the temple of God, claiming that he is God" (2 Thessalonians 2:3–4). At what point does man realize that perhaps these seemingly incredible technologies and transhumanist capabilities are not a gift from God, but simply the great deception Satan tempts us with while promising no more pain, suffering, or death?

Futurist Arthur C. Clarke famously said, "A sufficiently advanced technology is indistinguishable from magic."[65] Right now it seems like those advanced technologies could very well be the magic of Satan and technological image of the beast that we're so strongly warned about in the last days.

The current and future technologies on the horizon will undoubtedly transform both humanity and the world of nature from a biological standpoint, as well as how biblical prophecy lays out an end-times scenario of global control and deception. There is firm reason to believe that artificial intelligence will pave the way for a leader and False Messiah to emerge and lead all of mankind to the ultimate battle against the True Messiah, Jesus Christ, famously labeled the Battle of Armageddon.

12

Two Witnesses Appear

Bible prophecy sometimes follows a straight line of progression. At other times, it seems convoluted and folds in upon itself. For example, it might flow like a newspaper report of the facts that will come to pass. Or, it might present a sense of flashbacks and flashforwards not unlike a novel or movie, requiring careful study. Always, though, God's Word is truth, and learning that Word will be assisted by the Holy Spirit as we earnestly attempt to understand. The study of the Bible—especially of prophecy—with intensity and purpose to gain comprehension of things to come is worth the effort and will be greatly rewarded. We are promised by Jesus, who gave the Revelation to John the prophet:

> The Revelation of Jesus Christ, which God gave unto him, to shew unto his servants things which must shortly come to pass; and he sent and signified it by his angel unto his servant John:
>
> Who bare record of the word of God, and of the testimony of Jesus Christ, and of all things that he saw.

Blessed is he that readeth, and they that hear the words of
this prophecy, and keep those things which are written therein:
for the time is at hand. (Revelation 1:1–3)

Jesus is saying that those who read, heed, and follow through on
obeying things written in His Word will receive blessings. The Lord here
is almost certainly promising a special blessing for those who give themselves to studying His prophetic Word.

Following the Rapture of the Church, the greatest time of trouble in
human history is coming upon the world scene. We've seen this many
times thus far. Sometimes we've seen a straight reporting of how things
will unfold, and at other times, we see the folding, flashbacks, and
flash-forwards.

So, it's somewhat difficult to establish exactly when the two dynamic
men of God—the two witnesses of Revelation 11—will appear. Theirs
will indeed be a ministry of dynamism never matched in the annals of
ministry, so far as forewarning others about what opposing God will
bring to earth's rebels. They will preach and prophesy with such fervency
that the anti-God forces will hate them and seek to kill them. Antichrist
will pursue them with the fervor with which he will pursue the fleeing
Jews following his claim to be god in the temple.

These two men will be untouchable for the time of their witness.
As a matter of fact, anyone who tries to kill them will be destroyed, the
prophecy says.

And I will give power unto my two witnesses, and they shall
prophesy a thousand two hundred and threescore days, clothed
in sackcloth.

These are the two olive trees, and the two candlesticks standing before the God of the earth.

And if any man will hurt them, fire proceedeth out of their
mouth, and devoureth their enemies: and if any man will hurt
them, he must in this manner be killed.

> These have power to shut heaven, that it rain not in the days
> of their prophecy: and have power over waters to turn them to
> blood, and to smite the earth with all plagues, as often as they
> will. (Revelation 11:3–6)

When their time of their mission is finished, Antichrist will at last be
allowed to kill them.

> And when they shall have finished their testimony, the beast that
> ascendeth out of the bottomless pit shall make war against them,
> and shall overcome them, and kill them.
> And their dead bodies shall lie in the street of the great city,
> which spiritually is called Sodom and Egypt, where also our
> Lord was crucified. (Revelation 11:7–8)

When these witnesses are finally slain, the world of rebellious earth
dwellers—as the Bible calls them—will rejoice.

> And they of the people and kindreds and tongues and nations
> shall see their dead bodies three days and a half, and shall not
> suffer their dead bodies to be put in graves.
> And they that dwell upon the earth shall rejoice over them,
> and make merry, and shall send gifts one to another; because
> these two prophets tormented them that dwelt on the earth.
> (Revelation 11:10–11)

These men will have pointed to the people of earth and accused
them of their blasphemous, rebellious, anti-God comportment. Like
Elijah and Moses of ancient days, these prophets will bring plagues upon
the world, each becoming more punishing than the next. When they
are finally murdered by Antichrist forces, news-gathering sources will no
doubt aim cameras on them and broadcast the image of them lying in
the streets of Jerusalem.

This prophecy used to make people wonder how it would be possible for all the world to see these dead men on the streets. But that long ago ceased to be a wonder. Satellite will instantly broadcast the sight to most every part of the world as they lie decomposing for three days.

People will throw great parties of congratulations: The preachers who pointed fingers and called for them to repent are no longer around to torment them! But that will come to an end with staggering suddenness.

> And after three days and an half the Spirit of life from God entered into them, and they stood upon their feet; and great fear fell upon them which saw them.
>
> And they heard a great voice from heaven saying unto them, Come up hither. And they ascended up to heaven in a cloud; and their enemies beheld them. (Revelation 11:11–12)

When these dead men suddenly stir upon the screens of computer monitors and televisions across the world, the shock will be stunning to the gawkers. The resurrected men will stand upon their feet, and a voice will be heard beckoning them to come into heaven. No doubt there will be fatal heart attacks in some of the onlookers as God manifests His great power to resurrect the dead, then calls them to Himself.

Just after the moment the witnesses rise into the clouds, an earthquake of one of the most powerful magnitudes ever will shake the city and the world, as God's power continues to manifest before the eyes of those who have shown their hatred for Him and His governance.

> And the same hour was there a great earthquake, and the tenth part of the city fell, and in the earthquake were slain of men seven thousand: and the remnant were affrighted, and gave glory to the God of heaven. (Revelation 11:13)

This will so frighten those watching—those who see seven thousand men die in the quake—that the "remnant" (the term for the Jews who are or will become believers) will, the prophecy says, give glory to the True God of Heaven. It is likely that many Gentiles who watch these astonishing things will also be so frightened as to be moved to reconsider their rebellion and following Antichrist.

Whether this means they will instantly believe and be saved, we can't say for certain. If the mark of Revelation 13:16–18 has been instituted, those who have received it cannot repent and be saved, according to Revelation 14. But one has to think that many, if they haven't taken the mark at this time, will turn to God at that stupefying moment.

Some scholars of Bible prophecy believe the seven thousand men mentioned as being slain by the earthquake represent the most notable men of Jerusalem—likely some of the top men under Antichrist. They are probably suddenly swallowed up as the earth gives way, much like what happened to the rebellious Israelites and Egyptian people who fled Pharaoh in the Exodus, but who turned to idol worship while Moses received the Ten Commandments atop Mount Sinai.

Identity of the Two Witnesses

There has always been much controversy over who these two prophets are who so upset the inhabitants of Tribulation-era earth. Indeed, there are good arguments from a number of viewpoints.

Most prophecy students and scholars believe that Elijah is one of the two. This Old Testament prophet performed many of the plague-like judgments, under God's authority and power, that the two witnesses will perform. Elijah never died, but was lifted into the heavenly dimension by a fiery chariot while his successor, Elisha, stood mesmerized while watching. This, many believe, gives good reason to think Elijah will be one of the two.

Another reason for this thinking is that the Jewish people are promised that Elijah will again come back to them before the "great and terrible Day of the Lord"—i.e., he will return to assist God's chosen people in their time of trouble. Jews today, some orthodox believers and some secular types who simply like tradition, provide an empty chair and plate at their tables in remembrance of God's promise to send the prophet at some point near the time of the Messiah's coming.

Moses is another thought to be one of the two witnesses. His body was never discovered, because God, Himself, buried him (see Deuteronomy 34:5–7). Moses, too, was given authority and power to bring down plagues on Pharaoh's kingdom while convincing the Egyptian king to release the Israelites in the Exodus.

Another candidate is Enoch. He was taken by God in a Rapture-like translation by God, because he walked so closely to the Lord. Some think this means Enoch might be returned to serve as one of the two witnesses during the mid-Tribulation point, just before that point, or right after it.

Dr. J. Dwight Pentecost, in his book *Things to Come,* presented the following from an author who weighed in on the two witnesses. It is yet another view of who they might be.

It would seem best to conclude that the identity of these men is uncertain. They, in all probability, are not men who lived before and have been restored, but are two men raised up as a special witness, to whom sign-working power is given. Their ministry is one of judgment, as their sackcloth clothing indicates. They are slain by the beast (Rev. 13:1–10). Concerning the time of their death the same author says:

Mental arithmetic will quickly reveal that the period of prophecy entrusted to the two witnesses, twelve hundred and sixty days, is three and one-half years in duration. In which half of the Tribulation, then, will these witnesses prophesy? Or will their witness not be limited by either half of the seven years, but run from one half into the other? I do not think we can be dogmatic about it. There is thought-provoking logic in the argument that their testimony will be given during the first half of

Daniel's prophetic week, and that their martyrdom will be the first persecuting act of the Beast, after he breaks his covenant with the Jews (Dan. 9:27). Their ministry will be attended with power over their enemies, whereas, according to Daniel 7:21, the "little horn" (who is this Beast) will make war with the saints and prevail against them, and this will be in the last half of the week. On the other hand, in Revelation 11:2 the "forty and two months" undoubtedly refers to the second half of the Tribulation, and the period of the testimony of the two witnesses seems to be synchronous with this. Further, their witness is recorded just prior to the blowing of the Seventh Trumpet, and this event takes us right on into the Millennial Kingdom. But the exact period when the testimony will take place is unimportant to believers of this age—it will be in God's time, that we know, and that will be the proper time.[66]

So, it is unclear who these men will be and exactly when their time of ministry will begin. They will obviously dominate the news of that time and cause Antichrist's rage to grow by the minute as they proclaim the glory of God and urge the son of perdition's victims to turn to the Lord for salvation.

Their message will be punctuated mightily by the tremendous feats they perform. There can be no doubt that they'll be unleashed with supernatural abilities that surpass even those of the False Prophet, Antichrist's Goebbels-type propagandist.

Bill Salus, in his book *The LAST Prophecies: The Prophecies in the First 3½ Years of the Tribulation*, writes the following on these witnesses' time on earth and the powerful forces of judgment they will call down upon Antichrist and rebellious people living on earth at that time:

These Two Witnesses will:
1. Have power to prevent rainfall, turn waters to blood and create plagues (v 3, 6),

2. Prophesy for one thousand two hundred and sixty days clothed in sackcloth (v 3),
3. Live constantly in harm's way (v 5),
4. Kill those who attempt to harm them (v 5),
5. Successfully profess their testimonies (v 7),
6. Be killed by the Antichrist (v 7),
7. Lie dead in the streets of Jerusalem for three-and-a-half days (v 8–9),
8. Torment those (unbelievers) who dwell on the earth (v 10),
9. Resurrect from the dead (v 11),
10. Ascend to heaven (v 12),
11. Be instrumental in causing (some) Jews to recognize God (v 13).

The Identities of the Two Witnesses

Is it possible, from the clues provided in Revelation 11:3–13, to make an educated guess as to who are these Two Witnesses? Some believe that they are Moses and Elijah. Others suggest they are Elijah and Enoch. Some have posited that they could be none of the above, but might be two entirely new faces. The strong arguments that favor Moses and Elijah as the Two Witnesses are explained below.

1. Moses and Elijah appeared together on the mount of transfiguration. (Matthew 17:3–4). If they appeared together in a significant event of the past, they will likely appear together in the future as well.

2. Moses and Elijah possessed in the past the similar supernatural powers that the Two Witnesses possess in the future. These powers include:

- Fire that proceeds from the mouth and devours their enemies (v 5),

- Power to shut heaven so that no rain falls in the day of their prophecy (v 6),
- Power over waters to turn them to blood (v 6),
- The ability to strike the earth with ALL PLAGUES, as often as they desire (v 6).

Elijah's former powers concerning rain are documented in 1 Kings 17:1, 1 Kings 18:1, James 5:17–18. Elijah also called down fire from heaven in 1 Kings 18:38, and 2 Kings 1:10. Moses turned the waters to blood in Exodus 7:20–21. Concerning Moses and his ability to strike the earth will all plagues, he struck Egypt with ten plagues, which led to the Exodus of the Hebrews out of Egyptian bondage. The plagues were:

- First Plague: Water turned to blood, (Exodus 7:20–21),
- Second Plague: Frog infestation throughout Egypt, (Exodus 8:2–4),
- Third Plague: Gnats or lice infestation throughout Egypt, (Exodus 8:16–17),
- Fourth Plague: Swarms of flies on the people and in their houses, (Exodus 8:21),
- Fifth Plague: Livestock diseased, (Exodus 9:3),
- Sixth Plague: Boil infections upon the Egyptians, (Exodus 9:8–11),
- Seventh Plague: Hailstones rain down upon Egypt, (Exodus 9:18),
- Eighth Plague: Locusts cover the face of the earth, (Exodus 10:4–5),
- Ninth Plague: Thick blanket of darkness over Egypt, (Exodus 10:21–22),
- Tenth Plague: Deaths of the firstborn in Egypt, (Exodus 11:4–5).

Observation: The Plagues of the Two Witnesses
and the Trumpet Judgments

It's worthy to note, that some of the plagues performed by the Two Witnesses seem to be repeated in some variation within some of the trumpet judgments detailed in Revelation 8–9. The first trumpet involves hail and fire mingled with blood (Rev. 8:7). The second trumpet predicts that one-third of the seas will turn into blood (Rev. 8:8). The fourth trumpet says that one-third of the sun, moon and stars become darkened (Rev. 8:12). The fifth trumpet involves a plague of locusts (Rev. 9:3).

It is probable that the trumpet judgments are occurring within the same time-period that the Two Witnesses are ministering on the earth. Although, the trumpet judgments are cast upon the earth via the means of seven angels, and not the two witnesses, the affected populations will not likely be cognizant of that distinction. The verse below points out that the Two Witnesses are tormenting those who dwell on the earth.

"And those who dwell on the earth will rejoice over them, make merry, and send gifts to one another, because these two prophets tormented those who dwell on the earth." (Rev. 11:10)

It can be assumed that the tormenting is primarily the result of the Two Witnesses executing their powers, which includes the ability to strike the earth with ALL PLAGUES in Rev. 11:6. When these Two Witnesses lie dead in the streets of Jerusalem, *"those who dwell on the earth will rejoice, make merry and send gifts to one another."* This merriment is likely because the gift-givers could be under the impression that ALL the PLAGUES end with their deaths. It wouldn't be surprising if at that time the Antichrist, who kills these Two Witnesses, comes out publicly and declares that the plagues have ended. However, the plagues will continue to happen as the bowl judgments are poured out in the Great Tribulation.

More Reasons to Favor Moses and Elijah as the Two Witnesses
3. Elijah was caught up in a whirlwind to heaven and never experienced death, (2 Kings 2:11–12). This fact implies that Elijah is alive, available and ready to return to the earth as one of the Two Witnesses. Enoch was also caught up to heaven, which is why some believe that he could also return as one of the Two Witnesses, (Genesis 5:24).

4. The Old Testament prophet Malachi predicts the return of Elijah.

"Behold, I will send you Elijah the prophet Before the coming of the great and dreadful day of the Lord. And he will turn The hearts of the fathers to the children, And the hearts of the children to their fathers, Lest I come and strike the earth with a curse." (Malachi 4:5–6)

5. Moses represents the Law and Elijah the Prophets. When the Two Witnesses are on the earth, the Jews are reinstating the Mosaic Law and its animal sacrificial system. Moses and Elijah would be prime candidates to rebuke this effort. Both know that Jesus Christ is the Messiah. This was evidenced clearly to them at the mount of Transfiguration when the Lord said, "This is My beloved Son, in whom I am well pleased. Hear Him!" (Matthew 17:5). Jesus Christ fulfilled the Law, (Matthew 5:17), and in so doing, He rendered it inoperative. Galatians 3:24 clarifies the purpose of the law. It reads, "Therefore the law was our tutor to bring us to Christ, that we might be justified by faith."

6. There was a dispute between Satan and Michael the archangel over the body of Moses. This could imply that Satan is

concerned about Moses returning to the earth again as one of the Two Witnesses, (Jude 1:9). According to some midrashim accounts, God grants Moses a beautiful death. Below is a quote from an article entitled, "The Divine Kiss."

"At the end, God leans down from the heavens and ends Moses' life with a soft, gentle kiss. This is derived from Deuteronomy 34:5, where it is written, 'So Moses, the servant of the Eternal, died there, in the land of Moab, at the command of the Eternal.' The Hebrew reads, al pi Adonai, 'by the mouth of the Eternal.' Hence the legend about God kissing Moses at his moment of death. According to the Midrash, God wept after Moses died, as did the heavens and the earth. Deuteronomy 34:6 tells us that "God buried him in the valley in the land of Moab, near Beth-peor; and no one knows his burial place to this day."

How did a soft and gentle kiss from the Lord bring an end to the life of Moses? Where is the undisclosed location of his grave? Did Moses truly die and was he buried? The answers to these two questions appear to be yes and yes, but his appearance at the "Mount of Transfiguration" about 1200 years after his death, established the biblical and historical precedent for his potential return as one of the Two Witnesses.

The Timing of the Two Witnesses

There is a debate about whether these Two Witnesses prophesy in the first or second half of the Tribulation Period. Below is a quote on this timing topic from Dr. Ron Rhodes. He writes the following in his book entitled, *The End Times in Chronological Order.*

"Scholars debate whether the ministry of the two witnesses belongs in the first half or the second half of the tribulation. Their ministry will last 1260 days, which measures out to precisely three and a half years."… "Most prophecy scholars conclude that the two witnesses do their miraculous work during the first three and a half years."[67]

The massive earthquake will shake things as never before, but the things that will come upon the earth soon after that quaking will be much, much more destructive. The next chapter of Revelation opens with a frightening event:

> And there was war in heaven: Michael and his angels fought against the dragon; and the dragon fought and his angels, And prevailed not; neither was their place found any more in heaven.
>
> And the great dragon was cast out, that old serpent, called the Devil, and Satan, which deceiveth the whole world: he was cast out into the earth, and his angels were cast out with him.
>
> And I heard a loud voice saying in heaven, Now is come salvation, and strength, and the kingdom of our God, and the power of his Christ: for the accuser of our brethren is cast down, which accused them before our God day and night.
>
> And they overcame him by the blood of the Lamb, and by the word of their testimony; and they loved not their lives unto the death. Therefore rejoice, ye heavens, and ye that dwell in them.
>
> Woe to the inhabiters of the earth and of the sea! for the devil is come down unto you, having great wrath, because he knoweth that he hath but a short time.
>
> And when the dragon saw that he was cast unto the earth, he persecuted the woman which brought forth the man child. (Revelation 12:7–13)

Lucifer will truly be fallen at this point. He will be restricted from ever being able to move about the heavens or to come before the throne of God and accuse believers. Heaven will be blessed, but the earth will be in for unprecedented trouble.

Satan will add to the Antichrist's human minions his superhuman ones. The devil will know that his time is almost up, so he will rage as never before to cause as much death and destruction to the human race, particularly to the Jewish race, as possible.

God's wrath, too, will fall in greater power than ever before. Rebels against God upon this condemned sphere will truly experience hell on earth.

13

Seven Seals, Seven Trumpets, Seven Bowls

e again look at where the rebellious people of post-Rapture earth have been to understand what happens next in the progression of Bible prophecy and why. In thinking on Antichrist and the implementation of his Final Solution, it is necessary to revisit very briefly the prophetic stage-setting we have observed.

After a time of worldwide panic and chaos, the earth, as we have seen, will throw a party of sorts following Christ's saints' Rapture into heaven. Earth-dwellers will be deluded into thinking, at some point, that the evil influences that have held back progress have been removed. Now they can at last achieve their utopia, long promised by the one-world order gurus. That thought will be at the heart of their jubilation.

There will doubtless be explanations that will eventually calm fears. Those left behind following the great vanishing will likely be told that their loved ones who have disappeared were removed by "space brothers" or some other force to take them to an ethereal location of some sort for reeducation into the ways necessary for them to become productive citizens of the emerging New World Order.

The children—*all* children, even infants and those yet unborn—were taken away, those left behind will be told, to see to it they are properly inculcated from their earliest days as people of the new paradigm.

Already, today, we're seeing in the high places of academia the abandonment of evolution as a plausible theory for how mankind came to be. There are growing disputes among the scientific community that Darwin and the various derivatives of his "origins of mankind" are coming apart. There are too many inconsistencies and incongruities in the outdated, outmoded theory of evolution.

It is well within the realm of plausibility to consider that those left behind will fall victim to the deception that corrupted those of the antediluvian world. The pre-Flood people were seduced by the angels who "left their first estate" (the heavenly realm) when the "sons of god" (fallen angels) "came to earth" and took "daughters of men" (human women) and produced offspring. These offspring, it is almost certain, became the giants and titans from which the legends of super-beings like Hercules and the Titans come.

It is more than interesting to ask if there might not be a similar visitation when, for example, Revelation 12 is fulfilled and the devil and his angels are cast out of heaven, never to be allowed there again.

The so-called seed theory, which seems to fit this prophetic scenario, is well into the process of coming to the forefront as explanation of human development. "Space brothers," it is increasingly postulated, long ago "seeded" this big, blue marble with their biological material. Now, they have returned to keep the planet from destroying itself, those left behind will be deluded into thinking.

If not this spellbinding answer to the mind-terrorizing question of why these—especially all small children and even fetuses—vanished in a microsecond, it will be some other mesmerizing answer. Whatever the seductive explanation, that deception will set those left behind ablaze with excitement in anticipation of their promised, glorious future. But within a relatively short time, their frenzied elation will turn to uncertainty, then to fear, then to terror beyond ability to describe.

God's Cup of Wrath Overflows

God's cup of judgment has been filling since the time He poured it out the first time—during the Flood that covered the whole earth, when only Noah and seven of his family members went into the ark, and God, Himself, shut and sealed the door. His saints (Noah and his family) rose above the judgment; they were saved out of the carnage.

Saints Will Rise!

One day—perhaps today—God's saints will be taken from the planet's surface, and, ultimately, God's judgment will again flood the earth. Billions will die, but not from an inundation of waters. It will be a deluge of twenty-one specific judgments, which God's Word describes as being sent in a three-part series: 1) scroll, 2) trumpet, and 3) vials (bowls)—with seven judgments coming from each of the series.

Twofold Purpose of Judgments

Earth's party won't get too far into the celebrations before things will begin to go wrong—terribly wrong. As we've seen, the great world leader will step forward and offer a plan that will astound the people of the planet. Peace between Israel and its hatred-filled, blood-vowed enemies will be at the heart of the great man's blueprint for beginning (again) the earth's drive toward heaven on earth. But his *real* design will be the establishment of his Fourth Reich. He will soon bring forth his Final Solution.

Peace That Destroys

The peace that the leader assures by signing the covenant that guarantees Israel's security will be the very thing that fills God's cup of wrath to overflowing. Israel's acceptance of Antichrist, having rejected Jesus Christ, their Messiah, at least two millennia earlier, will cause God's fury to become full-blown. Jesus, Himself, said of Israel's rejection and of that time when Israel will accept Antichrist:

> I am come in my Father's name, and ye receive me not: if another shall come in his own name, him ye will receive. (John 5:43)

God's anger will flow in increasing volume upon the those who won't turn from their sin against Him. Daniel, the great prophet, described the whole end-time scenario, from the moment Israel rejected its Messiah through the very end of the terrible judgments that will end the Tribulation and bring Christ's Second Coming in power and glory. Let's look at Daniel's words again:

> And after threescore and two weeks shall Messiah be cut off, but not for himself: and the people of the prince that shall come shall destroy the city and the sanctuary; and the end thereof shall be with a flood, and unto the end of the war desolations are determined.
>   And he shall confirm the covenant with many for one week: and in the midst of the week he shall cause the sacrifice and the oblation to cease, and for the overspreading of abominations he shall make it desolate, even until the consummation, and that determined shall be poured upon the desolate. (Daniel 9:26–27)

Purpose Behind Judgments

The purpose of these righteous judgments for the entire Tribulation is to purge a remnant of Israel to love and obey God and be His people forever and bring a vast number of people out of the Gentile world to be His for eternity.

Purging Israel

The first reason God sends judgment upon the earth, once Antichrist confirms the covenant of security (peace), is to call out a remnant of His chosen people, the Jews, as people who love Him and will obey Him. Dr. Dave Breese presented this process in the following:

> The Tribulation is, therefore, the time of Jacob's trouble. Jeremiah says, "Alas! for that day is great, so that none is like it: it is even the time of Jacob's trouble; but he shall be saved out of it" (Jeremiah 30:7).
>
> Israel is held responsible by the Lord, along with the Gentiles, for the crucifixion of Christ. This is the reason for the awesome silence of Jehovah in relating to His people during the two millennia that have transpired since the death of Christ. Clearly, however, the Word of God declares that God has not finally and completely cast away His people.
>
> Indeed, the Scripture speaks of the casting away of Israel and announced that that [casting away] produced the reconciling of the world. The Scripture then speaks of the receiving of Israel, which will be life from the dead for the nations. Israel moved into a period of blindness and estrangement from God until a point of time called the fullness of the Gentiles (Romans 11:25).
>
> At this point, God promises to work in goodness and severity with His people so that...Israel will be brought to a place of decision and faith. This is always the intention of divine discipline for His own, in any era of history.
>
> The Tribulation, then, will be a time of the conversion of Israel. Most boldly, the Scripture announces:
>
> And so all Israel shall be saved: as it is written, There shall come out of Zion the Deliverer, and shall turn away ungodliness from Jacob; For this is my covenant unto them, when I shall take away their sins. (Romans 11:26–27)

Spiritual Revival

The Tribulation will, therefore, be a time of great spiritual revival. It will mark the conversion of Israel and great activity by Israel for the conversion of the world.

The Book of the Revelation, therefore, announces an amazing multitude of 144,000 witnesses who represent the twelve tribes of Israel. These will have been converted during the days of the Tribulation and will have a profound effect upon the world. When one remembers that there is only a fraction of this number of Christian missionaries in the world today, one is impressed with the zealous response that will come out of Israel in the form of faith in Jesus Christ as its Messiah. "The gospel of the Kingdom" will be preached with great zeal by them to the world.

Bringing Forth Gentile Saints

God's second reason for the period of judgments known as the Tribulation is to save, through their belief in Jesus, a great host of Gentile people to be a part of His family for eternity. Again, Breese explains:

The Tribulation will also be a time of massive conversion of Gentile multitudes. The Revelation says, after this I beheld, and, lo, a great multitude, which no man could number, of all nations, and kindreds, and people, and tongues, stood before the throne, and before the Lamb, clothed with white robes, and palms in their hands (Revelation 7:9).

So remarkable is this sight that one of the elders around God's throne asked who these people are. The answer from the Word of God is: "These are they who came out of the great tribulation, and have washed their robes, and made them white in the blood of the Lamb" (Revelation 7:14).

Amazing spiritual results occur when the world comes to the end of itself, realizing that nothing on earth is of any value. It then turns in great numbers to faith in Christ as Messiah, bringing in a time of evangelism that will be one of the largest and most effective in the history of the world. The anguish of the Tribulation produces a most salutary result. But a fearful time it will be!

Overview of Tribulation Terrors

It is wonderful to consider that we who are Christians will be in heaven with our Lord Jesus while all the prophesied horrors of the Tribulation are unfolding on earth. The Rapture is mockingly called "pie in the sky," "in the sweet by and by," and "wishful escapism" by those who don't believe in a Rapture or who believe Christians must prove how brave and strong we are by standing up to Antichrist in going through what Jesus called the worst time that has ever been.

There are some things Jesus indicated that are well worth escaping. We'll look more in depth at the most horrendous of the judgments shortly. For now, this might be a good place to put the things scheduled following the Rapture, according to prophecy, in a nutshell for quick review.

- Antichrist and the False Prophet will also have all the new believers they can find rounded up, tortured, then murdered.
- While Antichrist hunts down and murders people by the millions, God's judgments will begin to fall directly on the rebellious people of the earth.
- Millions upon millions will die while God's wrath pours out in a series of three types of judgments, each consisting of seven specific judgments, for a total of twenty-one.

- When all is said and done, more than half, possibly as much as two-thirds, of all human life on earth will die of the plagues.
- God will prepare, and the Jewish remnant will flee to, a hiding place, probably Petra, the ancient city carved in the rose-red-colored rocks of the Jordanian wilderness.
- Antichrist and his forces, led by Satan, will pursue the Jewish people and try to murder them, but the pursuing forces will be swallowed up by the earth.
- While the Jewish and many of the Gentile people still alive remain safely protected, God's wrath will fall in greater force.
- The sun will go partly dark, while at the same time heating up to seven times hotter than normal.
- A great object will fall into the ocean from space. Its impact will kill life in the sea, and most likely will destroy coastal areas with tidal waves.
- Another asteroid or other mass from space will strike earth and poison much of the planet's freshwater sources.
- Great, unprecedented earthquakes will happen simultaneously all over the world.
- People will be so frightened they will have heart attacks, just from the things they see are yet to come.
- A supernatural plague of huge, insect-like creatures will be released from the abyss, and they will sting all who have the mark of the beast. Men and women will try to commit suicide because of their great pain from the stings and bites of these demonic creatures.
- God will then move in the minds of all military forces on earth to gather in the valley of Jezreel, the plains of Esdraelon, near the ancient city of Megiddo. This is Armageddon.
- The "kings of the east," a huge army out of the Orient numbering more than two hundred million troops, will invade to make war with the forces of Antichrist.

- Jesus said of this time that if He didn't come back, everyone and everything would die because of the fighting about to take place.
- Jesus will return with the armies of heaven. His armies consist of the mighty angels and Jesus' Church, which will have been raptured at least seven years earlier.
- Antichrist's armies and all others will try to prevent Christ's return.
- Jesus will simply speak, and all armies on earth will be rendered helpless, with most killed.

Scary stuff, huh? But it will all happen. You have God's Word on that. A bunch of good reasons to be "Rapture ready," and to be found worthy to stand before Jesus, don't you think?

Again, Dave Breese informs us about the coming time of Tribulation.

The Tribulation is the time of the outpouring of the wrath of God upon a wicked world. In the account of the horsemen of the Apocalypse, when the fourth horseman rides forth, the Scripture says, power was given unto them over the fourth part of earth to kill with sword, and with hunger, and with death, and with the beasts of the earth (Revelation 6:8).

In the beginning days of the Revelation, therefore, approximately 25 percent of the world is killed in the opening wars pestilences of days. Very quickly, the Scripture says,

"And thus I saw the horses in the vision, and them that sat on them, having breastplates of fire, and of jacinth, and brimstone: and the heads of the horses were as the heads of lions; and out of their mouths issued fire and smoke and brimstone. By these three was the third part of men killed, by the fire, and by the smoke, and by the brimstone, which issued out of their mouths" (Revelation 9:17–18).

A third part of men killed! This already mounts up to one half of the world's population, and beyond this point in the Revelation many other natural catastrophes take place. As the Tribulation unfolds, there are mighty earthquakes, occasions of scorching heat, the advent of the Antichrist, world occult religious organization, and finally, the Battle of Armageddon, which will be fatal to scores of millions of soldiers. This time of natural catastrophe combined with divine judgment will bring awesome carnage across the face of the earth.

Words of Comfort

Just a quick look around today lets us know that the darkest hours of human history loom not too far in the distance. What tremendous power there is in knowing that born-again Christians will not have to endure the things that are coming to a world in rebellion against our Mighty God. Again, we know we won't have to face God's anger and judgment for sin, based upon—for one example—the prophetic words of Paul to us through the Thessalonian Christians nearly two millennia ago:

> For God hath not appointed us to wrath, but to obtain salvation by our Lord Jesus Christ,
>
> Who died for us, that, whether we wake or sleep, we should live together with him.
>
> Wherefore comfort yourselves together, and edify one another, even as also ye do. (1 Thessalonians 5:9–11)

Let us indeed comfort ourselves with these words. Let us, at the same time, do all within our power—and that power, through Jesus, is considerable—to reach the lost before it's too late for them to avoid the horrors coming upon the earth.

God as World Champion!

We've seen through Bible study that the apostle Paul often used sports terms to teach principles of godly living. We're told we don't "wrestle against flesh and blood," we "run" in the race of life, and we must not "beat" the air, as a boxer does when shadowboxing.

Paul's sports analogies fit very well while we consider the final years, months, days, and hours of human history just before Jesus' Second Coming. We will look at the Tribulation as the great climax in the battle of good versus evil. It will be a fight to determine the real champion for eternity. Although it won't be much of a fight, from the standpoint of competition, it will be the bloodiest of all conflicts ever.

The Seal Judgments

God calls on Jesus, the Lamb of God, to open the seals that will unleash righteous judgment upon a world that has totally rejected the Father's call to salvation. With Jesus releasing the judgments of God from the very first scroll, we know that it's God's wrath from the very beginning of the seven years of Tribulation.

The championship battle to prove who is and is not the champion for eternity begins…

The four horsemen of the apocalypse will ride forth upon command by Jesus, as He unrolls each of the first four sealed scrolls. These will be the opening rounds of this bloody battle.

Round One: White Horse of False Peace

The first rider, on the white horse, is Antichrist, who will come offering peace (Revelation 6:2). As we've already discussed, he is really a deceiver and a conqueror, however. He will promise prosperity and freedom to do whatever feels good. But, the jubilation over the fact that the Christians are gone, thus can't preach to earth-dwellers, won't last long. Antichrist's true colors will begin to show. They will be blood red! The peace he offers will destroy millions (read Daniel 8:25).

Round Two: Red Horse of War

The second rider, on a red horse, is the rider of war (see Revelation 6:4). The false peace Antichrist promised will be broken, and millions will die from unprecedented wars—all of which will be a prelude to the ultimate war, Armageddon!

Round Three: Black Horse of Famine

The third rider, on a black horse, is famine (see Revelation 6:5). Millions upon millions will die of starvation and other results of the all-out war-making ushered in by the rider on the red horse.

We have only to consider the great world wars of the last century and all other wars to know that hunger and disease inevitably follow the carnage. Considering that some of the future wars will include nuclear, biological, and chemical weaponry, the probability of great hunger and disease multiplies many times.

Round Four: Pale Horse of Death

The fourth rider, on a pale horse, has a partner riding close behind. The front rider is death (Revelation 6:8). Sheol, the abode of the dead nonbelievers, will follow. These riders will account for the death of a fourth of the world's population. The disease and famine will continue to mount.

Round Five: Martyrs

When Jesus opens the fifth seal, the saints of the Tribulation era who have been martyred for Christ will be seen in their white robes of salvation before God's throne (Revelation 6:9–11). Many scholars believe that the Tribulation will produce the greatest soul-harvest ever. Many believe the numbers saved during this time will far surpass the number of people saved during the Age of Grace (Church Age).

Round Six: Earth-Shaking Events

As the sixth seal is opened, there will be a great earthquake, the sun will darken, and the moon will turn (see Revelation 6:12–14). These events will so frighten the world's leaders that they will beg the rocks and caves in which they are hiding to fall on them and conceal them from the furious God of heaven. No wonder the prophetic Scripture tells us that men's hearts will fail them for fear of the things they see coming upon the earth. Yet earth-dwellers still won't repent; they'll actually curse God.

Round Seven: Getting a Breather

Unlike human athletes, God needs no breaks to catch His breath. But, He seems to take a breather in anticipation of the next catastrophic set of judgments with the opening of the seventh seal: a thirty-minute period of silence in heaven (Revelation 8:1–2). Following that quiet time, seven angels standing before God will be given the seven trumpets.

Most prophecy scholars see that this is a pattern God always follows in rendering His judgments, or between taking action in a series. For example, in Genesis, He takes the seventh day off from all the work He had done in the creation. He, therefore, takes a short time out between the sixth and seventh seals. But the pause doesn't change the minds and hearts of the evil ones who oppose him.

The Trumpet Judgments

God then prepares to step up the pace as the trumpet judgments begin.

Round Eight (First Trumpet): Hail, Fire, and Blood

After the angel sounds the first trumpet, hail and fire mixed with blood will fall from heaven. The fire will cause all green grass and a third of the earth's trees to burn up (see Revelation 8:6–7). Certainly, it will already appear to be the end of the world as we know it. God will fire off a stunning blow to those who won't repent of their sin against Him. But this will be just the beginning of His body blows to the planet.

Round Nine (Second Trumpet): Burning Mountain

Something that looked, to John, like a burning mountain will be cast into the sea. A third of the sea will turn to blood, a third of all sea life will die, and a third of the ships at sea will be destroyed (Revelation 8:8–9).

This will be a stupendous blow to a planet already reeling because of God's judgments. Any time God's Word uses phrases like "as it were" (Revelation 8:8), it is a symbolic description of something that is literal. In other words, this will not be a physical mountain, but it will be "like" a mountain in size. It really will be a big rock that's on fire, and it sounds much like the asteroids, meteors, and other rocks from space that pose danger to our planet. This prophecy appears to forewarn that something like that will slam into one of the oceans.

This event will be catastrophic to earth's environment, because the Bible says that the sea will become like blood, thick and slimy. A third of sea life will die and a third of all ships will be destroyed by the tremendous tidal waves.

Round Ten (Third Trumpet): Star Called Wormwood

A heavenly object of some sort called "Wormwood" will cause another great blow to earth's water supplies as it crashes into the planet. This time, the fresh waters will be poisoned, and people who drink from the affected waters will die (Revelation 8:10–11).

As noted by many who write on prophetic matters, the word "wormwood" in the Ukrainian language is "Chernobyl." Sound familiar? This is the town in the Ukraine infamous for the worst nuclear power plant disaster to date. The object falling from space, as described in this judgment, might well be nuclear, perhaps a nuclear-tipped missile.

Round Eleven (Fourth Trumpet): Darkness

The earth's inhabitants will next receive a black eye, so to speak, so that their vision will be severely affected. The sun will darken by a third, so naturally the moon, a reflective body, will also have its light diminished by one-third. The stars also will be supernaturally darkened (Revelation 8:12).

God seems to step back and size up His opponent before moving in to punish the rebels of earth even more. The ringside announcer—an angel—will proclaim that the next judgments will be even worse than the first (Revelation 8:13).

Round Twelve (Fifth Trumpet): Plague of Locusts

God apparently allows an angelic being to open the abyss, or "bottomless pit," releasing the weirdest, most fearsome creatures ever seen (Revelation 9:1–5). They're described as being like scorpions whose stings hurt people for five months. Many prophecy scholars are convinced the angelic being is Satan, who will fall to earth when he is cast out of heaven during the Tribulation, and many believe that the creatures are a horde of demons.

Round Thirteen (Sixth Trumpet): Army of Evil Horsemen

God will order the unbinding of demonic beings whose habitation is somewhere beneath the Euphrates River (Revelation 9:15–21). These are angels who followed Lucifer in his original rebellion against the Lord. They apparently will enter and possess the two hundred million troops that come from the Orient, which is east of the Euphrates. These tremendous numbers are referred to as "the kings of the east" in Revelation 16:12.

The might of these forces will be awesome. They will inflict horrific damage on all in their path. Another third of the people left on the earth will die because of their war-making. Still, rebellious people will not repent and bow before God.

Round Fourteen (Seventh Trumpet): Heralding the Bowl Judgments

Again, God will pause in His assault on His evil opponents. He'll stop between the sixth and seventh trumpet judgments to tell all the things that will take place between the blowing of the sixth trumpet and the beginning of the vial, or bowl, judgments. These awesome prophetic events include the two witnesses' time on the Tribulation scene; the 144,000 sealed super-evangelists; the whole story of Satan's hatred for Jesus and the Jewish race; and the rise and fall of Antichrist.

Round Fifteen (Bowl One): Sores

The next assault will begin with the first of the seven deadly bowls pouring out the pure wrath of the living God. Unbelievably horrible sores will infect all who have rejected Him.

Round Sixteen (Bowl Two): Bloody Sea

Before they switched to twelve-rounders as maximum, the fifteenth round in a world championship fight was the last one. In this battle of the ages, the fight will just be heating up. And, it will be one-sided. Judgments from God are so frightful, the prophet John must have had to totally depend upon the Lord to provide the words to describe them:

> Then the second angel poured out his bowl on the sea, and it became blood as of a dead man; and every living creature in the sea died. (Revelation 16:3)

God's Word doesn't even attempt to describe what will be poured into the sea. But whatever it is, it will kill every living thing. The water will become like a dead man's blood. Imagine! Water with the viscosity and, apparently, the stench and grotesqueness of coagulating blood.

Round Seventeen (Bowl Three): Bloody Rivers

The third angel will pour out his bowl into the fresh waters and they will turn to blood (Revelation 16:4). The judgments are indeed fearsome, but God is totally righteous in inflicting them upon those who have rejected Him. We hear the voices from God's corner urging Him onward as the fight continues:

> You are righteous, O Lord, The one who is and who was and who is to be, Because You have judged these things.
>   For they have shed the blood of saints and prophets, And You have given them blood to drink. For it is their just due. (Revelation 16:5–6)

Round Eighteen (Bowl Four): Scorching Heat

God will pound the earth with heavier and heavier blows. As the fourth angel pours out his bowl on the sun, it apparently goes into partial nova. That is, it will shrink and grow darker. Yet at the same time, it will get much hotter. People can't escape the scorching, killing heat. Rather than beg for forgiveness, they will curse God's holy name (Revelation 16:8–9).

Round Nineteen (Bowl Five): Darkness and Pain

God pours His judgments directly upon the most rebellious of the rebels. Apparently, ultraviolet rays from the dying sun will laser through the unprotected atmosphere and cause skin eruptions on those who aren't sealed with God's protection. They will gnaw their tongues in agony, but when they do manage to speak intelligible words, they will spew curses against the Lord (Revelation 16:10–11).

Round Twenty (Bowl Six): Euphrates Dries Up

Next, God will allow total demonic activity to take place upon earth. The vilest spirits apparently will be unleashed in the area of the Euphrates River and will enter the military forces of the world; tremendous death and destruction from the great campaign called Armageddon (it is a war campaign, not just a single, final battle) will intensify by the minute (Revelation 16:12–14).

The kings of the east will be allowed easy access to the Middle East because the Euphrates River, a natural barrier to land forces, will have dried up.

Pause for the Big Finish

Before the seventh bowl will be poured out, Almighty God pauses to say something about those who are His own:

> Behold, I am coming as a thief. Blessed is he who watches, and keeps his garments, lest he walk naked and they see his shame. And they gathered them together to the place called, in Hebrew, Armageddon.

Then the seventh angel poured out his bowl into the air, and a loud voice came out of the temple of heaven, from the throne, saying, "It is done!" (Revelation 16:15–17)

He seems to cover all from the Church Age through the Tribulation who are Christians. His words for Church Age saints seem to commend them for watching for Christ's any-moment return. He says He will come unannounced and suddenly upon an unsuspecting world. He will come "as a thief" because it will be an unanticipated, unwelcome break-in upon the world of rebels who do not know or want Him.

His own, however, should be watching for Him. They shouldn't be surprised by an unwelcome break-in upon their lives. They should never be comfortable with living like the rest of the world.

He gives blessings to the Tribulation saints for keeping their robes of righteousness by being faithful to Him. They did so in the face of the rebels who wanted to see them disrobe—that is, to deny Christ.

Round Twenty-One (Bowl Seven): Earthquake and Hailstones

The final tremendous blow from God's great right hand of judgment—following His weighty words, "It is done," will come in the form of a devastating earthquake and giant hailstones that flatten every city on the planet. Jerusalem will split into three parts. Entire islands will disappear under the titanic blow (Revelation 16:18–20). What could stand under the pounding of hailstones that weigh more than a hundred pounds each? The rebels are literally pounded into submission in this final round of judgments. The Babylonian system of godless humanism, commercialism, and religion will come to an end (see Revelation 17 and 18).

This will be the fulfillment of the dream-vision Daniel the prophet interpreted for Nebuchadnezzar, king of Babylon. Jesus, symbolically the stone from heaven, will strike the metallic man-image on the feet and ten toes, and all of the Babylonian, humanistic governmental system of history will crumble and fall. The debris will be blown away by the winds of eternity (read Daniel 2).

It really isn't much of a fight, is it? To put it in juvenile fight language: "There wasn't really but two punches thrown." God hits His enemies, and His enemies hit the ground.

Powerful Promise

God, even while dispensing judgment, does so in steps and with His supreme love. He gives everyone a chance to turn to Him. Each of us who has trusted Him for salvation should appropriate the power that is in the promise of God that we won't face His wrath. That understanding should give each of us strength to live life to the fullest, knowing that ours is a God of might and of truth!

14

144,000 Jews Sealed

While Antichrist rages in his quest to carry out his Final Solution, God isn't standing idly by. The two witnesses, as we have seen, have preached and warned of the necessity to reject the satanic regime and its every facet. Many will doubtless come to saving repentance after watching these dead men come to life and be called into heaven.

This is especially true of many of the Jews, who see that dazzling demonstration of God's awesome power. And it is the chosen people who have the Lord's most rapt attention during this portion of the Tribulation, which has turned into the time of Jacob's trouble (Jeremiah 30:7). The second half of the Tribulation will bring a period of God drawing a remnant of the children of Abraham, Isaac, and Jacob into His heavenly family. He will do this to bring about flesh-and-blood offspring of those progenitors in order to move them into the millennial earth. The millennium will be the thousand years of earth's history when Jesus Christ will reign as King of all kings. He was the Lamb slain from the foundation of the world, and, following the Tribulation, He will sit on the throne of David to rule the entire earth.

God loves all of mankind, especially the Jews, whom, because of their unbelief, He has set aside for the moment. Just as Christians are said to be the Bride of Christ, Israel is considered the wife of Jehovah. God likens them to being an unfaithful wife; they've chosen another to join and to love in their wickedness and sinfulness.

God doesn't refer to the Jews as "my people" in their present condition as wayward and rebellious. But He will one day again call them "my people," when He reestablishes one-third of the Jews as His people—His "chosen people," to be sure. They will inherit the millennial kingdom on earth. Israel will then be the apex nation of all history.

So the Lord will shake the entire planet mightily during the time of the apocalypse—the Tribulation—to bring out this group from among those who are rebellious toward Him. His great, cataclysmic judgments will rock the entire universe, and He will do all necessary to see that this calling-out of His people is done.

While the twenty-one judgments we've looked at are taking place, God will bring 144,000 men from among the twelve tribes of Israel to perform evangelistic feats the likes of which have never been performed on earth. They will be the most powerful preachers ever to make an impact on earth's peoples. God's Word about these Jewish evangelists is stunning. Their work in bringing the salvation message will be a supernatural act of first order:

> And I saw another angel ascending from the east, having the seal of the living God: and he cried with a loud voice to the four angels, to whom it was given to hurt the earth and the sea, Saying, Hurt not the earth, neither the sea, nor the trees, till we have sealed the servants of our God in their foreheads.
>
> And I heard the number of them which were sealed: and there were sealed an hundred and forty and four thousand of all the tribes of the children of Israel.

Of the tribe of Juda were sealed twelve thousand. Of the tribe of Reuben were sealed twelve thousand. Of the tribe of Gad were sealed twelve thousand. Of the tribe of Aser were sealed twelve thousand. Of the tribe of Nepthalim were sealed twelve thousand.

Of the tribe of Manasses were sealed twelve thousand. Of the tribe of Simeon were sealed twelve thousand. Of the tribe of Levi were sealed twelve thousand. Of the tribe of Issachar were sealed twelve thousand. Of the tribe of Zabulon were sealed twelve thousand. Of the tribe of Joseph were sealed twelve thousand. Of the tribe of Benjamin were sealed twelve thousand.

After this I beheld, and, lo, a great multitude, which no man could number, of all nations, and kindreds, and people, and tongues, stood before the throne, and before the Lamb, clothed with white robes, and palms in their hands;

And cried with a loud voice, saying, Salvation to our God which sitteth upon the throne, and unto the Lamb. (Revelation 7:2–10)

These men will be specifically elected and anointed for ministering during the evilest time of human history. They'll be sealed by the very Spirit of God so that no harm can come to them. Verses 9 and 10, we believe, testify that they accomplish their mission. It tells of the millions who will become believers as a result of their ministry. The following passage tells of their great welcome into heaven when their mission is completed:

And I looked, and, lo, a Lamb stood on the mount Sion, and with him an hundred forty and four thousand, having his Father's name written in their foreheads.

And I heard a voice from heaven, as the voice of many waters, and as the voice of a great thunder: and I heard the voice of harpers harping with their harps: And they sung as it were a new song before the throne, and before the four beasts, and the elders: and no man could learn that song but the hundred and forty and four thousand, which were redeemed from the earth.

These are they which were not defiled with women; for they are virgins. These are they which follow the Lamb whithersoever he goeth.

These were redeemed from among men, being the firstfruits unto God and to the Lamb.

And in their mouth was found no guile: for they are without fault before the throne of God. (Revelation 14:1–5)

Dr. J. Dwight Pentecost further elucidates the exploits and rewards of the 144,000-member evangelistic force and the troubled time of their ministry.

When the nation Israel is brought back into her land after the rapture by the covenant enacted by the head of the Revived Roman Empire (Dan. 9:27) Israel is still in unbelief. God, however, is very definitely dealing with that nation to bring it to salvation. The whole seventieth week of Daniel is a period of preparation for the coming of the King. The gospel of the kingdom, which necessitates repentance, is being preached. There is a reception of this message. God uses many different means to bring "all Israel" to salvation during the seventieth week. The Word of God is available and may be used so that those Jews who are hungering and thirsting may search that Word for a knowledge of Christ. The Holy Spirit, while not indwelling a temple as He did in this age, is nevertheless operative and will do a work of convicting and enlightening. Signs will be given to point Israel to a knowledge of Jehovah. Such a sign is the destruction of the king of the north (Ezek. 39:21–29). There will be the ministry of the 144,000 sealed of Israel (Rev. 7) and the ministry of the two witnesses (Rev. 11), all with the intent of bringing the nation to repentance and salvation. The outpouring of the wrath of God is seen to be for the purpose of bringing men to repentance (Rev. 16:9–10). While the majority will not repent, some may be turned to Jehovah by these signs.

It would be concluded, then, that the nation, unsaved at the beginning of the tribulation, receives a multitude of witnesses of various kinds so that the individuals are experiencing salvation through the period and the nation will be saved finally at the second advent (Rom. 11:26–27). The fact that the brethren, referred to in Revelation 12:10–11, overcome by the blood of the Lamb and by the word of their testimony indicates that many will be saved during the tribulation period....

In chapter seven the 144,000 are sealed by God, set apart to a special ministry, before the great tribulation begins. They seem to be sealed at the very outset of the tribulation period. In all probability the multitude of Gentiles, described in the passage that follows (Rev. 7:9–17), has come to a knowledge of salvation through the ministry of this group. In chapter fourteen the same group is pictured at the termination of the tribulation, when the kingdom is established. The returning King is on Mt. Zion, as was predicted of Him (Zech 14:4). At His return the faithful witnesses gather unto Him, having been redeemed (Rev. 14:4) and having faithfully witnessed in the midst of apostasy (Rev. 14:4–5). They are called "the first-fruits unto God and to the Lamb" (Rev. 14:4), that is, they are the first of the harvest of the tribulation period that will come into the millennium to populate the millennial earth. As the judgments are about to be poured out upon Babylon (Rev. 14:8), upon the Beast (Rev. 14:9–12), upon the Gentiles (Rev. 14:14–17), and upon unbelieving Israel (Rev. 14:18–20), these 144,000 are viewed as being preserved through all that the earth experiences so that they may be the firstfruits of that period. Stevens well summarizes:

"It seems both natural and reasonable to find in this company of one hundred and forty-four thousand—now come off more than conquerors and standing, translated and glorified... the company of the same number introduced in chapter 7, a selected company from all the tribes of Israel, sealed in their foreheads with the 'seal of the living God' and as His 'servants.' It was as special standard-bearers of the faith beginning with the era of the seventh seal that these Israelites were seen to be commissioned. Now, in the fourteenth chapter, this company, it would seem, is presented again in the enjoyment of the reward and commendations which will be theirs after their course has been finished. It is noteworthy that not one of the number is seen to have failed."

...The *destiny* of the remnant. Speaking of those brought to the Lord through the ministry of the 144,000 in Revelation 7:15–16, John writes:

"Therefore are they before the throne of God and serve him day and night in his temple: and he that sitteth on the throne shall dwell among them.

"They shall hunger no more neither thirst any more neither shall the sun light on them, nor any heat.

"For the Lamb which is in the midst of the throne shall feed them, and shall lead them unto living fountains of waters: and God shall wipe away all tears from their eyes."

They are seen "before the throne" (Rev 14:3). Thus the destiny of this remnant is the kingdom over which Christ will rule from the "throne of David." These promises are not heavenly, but earthly, and will be fulfilled in the millennium.[68]

Comparison to today's world of evangelism with that future period when the pressures are horrific on everyone on earth to give in to Antichrist's brutal regime just to survive are unfair to make. It is thought by some that there will be in this present pre-Tribulation era another "Great Awakening," a great revival of the church with massive numbers of lost souls coming to Christ for salvation. We prayerfully hope so, but find no place in God's Word where that is promised this side of Rapture. All indicators are, however, that a vast number of souls will come to salvation as a result of these Jewish men and their fervor to bring souls to Christ. Dr. David Jeremiah, one of America's best known pastors and Christian broadcasters, writes the following about the 144,000 men of the House of Israel:

> The Bible says in Joel chapter 2 that "it shall come to pass afterward that I will pour out My Spirit on all flesh; Your sons and your daughters shall prophesy, your old men shall dream dreams, your young men shall see visions. And also on My menservants and on My maidservants I will pour out My Spirit in those days" (Joel 2:28–29).
>
> These 144,000 witnesses are selected from the twelve tribes of Israel. They are sealed on their foreheads and they are servants of the living God. And the Bible says they are also separated to God—that means they have a special calling from the Lord. Revelation 14:4 says, "these are the ones who were not defiled with women, for they are virgins."
>
> Now a lot of people have tried to spiritualize that and talk about the fact that they had not committed spiritual adultery, but that's reading too much into the text. I believe these men will be celibates who just run around the earth preaching the Gospel. And frankly, when you read about what goes on in the Tribulation, there won't be any time for these men to have families. They'll be on a journey and on a mission, and it will be a full-time task. When we understand the pressures of the Tribulation period, it's easy to comprehend why these preachers would have a difficult married life.

The 144,000 Are Spared from Judgment

They are also spared from the coming judgment. Notice it says, "do not harm the earth, the sea, or the trees till we have sealed the servants of our God on their foreheads" (Revelation 7:3). In other words, these men will not be able to be taken out. There will certainly be an anger against them because of their preaching. But the Bible says no one is going to be able to touch them because Almighty God is going to have His arms wrapped around them.

You know it's an interesting thing that even today we can practice that, can we not? I'm going to tell you a little secret. When I first started to travel as a young pastor, my kids were young. I used to get on airplanes flying out of Fort Wayne, Indiana, and have a little pang of fear that would come into my heart. Now I wasn't afraid to die—I wasn't *anxious* to die, but I wasn't afraid to. But I had a great fear for my kids, for my wife, and my little children. And one day an older pastor came to me and gave me this little saying, and I wrote it in my Bible. Here's what it says, "God's man, in the center of God's will, is immortal until God is done with him."[69]

The man of sin, the most brutal dictator to ever exist, will no doubt be desperate to somehow stop these men of the Jewish race who are supernaturally endowed for service. As Dr. Jeremiah says, he will have no success. They, as we have seen, are "sealed" and can't be touched by Satan's man or his forces.

They'll apparently be able to move about instantaneously, much like Philip was removed far away from the Ethiopian eunuch once he had converted him and baptized him. These evangelists will be able to mesmerize with the powerful way they tell of the love of God and the salvation He wants for them. It will be like all of Billy Graham's crusades rolled up into one when they speak to the lost souls of the Tribulation era.

Here, we will break into all of the gloominess of this horrendous time with a bit of levity. We remember the stories of our two friends, Dr. David Reagan of Lamb and Lion Ministries and Christ in Prophecy Television program, and our dear brother, Zola Levitt, now in heaven where he longed to be.

Dave Reagan tells the story about how he wanted to know Zola's thoughts on the 144,000 Jewish evangelists of the time of the Tribulation. Zola, a Messianic Jew with a powerful ministry and television program for many years—*Zola Levitt Presents*—as always, was glad to answer Dave's question. The following is Dave's account of that back and forth.

I once called Zola Levitt and asked his opinion on this matter. Zola is a Messianic Jew who has a Bible prophecy ministry. When I asked if he believed that the 144,000 Jews of Revelation 7 would serve as evangelists trying to convert the world to Jesus, he said, "Of course! Why do you think the Lord has given us the kind of personality that we have?"

I wasn't about to touch that question with a ten-foot pole, so I played dumb. "What are you talking about?" I asked.

"Haven't you ever noticed," asked Zola, "that Jews are very pushy people?"

"Well yes," I responded, "now that you mention it, I must say that I have."

"Well," said Zola, "God has given us that kind of personality so that we can be the world's greatest salesmen. And one day, during the Tribulation, 144,000 believing Jews are going to use those skills to convert a great host of Gentiles to Jesus. We are going to push people up against the wall and hold them by the throat until they say, 'Jesus!' Before the Tribulation is over, we are going to convert more people to Jesus than you Gentiles have done in the past 2,000 years."

All I could say was, "I hope you are right."[70]

Zola, a long time and dear friend, is very much missed, as is his zeal for reaching out with God's Word to evangelize the world. If the 144,000 have the kind of infectious zeal exhibited by Zola Levitt, we can begin to understand why the Tribulation will be probably the greatest time of salvation of souls in human history.

15

Nephilim Giants Rise

English theologian George Hawkins Pember, in his 1876 masterpiece, *Earth's Earliest Ages*, analyzed the prophecy of Jesus Christ that says the end times would be a repeat of "the days of Noah." Pember outlined the seven great causes of the antediluvian destruction and documented their developmental beginnings in his lifetime. The seventh and most fearful sign, Pember wrote, would be the return of the spirits of Nephilim, "the appearance upon earth of beings from the Principality of the Air, and their unlawful intercourse with the human race."

Jesus Himself, in answering His disciples concerning the signs of His coming and of the end of the world, said it would be "as the days of Noah were" (Matthew 24:37). The implication is, just as it was before the Flood when the spirits of Nephilim were powerful upon earth (Genesis 6:4), mankind would experience an end-times renaissance of the influence of these entities. From Scripture we are made to understand that the purpose of this latter-day wave of supernaturalism includes deception (2 Timothy 3:13), and the effect upon mankind would be so successful that heresy and delusion would become firmly entrenched—

even within institutionalized Christianity. In writing of this scenario, Paul prophesied to Timothy that "in the latter times, some shall depart from the faith, giving heed to seducing spirits, and doctrines of devils" (1 Timothy 4:1).

Based on contemporary developments, the foretold increase in demonism and its influence within secular and religious society is rapidly unfolding in this century—abruptly, dramatically, and suspiciously. Biblical scholar Gary Stearman agrees, stating in disturbing language how the manifestation of these powers is quickening now because the world is under conditions "in which the influence of God's Holy Spirit is diminishing."[71] This is apparent not only in metaphysics, but within science and technology, where genetic engineering and transhumanist aspirations seem literally hell-bent on repeating what the Watchers did in giving birth to the spirits of Nephilim as in the days of Noah.

The First Time Nephilim Appeared on Earth

As far back as the beginning of time and within every major culture of the ancient world, the astonishingly consistent story is told of "gods" that descended from heaven and materialized in bodies of flesh. From Rome to Greece—and before that, to Egypt, Persia, Assyria, Babylonia, and Sumer—the earliest records of civilization tell of the era when powerful beings known to the Hebrews as "Watchers" and in the book of Genesis as the *benei ha-elohim* ("sons of God") mingled with humans, giving birth to part-celestial, part-terrestrial hybrids known as "Nephilim." The Bible says this happened when men began to increase on earth and daughters were born to them. When the sons of God saw the women's beauty, they took wives from among them to sire their unusual offspring. In Genesis 6:4, we read the following:

There were giants [Nephilim] in the earth in those days; and also after that, when the sons of God came in unto the daughters of men, and they bare children to them, the same became mighty men which were of old, men of renown.

When this Scripture is compared with other ancient texts, including Enoch, Jubilees, Baruch, Genesis Apocryphon, Philo, Josephus, Jasher, and others, it unfolds to some that the giants of the Old Testament such as Goliath were the part-human, part-animal, part-angelic offspring of a supernatural interruption into the divine order and natural development of the species. Enoch was the son of Jared, father of Methuselah, and great-grandfather of Noah, whose writings provide the most detailed account of the fall of the Watchers, the angels who fathered the infamous Nephilim. While the book of Enoch is no longer included in most versions of the Bible, Enoch's writings are quoted in the New Testament in at least two places, and he is mentioned by name in both the Old and New Testaments, including Jude 14–15, where one of his prophecies is cited. During the discovery of the Dead Sea Scrolls, pre-Maccabean fragments of Enoch were found, helping scholars verify the book's antiquity while also illustrating that the ancients held these texts to be inspired. Many early church fathers likewise considered the book of Enoch to be sacred, including Tertullian, Justin Martyr, Irenaeus, Origen, and Clement of Alexandria. Dr. Michael Heiser is now speaking out on why YOU should understand this ancient text, which, among other things, gives a name to the angels involved in this cosmic conspiracy, calling them "Watchers." We read:

And I Enoch was blessing the Lord of majesty and the King of the ages, and lo! the Watchers called me—Enoch the scribe—and said to me: "Enoch, thou scribe of righteousness, go, declare to the Watchers of the heaven who have left the high heaven, the holy eternal place, and have defiled themselves with women, and have done as the children of earth do, and have taken unto themselves wives: Ye have wrought great destruction on the earth: And ye shall have no peace nor forgiveness of sin:

and inasmuch as they delight themselves in their children [the Nephilim], The murder of their beloved ones shall they see, and over the destruction of their children shall they lament, and shall make supplication unto eternity, but mercy and peace shall ye not attain." (1 Enoch 10:3–8)

According to Enoch, two hundred of these powerful angels departed "high heaven" and used women (among other things) to extend their progeny into mankind's plane of existence. An Interlinear Hebrew Bible features an interesting interpretation of Genesis 6:2 in this regard. Where the King James Version of the Bible says, "The sons of God saw the daughters of men that they [were] fair," the IHN interpreted this as, "The benei Elohim saw the daughters of Adam, that they were *fit extensions*" (emphasis added). The term "fit extensions" seems applicable when the whole of the ancient record is understood to mean that the Watchers wanted to leave their proper sphere of existence in order to enter earth's three-dimensional reality. They viewed women—or at least their genetic material—as part of the formula for accomplishing this task. Departing the proper habitation that God had assigned them was grievous to the Lord and led to divine penalization. Jude described it this way: The "angels which kept not their first estate, but left their own habitation, he hath reserved in everlasting chains under darkness unto the judgment of the great day" (Jude 6).

Besides apocryphal, pseudepigraphic, and Jewish traditions related to the legend of the Watchers and the "mighty men" born of their union with humans, mythologized accounts tell the stories of "gods" using humans to produce heroes or demigods (half-gods). When the ancient Greek version of the Hebrew Old Testament (the LXX or Septuagint) was made, the word "Nephilim"—referring to the part-human offspring of the Watchers—was translated *gegenes*, a word implying "earth born." This same terminology was used to describe the Greek Titans and other legendary heroes of partly celestial and partly terrestrial origin, such as Hercules (born of Zeus and the mortal Alcmena), Achilles (the Trojan hero son of Thetis and Peleus), and Gilgamesh (the two-thirds god and one-third human child of Lugalbanda and Ninsun).

These demigods were likewise accompanied in texts and idol representation by half-animal and half-human creatures like centaurs (the part-human, part-horse offspring of Apollo's son, Centaurus), chimeras, furies, satyrs, gorgons, nymphs, Minotaurs, and other genetic aberrations. All of this seems to indicate that the Watchers not only modified human DNA during the construction of Nephilim, but the DNA of animals as well, a point the book of Enoch supports, saying in the seventh chapter that the fallen angels "sinned" against animals as well as humans. Other books such as Jubilees add that this interspecies mingling eventually resulted in mutations among normal humans and animals whose "flesh" (genetic makeup) was "corrupted" by the activity, presumably through crossbreeding (see 5:1–5; 7:21–25). Even the Old Testament contains reference to the genetic mutations that developed among humans following this time frame, including "men" of unusual size, physical strength, six fingers, six toes, animal appetite for blood, and even lion-like features (2 Samuel 21:20, 23:20).

But of all the ancient records, the most telling extrabiblical script is from the disputed book of Jasher, a mostly forgotten text referred to in the Bible in Joshua 10:13 and 2 Samuel 1:18. Jasher records the familiar story of the fall of the Watchers, then adds an exceptional detail that none of the other texts is as unequivocal about, something that can only be understood in modern language to mean advanced biotechnology, genetic engineering, or "transgenic modification" of species. After the Watchers had instructed humans "in the secrets of heaven," note what Jasher says occurred: "[Then] the sons of men [began teaching] the mixture of animals of one species with the other, in order therewith to provoke the Lord" (4:18).

The phrase "the mixture of animals of one species with the other" doesn't mean Watchers had taught men hybridization, as this wouldn't have "provoked the Lord." God made like animals of different breeds capable of reproducing. For example, horses can propagate with other mammals of the equidae classification (the taxonomic "horse family"), including donkeys and zebras. It would not have "provoked the Lord" for this type of animal breeding to have taken place, as God Himself made the animals able to do this.

If, on the other hand, the Watchers were crossing species boundaries by mixing incompatible animals of one species with the other, such as a horse with a human (a centaur), this would have been a different matter and may cast light on the numerous ancient stories of mythical beings of variant-species manufacturing that fit perfectly within the records of what the Watchers were accomplishing. Understandably, this kind of chimera-making would have "provoked the Lord" and raises the serious question of why the Watchers would have risked eternal damnation by tinkering with God's creation in this way. Yahweh had placed boundaries between the species and strictly ordered that "each kind" reproduce only after its "own kind." Was the motive of the Watchers to break these rules simply the desire to rebel, to assault God's creative genius through biologically altering what He had made? Or was something of deeper significance behind the activity?

Some believe the corruption of antediluvian DNA by Watchers was an effort to cut off the birth line of the Messiah. This theory posits that Satan understood the protoevangelium—the promise in Genesis 3:15 that a Savior would be born, the seed of the woman, and that He would destroy the fallen angel's power. Satan's followers therefore intermingled with the human race in a conspiracy to stop the birth of Christ. If human DNA could be universally corrupted or "demonized," they reasoned, no Savior would be born and mankind would be lost forever. Those who support this theory believe this is why God ordered His people to maintain a pure bloodline and not to intermarry with the other nations. When men breached this command and the mutated DNA began rapidly spreading among humans and animals, God instructed Noah to build an ark and prepare for a deluge that would destroy every living thing. That God had to send such a universal fiat like the Flood illustrates how widespread the altered DNA eventually became. In fact, the Bible says in Genesis 6:9 that only Noah—and by extension, his children—were found "perfect" in their generation. The Hebrew word for "perfect" in this case is *tamiym*, which means "without blemish" or "healthy," the same word used in Leviticus to describe an unblemished sacrificial lamb. The meaning was not that Noah was morally perfect, but that his physical makeup—his DNA—had not been contaminated with Nephilim descent, as apparently the rest of the world had become. In order to preserve mankind as He had made them, God destroyed all but Noah's family in the Flood. The ancient records including those of the Bible appear to agree with this theology, consistently describing the cause of the Flood as happening in response to "all flesh" having become "corrupted, both man and beast."

While the theory of DNA corruption as an intended method for halting the coming of Christ has merit, an alternative or additional reason the Watchers may have blended living organisms exists in a theory Tom Horn postulated in his book, *Zenith 2016*. In that book, Horn speculated that the manipulation of DNA may have had a deeper purpose—namely to create a hybrid form that neither the spirit of man nor God would inhabit, because it was neither man nor beast, and thus provided an unusual body made up of human, animal, and plant genetics known as Nephilim, an earth-born facsimile or "fit extension" into which the Watchers could extend themselves.[72]

Signs of "the Days of Noah" in Modern Science?

Watcher technology is echoed today in recombinant DNA science, where a transgenic organism is created when the genetic structure of one species is altered by the transfer of a gene or genes from another. Given that molecular biologists classify the functions of genes within native species but are unsure in many cases how a gene's coding might react from one species to another, not only could the genetic structure of the modified animal and its offspring be changed in physical appearance as a result of transgenics, but its sensory modalities, disease propensity such as with Covid-19, personality, behavior traits, and more could be changed as well.

Many readers will be astonished to learn that in spite of these unknowns, such transgenic tinkering is actively taking place in most parts of the world, including the United States, Britain, and Australia, where animal eggs are being used to create hybrid human embryos from which stem-cell lines can be produced for medical research. President Barack Obama signed several executive orders providing federal funding to expand this type of embryonic research in the United States. Not counting synthetic biology, where entirely new forms of life are being brewed, there is no limit to the number of human-animal concoctions currently under development in laboratories around the world. A team at Newcastle and Durham universities in the United Kingdom recently announced plans to create "hybrid rabbit and human embryos, as well as other 'chimera' embryos mixing human and cow genes." The same researchers more alarmingly have already managed to reanimate tissue "from dead human cells in another breakthrough that was heralded as a way of overcoming ethical dilemmas over using living embryos for medical research."[73] In the United States, similar studies led Irv Weissman, director of Stanford University's Institute of Cancer/Stem Cell Biology and Medicine in California, to create mice with partly human brains, causing some ethicists to raise the issue of "humanized animals" in the future that could become "self-aware" as a result of genetic modification. Even former president of the United States, George W. Bush, in his January 31, 2006, State of the Union address, called for legislation to "prohibit...creating human-animal hybrids, and buying, selling, or patenting human embryos." His words fell on deaf ears, and now "the chimera, or combination of species, is a subject of serious discussion in certain scientific circles," writes Joseph Infranco, senior counsel for the Alliance Defense Fund. "We are well beyond the science fiction of H. G. Wells' tormented hybrids in *The Island of Doctor Moreau*; we are in a time where scientists are seriously contemplating the creation of human-animal hybrids."[74]

Not everybody shares Infranco's concerns. A radical, international, intellectual, and quickly growing cultural movement known as "transhumanism" supports the use of new sciences, including genetic modification, to enhance human mental and physical abilities and aptitudes so that "human beings will eventually be transformed into beings with such greatly expanded abilities as to merit the label 'posthuman.'"[75]

Tom Horn has personally been the subject of international concern among transhumanists, and not long ago, *Zygon: Journal of Religion and Science* featured a piece written by Professor S. Jonathon O'Donnell in the Department of Religion and Philosophies at the University of London about him titled, "Secularizing Demons: Fundamentalist Navigations in Religion and Secularity."

O'Donnell's aim? According to the article's abstract, it was to explore at a deeper level than his peers the "anti-transhumanist apocalypticisms" of our day, the central voice behind which was identified as— "evangelical conspiracist Thomas Horn [and his] milieu [community gathering place]." Throughout the academic paper, O'Donnell simply refers to Horn and co-obstructionists as "Horn's Milieu."

In other words, the good University of London professor has determined that Horn and those who work with him at SkyWatch TV and Defender Publishing are the "leaders of the transhuman resistance" whom members of that community had better pay attention to. The peer-reviewed Zygon agreed, at least to the point that they found reason to promulgate O'Donnell's thesis.

Horn responded by publishing *The Milieu: Welcome to the Resistance*, in which he and other bioethicists and prophecy experts examined whether transhumanism's objectives reflect a renewal of the days of Noah by fallen angels.

Horn has also debated leading transhumanist Dr. James Hughes on his weekly syndicated talk show, *Changesurfer Radio*. Hughes is executive director of the Institute for Ethics and Emerging Technologies and teaches at Trinity College in Hartford, Connecticut. He is also the author of *Citizen Cyborg: Why Democratic Societies Must Respond to the*

Redesigned Human of the Future, a sort of bible for transhumanist values. Hughes is also featured in two-time Telly Award Winning documentary, *Inhuman* (produced by Horn and the Skywatch team's Defender Films) as part of a growing body of academics, bioethicists, and sociologists who support:

> ...large-scale genetic and neurological engineering of ourselves... [a] new chapter in evolution [as] the result of accelerating developments in the fields of genomics, stem-cell research, genetic enhancement, germ-line engineering, neuro-pharmacology, artificial intelligence, robotics, pattern recognition technologies, and nanotechnology...at the intersection of science and religion [which has begun to question] what it means to be human.[76]

While the transformation of man to posthuman is in its fledgling state, complete integration of the technological singularity necessary to replace existing Homo sapiens as the dominant life form on earth is approaching an exponential curve. In a Reuters article titled "Scientists Want Debate on Animals with Human Genes," just how far scientists have come and how far they intend to go was apparent. The news piece started out, "A mouse that can speak? A monkey with Down's Syndrome? Dogs with human hands or feet? British scientists want to know if such experiments are acceptable," and continued with revelations that scientists in Britain are comfortable now with up to 50 percent animal-human integration. The article hinted that not all of the research is being kept at the embryonic level and that fully mature monstrosities may be under study as "some scientists in some places may want to push boundaries." Legendary writer Vernor Vinge added that we are entering a period in history when questions like "What is the meaning of life?" will be nothing more than engineering questions. "[Soon] we will have the technological means to create superhuman intelligence," he told *H+ Magazine*. "Shortly thereafter, the human era will be ended."[77]

As the director of the Future of Humanity Institute and a professor of philosophy at Oxford University, Nick Bostrom (www.NickBostrom. com) is another leading advocate of transhumanism who, like the Watchers before him, envisions remanufacturing humans with animals, plants, and other synthetic life forms through the use of modern sciences. When describing the benefits of man-with-beast combinations in his online thesis, "Transhumanist Values," Bostrom cites how animals have "sonar, magnetic orientation, or sensors for electricity and vibration," among other extrahuman abilities. He goes on to include how the range of sensory modalities for transhumans wouldn't be limited to those among animals, and that there is "no fundamental block to adding say a capacity to see infrared radiation or to perceive radio signals and perhaps to add some kind of telepathic sense by augmenting our brains."[78]

Bostrom is correct in that the animal kingdom has levels of perception beyond human. Some animals can "sense" earthquakes and "smell" tumors. Others, like dogs, can hear sounds as high as forty thousand hertz—and dolphins can hear even higher. It is also known that at least some animals see wavelengths beyond normal human capacity. Incidentally, what Bostrom may also understand and anticipate is that, according to the biblical story of Balaam's donkey, certain animals see into the spirit world. Not long ago at Arizona State University, the Templeton Foundation funded a series of lectures titled "Facing the Challenges of Transhumanism: Religion, Science, Technology,"[79] in which transhumanism was viewed as possibly causing supernatural, not just physical, transformation. Called "the next epoch in human evolution," some of the lecturers at ASU believe radical alteration of Homo sapiens could open a door to unseen intelligence. As a result, ASU launched another study to explore communication with these "entities." Called the SOPHIA project (after the Greek goddess), the express purpose of the study was to verify communication "with deceased people, spirit guides, angels, other-worldly entities/extraterrestrials, and/or a universal intelligence/God."[80]

Imagine what this could mean if government laboratories with unlimited budgets working beyond congressional review were to decode the gene functions that lead animals to have preternatural capabilities of sense, smell, and sight, and then blended them with Homo sapiens. Among other things, the ultimate psychotronic weapon could be created for use against entire populations—genetically engineered "Nephilim agents" that appear to be human but who hypothetically see and even interact with invisible forces.

While the former chairman of the President's Council on Bioethics, Leon Kass, doesn't elaborate on the same type of issues, he provided a status report on how real and how frightening the dangers of such biotechnology could imminently be in the hands of transhumanists. In the introduction to his book, *Life, Liberty and the Defense of Dignity: The Challenges of Bioethics*, Kass warned:

> Human nature itself lies on the operating table, ready for alteration, for eugenic and psychic "enhancement," for wholesale redesign. In leading laboratories, academic and industrial, new creators are confidently amassing their powers and quietly honing their skills, while on the street their evangelists are zealously prophesying a posthuman future. For anyone who cares about preserving our humanity, the time has come for paying attention.[81]

The warning by Kass of the potential hazards of emerging technologies coupled with transhumanist aspirations is not an overreaction. One law school in the United Kingdom has already discussed the need to add classes in the future devoted to analyzing crime scenes committed by posthumans. The requirement for such specially trained law enforcement personnel will arise due to part-human, part-animal beings possessing behavior patterns not consistent with present-day profiling or forensics understanding. Add to this other unknowns, such as "memory transference" (an entirely new field of study showing that complex behavior patterns and even memories can be transferred from donors of large human organs to their recipients), and the potential for tomorrow's human-animal chimera issues multiplies. How would the memories, behavior patterns, or instincts, let's say, of a wolf affect the mind of a human? That such unprecedented questions will have to be dealt with sooner rather than later has already been illustrated in animal-to-animal experiments, including those conducted by Evan Balaban at McGill University in Montreal, where sections of brain from embryonic quails were transplanted into the brains of chickens and the resultant chickens exhibited head bobs and vocal trills unique to quail.[82] The implication from this field of study alone suggests transhumans will likely bear unintended behavior and appetite disorders that could literally produce lycanthropes (werewolves) and other nightmarish Nephilim traits.

As troubling as those thoughts are, even this contemplation could be just the tip of the iceberg. One-on-one, interpersonal malevolence by human-animals might quickly be overshadowed by global acts of swarm violence. The possibility of groups of "transhuman terrorists" in the conceivable future is real enough that a House Foreign Affairs (HFA) committee chaired by California Democrat Brad Sherman, best known for his expertise on the spread of nuclear weapons and terrorism, was among a number of government panels and think tanks studying the implications of genetic modification and human-transforming technologies related to future terrorism. *Congressional Quarterly* columnist Mark Stencel listened to the HFA committee hearings and wrote in his article, "Futurist: Genes Without Borders," that the conference "sounded more like a Hollywood pitch for a sci-fi thriller than a sober discussion of scientific reality…with talk of biotech's potential for creating supersoldiers, superintelligence, and superanimals [that could become] agents of unprecedented lethal force."[83] George Annas, Lori Andrews, and Rosario Isasi were even more apocalyptic in their *American Journal of Law and Medicine* article, "Protecting the Endangered Human: Toward an International Treaty Prohibiting Cloning and Inheritable Alterations," when they wrote:

The new species, or "posthuman," will likely view the old "normal" humans as inferior, even savages, and fit for slavery or slaughter. The normals, on the other hand, may see the posthumans as a threat and if they can, may engage in a preemptive strike by killing the posthumans before they themselves are killed or enslaved by them. It is ultimately this predictable potential for genocide that makes species-altering experiments potential weapons of mass destruction, and makes the unaccountable genetic engineer a potential bioterrorist.[84]

Observations like those of Annas, Andrews, and Isasi cause one to wonder if this is not how the servants of Antichrist move with such compassionless brutality in rounding up to destroy all who refuse to receive the mark of the beast.

In keeping with our study, imagine the staggering implications of such science if dead Nephilim tissue were discovered with intact DNA and a government somewhere was willing to clone or mingle the extracted organisms to make Homo-Nephilim. If one accepts the biblical story of the Nephilim as real, such discovery could actually be made someday—or perhaps already has been and was covered up. As an example of this possibility, in 2009, blood was extracted from the bone of a dinosaur that scientists insist is eighty million years old. Nephilim would have existed in relatively recent times comparably, making clonable material from dead biblical giants feasible. The technology to resurrect the extinct species is already in place, and cloning methods are being studied now for use with bringing back Tasmanian tigers, woolly mammoths, and other extinct creatures. *National Geographic* also confirmed this possibility in its special report, "Recipe for a Resurrection," quoting Hendrik Poinar of McMaster University in Ontario, an authority on ancient DNA who served as a scientific consultant for the movie Jurassic Park, saying: "I laughed when Steven Spielberg said that cloning extinct animals was inevitable. But I'm not laughing anymore.... This is going to happen. It's just a matter of working out the details."[85]

The ramifications of using science to revive extinct animals or Nephilim may also play a key role in the kingdom of Antichrist. This is because as interbreeding begins between transgenic animals, genetically modified humans, and species as God made them, the altered DNA will quickly migrate into the natural environment. When that happens (as is already occurring among genetically modified plants and animals), "alien" and/or animal characteristics will be introduced to the human gene pool and spread through intermarriage, altering the human genetic code and eventually eliminating humanity as we know it. This is what happened before the Great Flood, according to the book of Enoch, and perhaps that has been the whole idea for the end times as well—to create a generation of genetically altered "fit extensions" for the resurrection of underworld Nephilim-hordes in preparation of Armageddon.

Does a curious verse in the book of Daniel hint at this? Speaking of the last days of human government, Daniel said: "They shall mingle themselves with the seed of men: but they shall not cleave one to another, even as iron is not mixed with clay" (Daniel 2:43).

While Daniel doesn't explain who "they" that "mingle themselves with the seed of men" are, the personal pronoun "they" caused our old friend (now deceased) Chuck Missler in his book, *Alien Encounters*, to ask: "Just what (or who) are 'mingling with the seed of men?' Who are these non-seed? It staggers the mind to contemplate the potential significance of Daniel's passage and its implications for the future global governance."[86]

Daniel's verse troubled Missler because it seemed to indicate that the same phenomenon that occurred in Genesis chapter 6, where non-human species or "nonseed" mingled with human seed and produced Nephilim, would happen again in the end times. When this verse from Daniel is coupled with Genesis 3:15, which says, "And I will put enmity between thee and the woman, and between thy seed [*zera*, meaning 'offspring,' 'descendents,' or 'children'] and her seed," an incredible tenet emerges—that Satan has seed, and that it is at enmity with Christ.

Have We Entered the End-Times Days of Noah?

Christians cannot review the abbreviated information above without concluding that Satan is indeed engaged in an unprecedented conspiracy to revive supernaturalism such as existed in Noah's day. Though countless multitudes may never perceive them, these "principalities…powers… rulers of darkness…and spiritual wickedness in high places" (Ephesians 6:12) form the unseen arena under which unregenerate mankind (such as detailed in *Shadowland*[87] is currently organized. Within this demonic influence, scientists, politicians, philosophers, and even some preachers are being orchestrated within a great evil scheme toward an epic end-times event—the return of the days of Noah.

In more than thirty important biblical passages, the Greek New Testament employs the term *kosmos* describing the unseen government hard at work behind current earthly administrations. At Satan's desire, archons command this hidden, geopolitical sphere, dominating *kosmokrators* (rulers of darkness who work in and through their human counterparts) who, in turn, command spirits of lesser rank until every level of human government is touched by this influence. It is this dominion, not flesh and blood, that is building a world system under Satan's control (see Ephesians 6). If we could see through the veil into this invisible world, we would find there an underworld sphere writhing with Nephilim anticipating their return (see Job 26:5).

In the same way the ancient records say Watchers traded military and occult knowledge for use of human biology, today's humanist-scientific communities are striking a Faustian deal with the devil, whether they know it or not. This repeat performance by modern scientists to cross over the species barrier in direct violation of God's divine order is, in our opinion, the million-pound elephant standing at the center of modern prophecy research. It behooves the church to sit up, pay attention, and engage these issues while there is still time, as we are undoubtedly witnessing the unfolding of biblical prophecy in fulfillment of the days of Noah, the preeminent sign that the departure of the church is at hand.

16

Nations Cross Euphrates River Toward Israel

Bible prophecy tells that there will be a force to rival that of the great führer of the Fourth Reich. The power will come from the Oriental world. John the Revelator was given the prophecy about this by the angel assigned to relay the message from God's throne. We are told of this military juggernaut in two prophetic passages:

And the sixth angel sounded, and I heard a voice from the four horns of the golden altar which is before God,

Saying to the sixth angel which had the trumpet, Loose the four angels which are bound in the great river Euphrates.

And the four angels were loosed, which were prepared for an hour, and a day, and a month, and a year, for to slay the third part of men.

And the number of the army of the horsemen were two hundred thousand thousand: and I heard the number of them. (Revelation 9:13–16)

And the sixth angel poured out his vial upon the great river Euphrates; and the water thereof was dried up, that the way of the kings of the east might be prepared. (Revelation 16:12)

This huge military force will approach the Occidental world from the far reaches of the Oriental world. The numbers are staggering to consider.

It is difficult to understand how this gargantuan number of troops can be gathered for their assault toward the west. How the Antichrist will have been able to garner the power he has on such a wide basis, yet the kings of the east at the same time have been allowed to come forth is a sort of mystery.

Somehow, however, it seems that a supernatural force of some sort has kept the boundary between the Oriental and Occidental worlds separated. John's Revelation seems to indicate that the Euphrates River demarcates that boundary.

China has for years harbored the world's largest by far contingent of military ground troops. The Korean War of the early 1950s proves they have been formidable for decades. The red Chinese forces fought alongside North Korea to keep the North Korean dictatorship from being overrun once they attacked South Korea. America and the South Korean forces were moving the North Korean hordes back into their own territory and would have eventually destroyed the North Korean dictatorship, if not for the massive Chinese intervention.

It was turnabout in some ways as the Chinese completely overran even American forces in some battles. So the Chinese are not Johnny-come-latelies. A number of years ago, Dr. Tim LaHaye wrote the following:

The emergence of China onto the world scene as a powerful geopolitical force to be reckoned with during this generation has the attention of all the world leaders. It is not only the largest country of the world, with a population of 1.2 billion (almost five times that of the United States), but that vast empire is led by the most ruthless communist leaders. And they are looking hungrily at their Asian neighbors—Taiwan, India and the Philippines. They know the rest of the world is too cowardly to stand up to them with more than word threats. If they are not stopped, they will conquer the world, for communists are trained to envision imposing their brand of socialism on the entire globe.[88]

The late Dr. LaHaye could be said to have enjoyed a degree of prescience while writing back then about the behemoth China has become. We have witnessed its growth in ways only supernatural insight could provide.

America, among other Western democracies, has, through bad trade deals and other mishandling of relations with the Chinese communist regimes over the years, done exactly what LaHaye thought they might do in helping them build the lethal level of military they have now achieved. Dr. LaHaye wrote further:

Thanks to American capitalists who have invested heavily in developing this backward nation merely to gain incredible profits, China, which otherwise would never have been able to compete economically on the world scene, is experiencing its first real growth in hundreds of years. If allowed to go unchecked, those investors, or their grandchildren, will live to regret such profit motive investments without demanding internal social reforms that would have granted basic freedoms to the Chinese people. It will be interesting in the years ahead to see Russia and China contend for supremacy in the area. Without realizing it, they both could be fulfilling Bible prophecy.[89]

China's phenomenal rise to its current position of power has profound significance for Bible prophecy. Many believe it indicates a trend that global geopolitical conditions are shaping up for the world's last great conflict described more than 1,900 years ago by the apostle John. Again, here is the prophecy he was given:

> And the sixth angel poured out his bowl upon the great river, the Euphrates; and its water was dried up, that the way might be prepared for the kings from the east. (Revelation 16:12)

These kings from the east have befuddled Bible prophecy scholars for many years, for few mentioned anything about them until the communist takeover of China during World War II. Since then, it has become apparent that this nation has a prophetic role, however minor it may be, in end-time events. Although China has been content to stay within its vast borders for thousands of years and live pretty much to itself, its communist dictators have changed all that. They seem to have the same obsession that characterized communists before them—world conquest.

America in China's Crosshairs

Centuries ago, Napoleon Bonaparte said, "When China awakens, the world will tremble." One doesn't have to be a prophet to recognize that, at this moment in history, the time of trembling is here.

No longer is China, with the world's largest population and awesome economic and military power, the paper tiger it was considered to be prior to World War II. In our lifetime, it has startled the world and frightened many in the military complex with her enormous economic and military potential. Most who observe the Sino world of nations' juxtaposition know that China has reached a position at least as strong as that of the Soviet Union during the Cold War. China already has nuclear weapons, or soon will—and it has a delivery system feared by every country in the Orient. This country is trafficking in arms beyond belief by buying them from Russia and any of the formerly impoverished satellite countries that will sell them. Then it turns around and sells what it doesn't want to keep to any of the oil-rich allies that can afford them (such as Iran, Iraq, or even India).

China regained Hong Kong when the ninety-nine-year lease was up. Now its aggressive demand for Taiwan and the Spratly Islands indicates it has a strategy to control all of Asia. Whoever controls the Spratlys not only controls the oil checkpoints to the oil-dependent countries of the East, including Japan, Taiwan, and the Philippines, but also Australia, Indonesia, and Singapore, where 50 percent of the world's population lives. Basing claims to these almost-uninhabitable islands to centuries-old documents, China is probably more interested in the suspected rich oil fields under them than their location because no country can prosper today or in the foreseeable future without oil.

Their venture into the South China Sea, building entire islands and fortifying them with military assets, gives a clue to just where their thoughts are concentrated. They threaten even the vaunted American Navy with their newly created carriers and other fearful military arsenal.

Chinese interest, however, far exceeds merely the territories they can overpower in their part of the world. They look to points West to bully and take over; they have purchased many parcels of real estate and other economic assets in the United States and other areas. This is thanks to greedy American capitalists whose concern for profits exceeds their concern for the safety of our country. And, presidential administrations prior to that of Donald J. Trump seemed eager to make terrible trade deals. Apparently, in many cases they did so in order to get along and show the communist regime leaders that we mean them no harm.

That, of course, is complete insanity, as the Chinese communists' focus—like that of the Soviets and now the Russians—is to dominate the world. America stands in the way of that quest, and so is their enemy and must be dealt with treacherously. President Trump recognizes this and has moved to rectify the situations in terms of military preparedness and economic acumen. This, we believe, has set the teeth of the global-ists on edge. They don't want to confront China, but want to somehow cajole it into becoming a tranquil, good, global citizen.

Bible prophecy says this will not happen. Every day, China, by its comportment, shows this is not going to happen. It's on a course for collision with the Western nations and America.

John the Revelator has told us that the kings of the east will come to the Euphrates River during the last part of the Tribulation and will then cross it. That supernatural barrier represented by the river in some way, apparently, will be breached at that time:

> And the sixth angel poured out his vial upon the great river Euphrates; and the water thereof was dried up, that the way of the kings of the east might be prepared. (Revelation 16:12)

While many who read this prophecy believe that the drying-up of the Euphrates will come from the destruction of a dam to the north or the turning off of the water, we believe the Word of God makes it clear that this is supernatural. There are apparently demonic spirits somewhere beneath the Euphrates that are kept reserved until the time of this army's approach.

It seems apparent that these demon spirits will actually enter and indwell these human forces as they cross the river. The heaven-established barrier that somehow separates the Oriental world from the Occidental will fall, and the two-hundred-million-man army, possessed by truly evil spiritual beings, will move into the western world to kill, the prophecy says, one-third of the world's population.

So, what about the Fourth Reich's führer? Isn't he supposed to control the world?

Again, it's hard to give a definitive answer in considering the great power Antichrist will possess at this time. The only logical conclusion might lie in the supernatural barrier of the Euphrates River. It seems like this demon-guarded obstruction has been in place—because of God's restraining power—until the kings of the east are prepared for an hour and a day, as prophecy foretells.

When the two-hundred-million troop army has arrived, the demons are released to flow into the human armies. The river is supernaturally dried up.

Is it any stretch to say that if God could hold back two enormous sides of the Red Sea while three or four million Israelites passed through a dried-up sea bed, He can dry up the Euphrates with a mere movement of His mighty hand?

So, the massive military force from the Oriental world combines to make their move toward world domination. They are convinced, apparently, by satanic inspiration, that this is the time to make their move. They will do so and the Antichrist will take note as he gets reports of what's happening in the area we know as Iraq today.

> But tidings out of the east and out of the north shall trouble
> him: therefore he shall go forth with great fury to destroy, and
> utterly to make away many. (Daniel 11:44)

The next thing the prophecy tells us about the beast's actions reminds us of Adolf Hitler. Antichrist will apparently go a bit insane, learning that anyone would dare to challenge his right to complete power. Again, we're told: "Therefore he shall go forth with great fury to destroy, and utterly to make away many."

Antichrist will begin slaughtering as many as his forces confront. Meantime, the kings of the east, led by China, undoubtedly will do the same. That they kill a third of the people of earth almost certainly indicates the use of nuclear weaponry.

Why this degree of lethality isn't unleashed as the kings of the east drive toward the killing fields of Armageddon is a mystery. Perhaps it's because the eastern horde doesn't want to make the plunder they lust after in the Middle East to be made radioactive. The one thing we know for certain is that all of this carnage *will take place*. God has said so.

China and the Bible

China isn't mentioned to any great extent in the Bible. In fact, the reference to China, "kings of the east," includes more than just China. That phrase really means "kings of the rising sun," which would include Japan and possibly other Asian countries. As Dr. LaHaye wrote of this expression:

> There has been some tendency to take the expression "the kings of the east" literally, "the kings of the sunrise" as referring specifically to Japan where the rising sun is a symbol of its political power. However, it is more natural to consider the term, "rising sun" as a synonym for east.[90]

Some Bible teachers suggest that "the Sinites" referred to in Genesis 10:17, and again in Isaiah 49:12, are where the "land of Sinim" is located. After God scattered the Sinites from the tower of Babel, they evidently settled in the east in what we know today as China. Then they became isolated from the rest of the world.

After the Great Flood, the earliest settlers carried with them the stories of creation and the one true God. Early missionaries to China pointed out the truth of God in the Chinese pictographic language.

Dr. LaHaye reported:

> My brother-in-law, a missionary to Taiwan for more than 20 years, told me the Chinese name for God is "ShangTi," which is made up of two pictographic symbols: "above" (or heavenly) and "emperor." Together, they mean "Heavenly Emperor." In a country that worships many gods, it is interesting that the earliest of Chinese characters (going back as far as 4,500 years) indicate that they recognized one God above all the emperors and other gods.[91]

Chuck Missler gives other illustrations of Chinese pictographs:

For example, the word "boat" is made up of three Chinese characters: vessel, eight and mouth, which could be a carryover from the eight mouths on the ark. The word "beginning" (of sin) combines the pictographs for "woman, secretly and mouth." The Chinese word for "devil" combines four words: motion, garden, man, and privately. Even more obvious is the word for "desire or covet." It is made up of two trees and the symbol for woman. Doubtless there are many other Chinese characters that could be traced to Genesis before the Tower of Babel.

Another interesting factor students of China find is that the most ancient Chinese calendars are seven-day calendars. Given their pagan background, we can only speculate that this, too, is a carryover from the book of Genesis. Geographically, the Euphrates River, one of the first rivers mentioned in the Bible, has served for centuries as the natural dividing line between East and West. It is evident to Bible scholars that Judaism and Christianity had an enormous impact on the world west of the Euphrates River, but very little influence on the East. Instead, the master deceiver has condemned the billions of souls of the peoples of the East with a succession of false religions such as Buddhism, Hinduism, Taoism and combinations of all of them. The dragon, the official, symbol of China, overpowered the primitive biblical teachings possessed by the first settlers with the polytheistic pantheism they have today. The idea that "god is all and all is god" is really a rejection of the God of the Bible.[92]

China's Threat Today

Again, Tim LaHaye's words on the ominous nation from the Far East rings in our ears at present. They give warning of things to come.

Keep in mind that China is not controlled by democracy-loving liberals like most countries in the world. Chinese leaders are among the most dedicated communists in the world. They are not "agrarian reformers" or "progressives," as our media tried to represent them a few years ago. Rather, they are a ruthless group of elite leaders who have stolen the opportunity for freedom from the 1.2 billion freedom-loving Chinese people, and they have never wavered in their plan to use China as a military platform from which to conquer the world. The events of the next two decades, if indeed we have that long, will prove that point.[93]

China's Sudden Emergence

Our heading here might make one ask: "What do you mean, 'sudden emergence?'" By this question—to carry the supposition further—the questioner might follow up with: "The Chinese have been front and center and a growing item in the news for decades."

China has indeed been moving from its Far East shadows behind that long wall that can be seen from satellites in space. Their emergence continues on an hour-by-hour basis. All we have to do is to listen to any news report at the moment these days. In fact, China is even at the center of controversy in the matter of the COVID-19 crisis.

Top administration officials charged with national security are looking with accusatory thoughts toward the communist government of China. Almost certainly, many are saying, that nation is guilty of releasing the virus once it escaped from one of their labs somewhere near Wuhan.

The city—larger in population than New York City—was shut down for some time right at the beginning of the virus' release, experts are saying. Somehow, we can't remember exactly how, according to the report, the intelligence from the area showed that many roads for heavy traffic were completely closed for more than a week at one point. It was something that had never been done. There was no explanation for the shutdown, the report said.

The inference made was that the streets and roads were shut down, disallowing the city's millions of people to traverse them. This means, they believe, that something of a highly dangerous nature caused the dictator, Xi Jinping, to totally disrupt life in the area.

Shortly after the shutdown, US intelligence agencies reported that Chinese military removed hundreds, if not thousands, from their apartments. These same people haven't been heard from since. The thinking among the people who gather intelligence is that they were taken and killed in some manner, and attempts were made to erase the fact that they ever existed.

Why? Apparently those removed were sick with the virus. They were removed, the thinking goes, so that the Chinese government could hide that the virus broke out in Wuhan and vicinity.

This "theory" is based in fact, in that US intelligence authorities have made no effort to discount the report. Apparently, electronic devices that monitor the area of Wuhan and the military weapons laboratory picked up on all these doings in and around the area.

The reports discount the theory that the virus spread from the so-called wet markets—the places where meats are bought by grocery shoppers. They apparently, in some cases, choose live animals—exotic animals at that. Bats were thought to be the "meat" from which the virus came.

Now the question is whether the virus escaped the labs accidentally or was deliberately released. The former thinking seems to be what most of the intelligence people have concluded.

Now the accusations are that Xi Jinping and his cadre of underlings decided that the accidental release was not going to bring only China's economic circumstance to a standstill. They wanted all economies to suffer so China can maintain its relatively close to number-one economic position as it comes out of the crisis. The virus, the thinking goes, was put on planes by the Chinese government, with people carrying it to major cities around the world.

This certainly seems to be the plausible explanation of what has happened. It is much more than just doubtful that this could have been contrived as part of a plan to do the damage it has done. The Chinese have simply—maybe not so simply—taken advantage of the virus' accidental release. Their strategy, if so, is brilliantly evil.

We believe it *was* planned by the greatest schemer there is—Lucifer, the fallen one. He, we conjecture, started it from the beginning and continues to carry out the devilish plan. So the American administration cast a suspicious glare at the Chinese communist regime and pointed an accusatory finger, based on electronic and on-the-ground intelligence.

What does this all mean, prophetically speaking? Our thoughts are that while Satan has planned it all from its inception, it is, of course, under the complete control of God, whose omniscience nothing and no one escapes. We believe it is yet another signal of the stage being set for the Tribulation era and the ultimate return of His Son, the Lord Jesus, to clean up the planet of all sin and rebellion.

It is almost certain that China will be a primary player in the Tribulation era. The virus and China's part in the release of its deadly and destructive effects could well be the Lord grabbing the old Chinese dragon by its neck and pulling it to the surface of earth's bubbling cauldron of rebellion against God—thus to make known its evil intentions. China is showing itself to be the hegemonic force that consistently proves it not only wants to dominate the South China Sea and its sphere of influence, but wants to become the world's number-one economic and military superpower.

The coronavirus might be a pandemic—a much-overblown one, in terms of its potential deadly effects, in our estimation. It is likely that Satan, however, has brought it about to the degree that it has inflicted its havoc upon the world. But the God of heaven controls it, like He controls everything in the ultimate sense.

Could China now have been "outed" in alerting all observers to its genocidal evil? Could the Lord be seeing to it that the Chinese dragon is shown to be in cahoots with the old red dragon, Satan, so that there can be no excuse that the world hasn't been warned?

That Chinese dragon will be the king of the kings of the East; *we* have little doubt. Again, they and their Near-East and Far-East Asian cohorts will be responsible for killing fully one-third of earth's inhabitants at the later stages of the movement of nations toward the killing fields of Armageddon.

17

Mystery Babylon

While the Fourth Reich's führer consolidates power, an offer of benevolence to those under his rule will be instituted for a time. The great leader will, as Hitler in the 1930s, reach out to various groups and convince them that if they support him completely, they'll eventually be restored to normality.

This promise will be greatly desired because, as we have seen, chaos will certainly follow the disappearance of millions. It will be the greatest crisis of human history to that point. COVID-19 and all other crises through the ages will seem as nothing. The vanishing will haunt every waking moment of the people alive at that time. Their worst nightmares will have come to life. They'll gladly give the leader whatever he asks as he promises to turn their world right-side up again.

Whether we recognize it or not, we have in our very soul a God-shaped void, a deep need for the God who created us. The Fall in the Garden of Eden separated God and mankind. Only a reunification with the Creator-God can satisfy that emptiness. People of the post-Rapture world will sense in their core beings the need for the comfort and reassurance only God will be able to fill. They will, therefore, search for that level of comfort. They will think they have found it when a man appears on the scene who comes alongside the great political leader who promises that if they obey his edicts, they'll ultimately have heaven on earth.

False Prophet's Appeal

The man will come wearing the clerical robes of high ecclesiastical prominence. He will be near the great leader and will promote the political agenda as righteous...even godly. He will manage to meld many religions and cults into the geopolitical system—a truly ecumenical orchestration that will synthesize all ways to get to heaven the world's rebellious populations have long desired to be promised. The great religions of the world will for the most part eagerly join the new religious amalgamation.

For the time being, the rising leader of the Fourth Reich will be content to allow the religious hybrid entity to ride atop the swelling tide of his rise to full power. The religious fervor will be like that of the Nuremberg rallies during Hitler's time. The new religion will give all honor to the political elements of the regime, while giving the people under its thumb of rule the sense that the "God void" in their souls is being filled.

God's prophetic Word has an entirely different view of this religion that will rise alongside the first beast of Revelation 13, under the second beast's mesmerizing orchestration. Here is God's portrait of the system that will develop soon after the Rapture. Revelation 17 describes the great scarlet whore, a word picture of the decadence, debauchery, and prostitution of that coming religious entity, as John is shown this monstrosity by the angel:

So he carried me away in the spirit into the wilderness: and I saw a woman sit upon a scarlet coloured beast, full of names of blasphemy, having seven heads and ten horns.

And the woman was arrayed in purple and scarlet colour, and decked with gold and precious stones and pearls, having a golden cup in her hand full of abominations and filthiness of her fornication: And upon her forehead was a name written, MYSTERY, BABYLON THE GREAT, THE MOTHER OF HARLOTS AND ABOMINATIONS OF THE EARTH.

And I saw the woman drunken with the blood of the saints, and with the blood of the martyrs of Jesus: and when I saw her, I wondered with great admiration. (Revelation 17:3–6)

The gaudily decked-out harlot riding upon the strange red beast is a picture of a religious system that is totally beholden to the political beast—the power that assures her existence. She has, this portrait tells, been responsible for sacrificing the people within her orbit to the ravenous monster she rides.

The scarlet beast is almost certainly the same one Daniel first saw (Daniel 8), and it is the same as the one John saw as it arose from the sea in Revelation chapter 13.

Arnold Fruchtenbaum, the Messianic Jewish scholar, identifies Babylon the harlot in Revelation 17:

Babylon the Harlot represents the one-world religious system that rules over the religious affairs during the first half of the Tribulation. She rules over the nations of the world (the many waters) fully controlling the religious affairs and has the reluctant support of the government. The headquarters of this one world religion will be the rebuilt city of Babylon, the "mother" of idolatry, for it was here that idolatry and false religion began (Genesis 11:1–9).[94]

One can only imagine what John thought as the vision played in front of his astonished eyes. He doubtless stood in stunned silence, muted by the gory scene before him.

The account of Daniel and the prophetic scenes he wondered over when the angel came states that he asked to know the meaning. We don't get that sense with John. It doesn't appear that he ever asked. So, the angel holding one of the seven vials of judgment took it upon himself to pull John out of his stupor.

And the angel said unto me, Wherefore didst thou marvel? I will tell thee the mystery of the woman, and of the beast that carrieth her, which hath the seven heads and ten horns.

The beast that thou sawest was, and is not; and shall ascend out of the bottomless pit, and go into perdition: and they that dwell on the earth shall wonder, whose names were not written in the book of life from the foundation of the world, when they behold the beast that was, and is not, and yet is. And here is the mind which hath wisdom.

The seven heads are seven mountains, on which the woman sitteth. And there are seven kings: five are fallen, and one is, and the other is not yet come; and when he cometh, he must continue a short space.

And the beast that was, and is not, even he is the eighth, and is of the seven, and goeth into perdition.

And the ten horns which thou sawest are ten kings, which have received no kingdom as yet; but receive power as kings one hour with the beast.

These have one mind, and shall give their power and strength unto the beast.

These shall make war with the Lamb, and the Lamb shall overcome them: for he is Lord of lords, and King of kings: and they that are with him are called, and chosen, and faithful.

And he saith unto me, The waters which thou sawest, where the whore sitteth, are peoples, and multitudes, and nations, and tongues.

And the ten horns which thou sawest upon the beast, these

shall hate the whore, and shall make her desolate and naked, and shall eat her flesh, and burn her with fire.

For God hath put in their hearts to fulfil his will, and to agree, and give their kingdom unto the beast, until the words of God shall be fulfilled.

And the woman which thou sawest is that great city, which reigneth over the kings of the earth. (Revelation 17:7–18)

It might seem that the description the angel gave John raises more questions than it answers. The prophecy certainly has been fodder for many biblical students, scholars, teachers, and preachers through the years to ponder and pontificate upon.

Dr. Mark Hitchcock gives the following statement in his book on Babylon:

But one thing is sure from this vision. Whatever the woman and the beast represent, they are very closely tied together. Beauty is riding on the beast.

Her riding the beast indicates that she controls him in some way, or exercises strong influence over him. Their relationship is one of both convenience and necessity.

I believe that the scarlet beast with seven heads and ten horns is the Antichrist and his ten-kingdom empire, as described in detail in Daniel 7 and Revelation 13. The harlot in Revelation 17 represents the false religious system, centered in the city of Babylon, which gives spiritual cohesion to the system.[95]

The angel's description of the harlot religious system that is supported and carried about by the scarlet-colored beast has been viewed in many different ways. The study is particularly problematic in trying to pin down where the angel speaks of the beast, his ascending out of the bottomless pit, and going into perdition.

Some believe it to mean that it represents the Roman Empire in some fashion. It never really died, and now comes back to revive and be the final version of the final empire. Others have interpreted it as the first beast of Revelation 13, who had the deadly wound and lived, which is a reference to a counterfeit resurrection. Dr. Walvoord wrote:

> 17:8 The beast that thou sawest was, and is not; and shall ascend out of the bottomless pit, and go into perdition: and they that dwell on the earth shall wonder, whose names were not written in the book of life from the foundation of the world, when they behold the beast that was, and is not, and yet is.
>
> The angel first gives a detailed description of the beast in his general character. The beast is explained chronologically as that which was, is not, and is about to ascend from the abyss and go into perdition. "The bottomless pit" (Gr., *abyssos,* meaning "bottomless," or "the abyss") is the home of Satan and demons and indicates that the power of the political empire is satanic in its origin as is plainly stated in 13:4. The word perdition…means "destruction" or "utter destruction," referring to eternal damnation. The power of the political empire in the last days is going to cause wonder as indicated in the questions in 13:4: "Who is like unto the beast? who is able to make war with him?" The overwhelming satanic power of the final political empire of the world will be most convincing to great masses of mankind.
>
> There is a confusing similarity between the descriptions afforded Satan who was apparently described as the king over the demons in the abyss (9:11), "the beast that ascendeth out of the bottomless pit" (11:7), the beast whose "deadly wound was healed" (13:3), and the beast of 17:8. The solution to this intricate problem is that there is an identification to some extent of Satan with the future world ruler and identification of the world ruler with his world government. Each of the three entities is described as a beast. Only Satan himself actually comes from the abyss. The world government which he promotes is entirely

satanic in its power and to this extent is identified with Satan. It is the beast as the world government which is revived. The man who is the world ruler, however, has power and great authority given to him by Satan. The fact that Satan and the world ruler are referred to in such similar terms indicates their close relationship one to the other.

While many have attempted to demonstrate from this verse that the final world ruler is some resurrected being such as Judas Iscariot, Nero, or one of the more recent world rulers, it would seem preferable to regard the "eighth" beast as the political power of the world government rather than its human ruler. What is revived is imperial government, not an imperial ruler (cf. Rev. 13:3). That which seemingly went out of existence in history never to be revived is thus miraculously resuscitated at the end of the age.[96]

The mysterious woman called the whore of Babylon has fornicated with the kings of the earth. She is given great wealth because of her wickedness as symbolic mistress of those in power during this final age of human history that leads to Christ's Second Advent.

She has been complicit in helping put a murderous end to true believers who come to Christ during this horrific era. She has also, undoubtedly, helped round up as many of the House of Israel as possible as Antichrist puts into effect his Final Solution.

This religious system is the culmination of all the false-worship entities of history. At the center of her apostasy is the many ways to God and heaven, as we've discussed previously.

It is of great interest to many that the current pope, as of this writing, fits the mold of the one who will be the False Prophet—the second beast of Revelation 13. Dr. Thomas Horn has written a tremendous volume explaining the possibilities of a future pope becoming that second beast. In *Petrus Romanus*, regarding the explanation of the prophecy about the last pope being the False Prophet of Revelation 13, Horn writes:

As the legend goes, Malachy experienced what is today considered a famous vision commonly called "The Prophecy of the Popes." The prophecy is a list of Latin verses predicting each of the Roman Catholic popes from Pope Celestine II to the final pope, "Peter the Roman," whose reign would end in the destruction of Rome. According to this ancient prophecy, the very next pope (following Benedict XVI) will be the final pontiff, Petrus Romanus or Peter the Roman.

The final segment of the prophecy reads:

In persecutione extrema S. R. E. sedebit Petrus Romanus, qui pascet oves in multis tribulationibus: quibus transactis civitas septicollis deruetur et judex tremendus judicabit populum. Finis.[97]

Which is rendered:

In the extreme persecution of the Holy Roman Church, there will sit Peter the Roman, who will nourish the sheep in many tribulations; when they are finished, the City of Seven Hills will be destroyed, and the dreadful judge will judge his people. The End.[98]

Babylon's Mystery Minister

This world system, so antithetical to God's blueprint for humanity, is winding up for the consummation of history by every measure examined by students of Bible prophecy who hold to a pre-Trib, premillennial view.

Global politics, government, and socioeconomics are gushing in the prophet Daniel's end-times flood (Daniel 9:26) toward the end of the Church Age. But no signal of the approaching apocalypse presents a more laser-like, focused view of the end-of-days dynamics than religious rearrangements taking place locally, nationally, and especially worldwide. The departure from biblical Christianity is so rampant and moving at such a furious pace in American neighborhoods and nationwide that even the most ardent, futurist students of end-times matters are sometimes stunned by developments.

Added to the departure from the faith was the recent closure of churches across America. The social distancing ordered because of the COVID-19 crisis took its toll on the "assembling of ourselves together," as the Lord admonished (see Hebrews 10:25). Whether the nation will come out of the crisis anywhere near as strong in adherence to Christian worship is a matter of great concern.

Preparations for the harlot system that will hold all within the Fourth Reich captive in its hellish false-worship system is well underway. The prediction of the last pope being the False Prophet of Revelation 13 who will guide and direct that system is therefore worthy of consideration.

The story of St. Malachy injects intriguing speculations and possibilities into the world's rush into last-days ecumenism. The twelfth-century Irish bishop of the Roman Catholic Church, canonized by Pope Clement III in 1190, presented a fascinating line of predictions that many believe were visions leading to the man who will be the final pope.

St. Bernard of Clairvaux was St. Malachy's biographer. Clairvaux wrote in his book, *Life of Saint Malachy,* that Malachy was said to have the gift of prophecy. It is claimed that St. Malachy predicted the exact day and hour of his own death.

Hal Lindsey (author of *The Late, Great, Planet Earth*) wrote for WorldNet Daily (WND) upon the death of Pope John-Paul II, in 2005, regarding St. Malachy's papal predictions:

> According to his biographer, St. Malachy was visiting Rome in 1139 when he went into a trance and received a vision. Malachy wrote down this extraordinary vision in which he claims to have foreseen all of the popes from the death of Innocent II until the destruction of the church and the return of Christ.
>
> St. Malachy wrote briefly, in Latin, on each succeeding pope of the future, and then gave the document to Pope Innocent II, who had it

placed in Vatican archives where it remained for several centuries. It was rediscovered in 1590 and published.

Lindsey wrote:

[Malachy] named exactly 112 popes from that time until the end. The interesting thing is that scholars have matched the brief 110 descriptive predictions with each of the 110 popes and anti-popes that there have been since Innocent II. Though they are a bit obscure, they have fit the general profile of each of the popes.

The bottom line is that the last two popes, John Paul II and Pope Benedict XVI, fit the profile that running string of papal succession seems to accurately predict. Number 112 is supposed to be the pope who will head the Roman Catholic Church during the great time of trouble—the Tribulation—according to the Malachy prophecy. He will be, the prediction says, Petrus Romanus (Peter the Roman). Pope Benedict XVI is number 111.

Hal Lindsey wrote further in 2005:

Now, if St. Malachy is accurate, there will be only two more popes before the end of this world, as we know it and the Second Coming of Christ. I do know that the whole prophetic scenario of signs that Jesus Christ and the prophets predicted would come together just before His return are now in view. So what St. Malachy predicted is certainly occurring in the right time frame.

Now, in 2020, we know that Pope Benedict became pontiff in 2005 and later resigned in 2013. This is a fact that Horn and Putnam astoundingly predicted in their book, *Petrus Romanus,* a year ahead of Benedict's resignation. Pope Francis was then elevated to the papal throne. He is number 112 of the list of the 112 popes Malachy gave leading to the final pontiff—the pope who will be the False Prophet, according to his reckoning.

18

Armageddon

rmageddon is a term that encompasses the direst connotation possible. It is sometimes used rather lightly to describe various situations that seem hopeless. During the COVID-19 pandemic crisis, for example, some have termed the financial disaster it portends "economic Armageddon." By that, is meant that there is no hope. It is the end of any hope. Complete defeat and destruction is in the offing.

The term comes, of course, from biblical prophecy. Armageddon is the place of the great, final battle of human history. Actually, it is the end of a continuing war that will have begun with the gathering of armies during the Tribulation, as we've looked at before.

The Armageddon campaign will have its starting point with the sixth bowl judgment, as recorded in Revelation:

And the sixth poured out his bowl upon the great river, the river Euphrates; and the water thereof was dried up, that the way might be made ready for the kings that come from the sunrising.

And I saw coming out of the mouth of the dragon, and out of the mouth of the beast, and out of the mouth of the false prophet, three unclean spirits, as it were frogs:

for they are spirits of demons, working signs; which go forth unto the kings of the whole world, to gather them together unto the war of the great day of God, the Almighty.

(Behold, I come as a thief. Blessed is he that watcheth, and keepeth his garments, lest he walk naked, and they see his shame.)

And they gathered them together into the place which is called in Hebrew Har-Magedon. (Revelation 16:12–16)

The great barrier between the Oriental and Occidental world will be dried up, as we've seen. Satan will thus begin gathering all the forces that oppose God for the final assault on His chosen land and people of Israel.

"Armageddon" is an English translation from the name "Mount of Megiddo." This is a geographic location in Israel's northern region. The vast area will be the center of earth's final world war.

This is where the climax of human history occurs, when Jesus Christ returns to put an end to Antichrist's genocidal madness. Events leading up to this war will be cataclysmic, according to Scripture. The stage-setting leading to this point will be earth-shaking, as Jesus outlined in His answer to the disciples' question: "What shall be the sign of thy coming, and of the end of the world?"

The Lord, while sitting atop the Mount of Olives still in human flesh, gave a number of signals that would be prevalent at the end of the age. These indicators, He later—as the resurrected, glorified Christ in heaven—revealed through an angel, will build in severity and intensity while the Tribulation years unfold. There will be, as we've discussed, twenty-one judgments that will take place in a series of seven seals, seven trumpets, and seven bowls. The climax of God's judgment and wrath upon a world of rebellious earth dwellers will be the final battle of Armageddon.

Dr. John Walvoord wrote the following regarding the buildup to Armageddon:

> According to 1 Thessalonians 5:1, 2, when the rapture occurs it begins a new period of time called "the day of the Lord." This is a familiar term in the Old Testament and applies to any period of time during which God dealt in direct judgment of Israel. This is described, for instance, in Isaiah 13:1–22 and is characterized as "a cruel day, with wrath and fierce anger" (Isaiah 13:9). The book of Joel almost entirely addresses this subject; it speaks of many days of the Lord as, for instance, in chapter 1, when the invasion of locusts causes starvation. Many descriptions of the day of the Lord go beyond what occurred in the Old Testament, for instance, Joel 2:30–3:3 with the verses that follow describe this terrible time of judgment which is still in the future. The day of the Lord beginning at the rapture will continue even through the thousand-year reign of Christ when there still will be direct judgment of open sin against God, fulfilling the prediction that Christ will rule with an "iron scepter." There will be a display of "the fury of the wrath of God Almighty" (Revelation 19:15). The major events of the judgment of God, however, may not be immediately fulfilled after the rapture but will gradually increase as the period between the rapture and the Second Coming is fulfilled.[99]

The war of Armageddon will be God bringing all satanic evil of world history since the Garden of Eden rebellion to account. It will especially mark His dealing with the tremendous evil and all of the carnage subsequent to it that the militaries of world history have inflicted.

Antichrist is representative of all anti-God tyrants and dictators of human history rolled into one. He will meet his doom, as we've seen as far back as 2 Thessalonians 2:8:

And then shall that wicked be revealed, whom the Lord shall consume with the spirit of his mouth, and shall destroy with the brightness of his coming.

We have seen how this will be the worst and most dangerous of all despots to have lived. His Fourth Reich, as we term it, will put into effect Satan's Final Solution in an effort to eradicate every last one of God's chosen people. This is primary to consider in thinking about the severity and completeness of the punishment in the Lord's dealing with humanity at Armageddon. His anger against the world of rebels will be instituted largely as a result of the harsh treatment of the people through whom He chose to bring the Savior into the world.

Hatred of the Chosen

Satan has fought through human armies and governments throughout the ages to try to negate God's promises to Abraham, Isaac, and Jacob. That promise, in part, follows:

The Lord said to Abraham, And I will make of thee a great nation, and I will bless thee, and make thy name great; and thou shalt be a blessing:

And I will bless them that bless thee, and curse him that curseth thee: and in thee shall all families of the earth be blessed. (Genesis 12:2–3)

If Lucifer can negate God's promises, he must think—in his reprobate, anti-God mindset—that he can contravene his own doom in the lake of fire. So the hatred is stepped up at every opportunity against God's chosen people.

Anti-Semitism has been the rule throughout the centuries among the nations of earth, and it's growing once again, as many news accounts report almost hourly. Not meaning to pick on any one area of today's world, we nonetheless need to illustrate how Satan is at work today in ramping up hatred against Israel and the Jewish people. We'll use Australia and news reports coming from there over the past several years. The headlines read:

- "Confronting Reality: Anti-Semitism in Australia Today," *Jewish Political Studies Review,* 16:3–4 (Fall 2004).[100]
- "Israel Arrests Woman Wanted on Child Sex Abuse Charges at Melbourne Jewish School," (February 13, 2018).[101]
- "Australian Jewish Leader Condemns Senator's Speech Calling for 'Final Solution,'" (August 15, 2018).[102]
- "Anti-Semitic Attacks of Boys Who Were Called 'Jewish Ape' and 'Dirty Jew' Shock Australia," (October 3, 2019).[103]
- "Australian Teenager Charged over Making Jewish Boy Kiss Another Student's Shoes," (October 25, 2019).[104]
- "We Cannot Let Anti-Semitism Spread Here," (November 21, 2019).[105]
- "Report Shows Anti-Semitism on the Rise Following Outrage over 'Party Nazis,'" (November 25, 2019).[106]
- "Anti-Semitic Assaults and Threats up by 30 Percent in Australia, New Report Finds," (November 26, 2019).[107]
- "Australia Sees 30 Percent Increase in Anti-Semitic Incidents," (November 26, 2019).[108]
- "Toxic Left-Wing Anti-Semitism: Australia, UK and the USA," (December 19, 2019).[109]
- "Global Anti-Semitism: Select Incidents in 2019," (December, 2019).[110]
- "Australian Jewish Survivors Recount How the Fire Swept into Their Home in 45 Minutes," (January 9, 2020).[111]
- "Holocaust Survivor 'Suffering Flashbacks' after Nazi Flag Flown Metres away from His Australian Home," (January 17, 2020).[112]

- "The BBC Has Shamed Itself with Orla Guerin's Holocaust Report," (January 33, 2020).[113]

Many other reports of anti-Semitism could be added from points around the globe. As mentioned before, all but a handful of countries that make up the United Nations show total disdain for Israel. They want Israel removed from being a nation. By this they are "cursing" Israel, the progeny of Abraham, Isaac, and Jacob.

God says He will bring all the world to account for this egregious treatment. He will bring them to the killing field, that triangular expanse in the Valley of Jezreel, on the plains of Esdraelon, beneath the mount called Megiddo. It is also known as the "valley of Jehoshaphat":

> For, behold, in those days, and in that time, when I shall bring again the captivity of Judah and Jerusalem, I will also gather all nations, and will bring them down into the valley of Jehoshaphat, and will plead with them there for my people and for my heritage Israel, whom they have scattered among the nations, and parted my land. (Joel 3:2)

Again, Dr. Walvoord gives us a look at history's world empires—combined into one beast—that will be dealt with at Armageddon. These will be the armies and peoples of history who have dealt treacherously with God and the House of Israel.

> The book of Daniel provides a broad prediction of how God is going to deal with the Gentile world, beginning with Babylon in the time of Daniel about 600 B.C. and continuing through the empires that followed, that of Medo- Persia, Greece, and Rome. The predictions of Babylon, Medo-Persia, and Greece have all been literally fulfilled and are now part of the historic past. The Roman empire, however, which was in power at the time of the first coming of Christ, is still a continuing part of God's purpose.

It continued for many centuries after Christ and then eventually disappeared, but, according to Scriptures, will be revived in the end times.

Daniel 7 pictures the four empires as ferocious beasts, with Babylon depicted as a lion, Medo-Persia as a bear, and Greece as a leopard. The fourth empire is described in different terminology in Daniel 7 as follows:

"After that, in my vision at night I looked, and there before me was a fourth beast-terrifying and frightening and very powerful. It had large iron teeth; it crushed and devoured its victims and trampled underfoot whatever was left. It was different from all the former beasts, and it had ten horns" (Daniel 7:7).

The Roman empire literally fulfilled the picture of a beast with great iron teeth, crushing and devouring everything before it. Its well-disciplined soldiers went into countries that were unprepared to fight. The soldiers then conquered the country, carried off the able-bodied men as slaves, left a detachment of soldiers to collect taxes, and moved on to the next country. As the greatest empire of the past, it was ruthless in its destruction of whatever opposed it. Most of Daniel 7:7 has already been fulfilled.

The final statement in verse 7, however, states, "it had ten horns." Nothing in history corresponds to this, and Bible expositors have been struggling for centuries to explain this prophecy that has not been fulfilled.

But Daniel 7:24 reveals that "The ten horns are ten kings who will come from this kingdom." How can this be explained in view of the fact that the Roman empire today is non-existent? In order to understand this period, one has to recognize that the Old Testament described the events leading up to the first coming of Christ, but then many Scriptures skip from the first coming to the Second Coming and omit reference to what we call the present age of grace…the present age is not in view.

While Old Testament Scriptures deal with the time of judgment preceding the Second Coming, they do not anticipate that the Roman empire will go out of existence for many centuries, only to be revived in the end time in the form of these ten kingdoms.

Scripture does not indicate exactly when this will happen, but as soon as the rapture occurs, the ten kingdoms are in the background and apparently the formation of the ten-kings power bloc will come together either just before or just after the rapture. The fact that the European Union is friendly today, geopolitically speaking—that is, the major players are not at odds with each other—provides fertile soil for producing a united Europe, which would fulfill, at least in part, this prophecy....

Steps in that direction-including implementing a common currency- have already taken place. Accordingly, the situation described at the rapture of ten nations banded together is something that could occur at any time and is strategic evidence that the rapture of the church could be near.[114]

So all nations will be brought to Armageddon for the conclusion of the Day of the Lord. It will be the most terrible moment of human history.

We can't look into the high councils of the third heaven and know the rendering of judgmental edicts. We can, however, look at God's Word of condemnation and examine evidence to get a pretty clear understanding of what that evidence points to. You can do the same. Does the God of Israel keep His promises? You be the judge.

While anti-Semitism rages in the continent down under, so do the geophysical elements. Australia has, in the very recent past, experienced plague-like affliction almost biblical in proportion:

In the midst of raging wildfires, hailstones the size of baseballs pounded Australia in a mix of elemental opposites echoing the Egyptian plague. As if that reminder of the Exodus were not enough, a massive dust storm turned day into night. These and other phenomena created a pre-Messiah show of wonders in the hard-hit continent down under conspicuously timed to coincide with the week when Jews around the world read the section of the Torah relating the story of the plagues in Egypt.

While the northern hemisphere hunkers down for winter, Australia enters its dry summer. This year, a stark drought brought on devastating wildfires that have, so far, burned an estimated 46 million acres of land. The fires destroyed over 5,900 buildings including approximately 2,683 homes, and killed at least 30 people. An estimated one billion animals were also killed and some endangered species may be driven to extinction.[115]

In a strange, horrifying mixture that can only be described as a biblical-type plague, hail the size of baseballs fell following catastrophic fire that ravaged the region.[116] The article further explains the devastating phenomenon:

As if a Biblical plague of hail was not enough, a massive dust storm engulfed the town of Narromine, some 250 miles northwest of Sydney. The 186-mile wide cloud of red dust was carried by wind gusts up to 66 miles per hour. The huge storm quickly plunged the area into darkness so complete the weather service described it as "Day turns into night!"

Again, this isn't just to pick on our good friends in Australia. The evidence, however, contrasting anti-Semitism's assault to the very elements crying out in such fury must be noted. "America, take notice!" is the message. That goes for the rest of the world as well.

God's chosen nation is front and center as the number-one sign of where we stand on His prophetic timeline. Although modern Israel is as evil in comportment as the nations of the rest of the world in many ways, its God neither slumbers nor sleeps. He has declared His absolute love and protection over this place he calls "the apple of my eye."

This is what the Lord says, "He who appoints the sun to shine by day, Who decrees the moon and stars to shine by night, Who stirs up the sea so that its waves roar—the Lord Almighty is His Name;

"Only if these ordinances vanish from My sight," declares the Lord, "will the descendants of Israel ever cease to be a nation before Me." (Jeremiah 31:35–36)

Armageddon forces are being gathered even now. The Lord of heaven knows exactly who the offenders are in exercising hatred for Israel—and for Him. A terrible price will be paid during the years ahead, particularly following the Rapture of the Church.

Dr. Arnold Fruchtenbaum gives additional description of what is entailed in the matter of Armageddon.

While the term, "Battle of Armageddon," has been commonly used, it is really a misnomer, for more than one battle will be taking place. For this reason, many prophetic teachers have stopped employing that term and are using the term, "Campaign of Armageddon…" But this, too, is a misnomer because there will be no fighting in Armageddon itself; all of the fighting will take place elsewhere. A more biblical name for this final conflict is found in the closing words of verse 14: *the war of the great day of God, the Almighty.* This is a more accurate description of the nature and extent of this final conflict.…

The train of thought is picked up again in verse 16, which names the place where the allies of the Antichrist will be gathered: *Har-Magedon.* As the ASV text shows, the word is a combination of two Hebrew words which mean, "the Mountain of Megiddo." Megiddo was a strategic city located at the western end of the Valley of Jezreel, guarding the famous Megiddo Pass into Israel's largest valley. One can see the entire Valley of Jezreel from the mount upon which the city of Megiddo stood. So what is known as the Valley of Armageddon in Christian circles is actually the biblical Valley of Jezreel. The term *Armageddon* is never applied to the valley itself, but only to the mount at the western end. Here, in this large valley of Lower Galilee, the armies of the world will gather for the purpose of destroying all the Jews still living.

It should be noted that the passage says nothing of a battle in this valley, for no fighting will take place here. The Valley of Jezreel, guarded by the Mountain of Megiddo, will merely serve as the gathering ground for the armies of the Antichrist. Armageddon will play the same role that England played in the closing stages of World War II. The allied forces gathered their armies together in England, but that is not where the final battle took place. The final conflict began on the beaches of Normandy, France, on D-Day. Armageddon will also serve as a gathering place, with the battle beginning elsewhere.[117]

God Laughs

Man will view this gathering of the armies of the world from the perspective that it is mainly Antichrist bringing them together for some great purpose—to finally rid the earth of the hated Jew, of Israel. It will be the Final Solution in action. All leaders of armies will know Antichrist's purpose and will be eager to make this final thrust into what the Bible has termed "my land."

God sees the gathering from an entirely different perspective:

Proclaim ye this among the nations; prepare war; stir up the mighty men; let all the men of war draw near, let them come up.

Beat your plowshares into swords, and your pruning-hooks into spears: let the weak say, I am strong.

Haste ye, and come, all ye nations round about, and gather

yourselves together: thither cause thy mighty ones to come down, O Jehovah. (Joel 3:9–11)

God's ironic sense of punitive humor against those opposed to Him comes to the forefront. He mockingly invites them to prepare for battle, to turn their farming equipment into weapons of war.

The leaders of these armies intend to destroy all vestiges of the Jewish race. God has quite another idea about why He has gathered them together. His taunting of this tremendous array of forces comes further into focus with the following:

Why do the nations rage, And the peoples meditate a vain thing?

The kings of the earth set themselves, And the rulers take counsel together, Against Jehovah, and against his anointed, saying, Let us break their bands asunder, And cast away their cords from us, He that sitteth in the heavens will laugh:

The Lord will have them in derision. Then will he speak unto them in his wrath, And vex them in his sore displeasure: Yet I have set my king upon my holy hill of Zion. (Psalm 2:1–6)

Dr. Fruchtenbaum further expounds on the gathering of God and Israel's enemies:

The gathering of the nations is presented as a gathering against God the Father and His Anointed, that is, the Messiah Jesus. By seeking to destroy the Jews, Satan is also seeking to break the cords of God's control of the world. How foolish! Then God is portrayed as sitting in the heavens and laughing, because He will soon have these nations in confusion. It is God who will set His own king upon Zion, and Satan and the Antichrist will not be able to prevent it. Although the nations will assemble to carry out the program of the counterfeit trinity, they will actually accomplish the purpose of the Triune God. This gathering of

the armies of the nations in the Valley of Jezreel will be the first
stage of the Campaign of Armageddon.[118]

We'll next look at the devastating defeat of Antichrist and the forces
arranged against God. All the military power on earth—neither conventional, nuclear, nor any other—can hold back the most anticipated
victory of the history of man.

19

Second Coming and the Judgment Seat

The Second Coming, also known as Christ's Second Advent, is the time prophesied in the Bible when Jesus Christ returns to the earth to put an end to Armageddon. Christ is called "the King of kings" in His glorious return, and will institute his millennial reign (thousand-year kingdom) on earth. He will rule the world from atop Zion (the place now occupied by Mount Moriah) at Jerusalem from the throne of David.

Christ's Second Coming is foretold by John, the writer of the Revelation:

And I saw heaven opened, and behold a white horse; and he that sat upon him was called Faithful and True, and in righteousness he doth judge and make war.

His eyes were as a flame of fire, and on his head were many crowns; and he had a name written, that no man knew, but he himself.

And he was clothed with a vesture dipped in blood: and his name is called The Word of God.

And the armies which were in heaven followed him upon white horses, clothed in fine linen, white and clean.

And out of his mouth goeth a sharp sword, that with it he should smite the nations: and he shall rule them with a rod of iron: and he treadeth the winepress of the fierceness and wrath of Almighty God.

And he hath on his vesture and on his thigh a name written, KING OF KINGS AND LORD OF LORDS. (Revelation 19:11–16)

A Dramatic Overview

Before getting into details of what the Second Coming is about, let's look at an overview of the stunning event. There has never been, nor ever will be, one more dramatic.

Leaders of the forces meet at Armageddon to battle each other and will turn to see the brightness that's broken through the darkness that has overcast earth's skies because of the judgments of God. Antichrist, supreme leader of much of the gathering military west of the Euphrates River, will recognize the invading power from heaven. Perhaps the leaders from the two hundred-million-man army from the Orient that has crossed the dried-up Euphrates from the east will also know what the brilliantly shining heavenly intrusion is all about. All hostile, earthly hordes will then turn to concentrate their fire at the descending heavenly army, led by Jesus Christ.

While the sea of humanity on the planet's surface viciously roars in an attempt to prevent the heavenly intervention, those warring forces will turn from battling with each other to curse God and all His righteousness. Then Jesus Christ, mounted upon a stunning white steed, will speak words sharper than a two-edged sword.

Master to Calm Storm

We are convinced they will be the same words Jesus of Nazareth spoke to that raging sea of Galilee nearly two millennia ago (read Mark 4:36–

41.) They are the same words He speaks today to everyone who turns to Him, acknowledging that nothing and no one but Christ can save them. He speaks those words to all who accept Him and trust Him to save them from their sins and to make them born-again children of God.

Just as His words instantly calmed that violent sea, saving the men in the little boat, Jesus' words will immediately end the warfare and rebellion at Armageddon. Christ's words to the troubled heart likewise bring tranquility and joy to the soul. A person is never the same when Jesus speaks those life-changing words, "Peace, be still" (Mark 4:39).

Bloody Peace

When Jesus speaks the words "Peace, be still" at Armageddon, His command will be against all the vileness that has been building in humanistic rebellion over the thousands of years since God last judged in such a mighty way. All people died in the Flood except Noah and seven others. Christ's words at Armageddon will apparently cause most, if not all, of the soldiers of the armies of the world gathered there to literally burst open, His command will be so powerful.

The plains of Armageddon will flow with a flood of blood. Scripture says:

> And the winepress was trodden without the city, and blood came
> out of the winepress, even unto the horse bridles, by the space of
> a thousand and six hundred furlongs. (Revelation 14:20)

The point is, when Jesus speaks, His words are sharper and more powerful than a two-edged sword. All opposition by earth's armies will instantly cease and desist. All will lie horribly bloody—but peacefully—upon the vast killing field called Armageddon.

Jesus on the Throne!

Jesus, following His stunning victory over the enemies of God, will proceed to get the people of Israel who have, during the Tribulation, come to believe in Him. He will rescue them from the place God has hidden them. This hiding of believing Israel (all Jewish people who will have accepted that Jesus is their Messiah) is revealed in the following:

> And when the dragon saw that he was cast unto the earth, he persecuted the woman which brought forth the man child.
>
> And to the woman were given two wings of a great eagle, that she might fly into the wilderness, into her place, where she is nourished for a time,
>
> and times, and half a time, from the face of the serpent.
>
> And the serpent cast out of his mouth water as a flood after the woman, that he might cause her to be carried away of the flood.
>
> And the earth helped the woman, and the earth opened her mouth, and swallowed up the flood which the dragon cast out of his mouth.
>
> And the dragon was wroth with the woman, and went to make war with the remnant of her seed, which keep the commandments of God, and have the testimony of Jesus Christ. (Revelation 12:13–17)

The Hiding Place

Satan's Antichrist forces will try to wipe the Jewish race from the face of the earth to fully implement Satan's Final Solution. But, God will intervene with great supernatural catastrophe and prevent the Antichrist from finding the Jews. As we've said, God will have hidden them somewhere; many prophetic scholars believe the hiding place will be in the Jordanian desert, in the "rose-red city" called Petra. Jesus will retrieve these believing Jews and use them to be His nation of Israel during the millennium.

Israel Saved!

The Bible says a third of Jews alive during the Tribulation will recognize their Messiah, Jesus Christ, at the moment He returns in the Second Coming. It will be a real eye-opener for them.

> And I will pour upon the house of David, and upon the inhabitants of Jerusalem, the spirit of grace and of supplications: and they shall look upon me whom they have pierced, and they shall mourn for him, as one mourneth for [his] only [son], and shall be in bitterness for him, as one that is in bitterness for [his] firstborn. (Zechariah 12:10)

Jesus will then move, with His saints of the Church Age and His chosen people (all of saved Israel) to Jerusalem. He will set up His throne upon a topographically changed Mount Moriah in the millennial temple He will build.

More Judgments

Antichrist and False Prophet Judgment

The Lord Jesus will judge Antichrist and the False Prophet, who will have persecuted Tribulation saints and, particularly, the Jewish race (Israel). We learn of the fate of these two beasts as follows:

> And the beast was taken, and with him the false prophet that wrought miracles before him, with which he deceived them that had received the mark of the beast, and them that worshipped

his image. These both were cast alive into a lake of fire burning with brimstone. (Revelation 19:20)

These two will be the first to be cast into hell. They'll have it to themselves until a thousand years later, after the white throne judgment, which we'll look at in a later chapter.

Satan's Confinement

Next, Satan will be grabbed and confined for the thousand years as well:

And I saw an angel come down from heaven, having the key of the bottomless pit and a great chain in his hand.

And he laid hold on the dragon, that old serpent, which is the Devil, and Satan, and bound him a thousand years,

And cast him into the bottomless pit, and shut him up, and set a seal upon him, that he should deceive the nations no more, till the thousand years should be fulfilled: and after that he must be loosed a little season. (Revelation 20:1–3)

The bottomless pit is the same place from where the rich man, in torment, looked into paradise to see Lazarus in Abraham's bosom, according to Jesus's teaching (read Luke 16:19–31).

Sheep and Goat Judgments

Christ will judge the nations. Their fate will hang upon how they treated His chosen people. The "goat" nations will stand on Christ's left while He judges, while the "sheep" nations will stand on His right.

All in the "goat" nations will be cast into everlasting darkness, lost for eternity. These nations consist of individually lost souls, each of whom will, apparently, be placed in nations that have persecuted Jews, and, most likely, Tribulation saints as well. The nations so judged will no longer be part of the nations of earth. (Read Matthew 25:32–46 to learn more about that judgment.)

It is logical to presume that the saved people who will have lived in the "goat" or lost nations will be put into the "sheep" nations, which will be allowed into the millennial kingdom. Likewise, the unsaved people who will have lived in the sheep nations will go into the goat nations to meet their eternal fate in outer darkness.

Dr. Walvoord's description of the Second Coming of Christ adds much to our understanding of that great event.

> The second coming of Christ is mentioned frequently in the Old and New Testaments' and many passages in the New Testament. The many passages devoted to this subject indicate how important it is. As the four gospels portray Christ in His first coming, so the book of Revelation portrays events before and after the future second coming of Christ. In Revelation 19:11–16, He is described as coming on a white horse, a symbol of victory, to judge the world; He is followed by the armies of heaven. He has the power to strike down the nations (verse 15), and the prediction is He will rule "with an iron scepter."
>
> His coming will express the wrath of God against wickedness in the human situation. It is clear that the heavens will be ablaze with the glory of God accompanied as He is by millions of holy angels and saints, who are moving from heaven to the Mount of Olives in preparation for the millennial kingdom. The descent will not be a rapid event but will undoubtedly take 24 hours so the earth can turn, permitting everyone to see the glory of Christ in the heavens. Satan and the unsaved alike will realize that this is the second coming of Christ, but it is too late for those who are not ready for His second coming.

The Destruction of the Armies of Earth

One of the first acts following the second coming is the destruction of the armies who will forget their differences and unite to fight the army from heaven.

This is described in graphic terms in Revelation 19:17–19 and is confirmed in verse 21 in the statement that all the wicked are killed on this occasion.

Christ captures the world ruler, the Antichrist (described as the beast), and his assistant (described as the false prophet) and casts them into the "fiery lake of burning sulfur" (Revelation 19:19, 20). This lake was previously described as the place for the ultimate end of the satanic world (Matthew 25:41–44).

While all the wicked who have died are in Hades, up to this point the lake of fire has not been occupied; the beast and the false prophet are the first occupants.

After the second coming a series of prophetic events will follow preparing the world for a future millennial kingdom. First of all, in Revelation 20:1–3 it is prophesied that Satan will be bound, rendered inactive and unable to deceive the nations in the future millennium.[119]

Dr. Dave Breese further enlightens us on the Second Coming of Jesus Christ:

Since the beginning of the Tribulation, where will the Church have been? In heaven. The Church will have gone through an experience called the Judgment Seat of Christ, and the Marriage Supper of the Lamb. At that time, it is "clothed in fine linen, white and clean." But then the announcement is made to Christians, the Church in heaven with God, that there's still a very serious piece of unfinished business that needs to be done in the world. That is to depose the Antichrist, and to pronounce the judgment of God upon the devil. They will be instruments in bringing that to pass.

So Jesus Christ comes back, not alone, but He brings the Church with Him. How do we know this? Well, Jude quotes Enoch as saying about Jesus: "Behold, the Lord cometh with ten thousands of his saints" (Jude 14).

Now a saint is a Christian. There is no such thing as Saint Somebody, or Saint Somebody Else, as unique Christians who are awarded sainthood through the vote of some committee. Rather, all of us who have been saved by grace, given the gift of imputed righteousness, are "hagios"—the holy ones, by virtue of the holiness of Jesus Christ. We are saints. These are saints returning with the Lord Jesus, the saints of God, "ten thousands of his saints."

By this time, the armies that surround the city of Jerusalem have every reason to expect that they will conquer the place. Yet, they look up, and see a massive military contingent coming back from heaven, sweeping down out of the skies, and taking them out of the way like nothing! They will be utterly destroyed. That army will be scattered all over the place. There will be millions who die. And there will be a special thing that is done with reference to the devil and the Antichrist. The Scripture says that the Antichrist will be thrown into the lake of fire (Revelation 19:20), and the devil will be thrown into the bottomless pit (Revelation 20:1-3). He is kept prisoner there for 1000 years.

You may say, "That's a lot of arrogant presumption. Christians returning with Jesus Christ? Who do you think you are to say that?" Well, the Scripture says that. In fact, did you know that the Bible says that the saints, that is, Christians, shall judge the world? Did you know that the Bible says that the saints shall judge angels (1 Corinthians 6:2–3)?

The devil, as you know, is an angel. Therefore, the devil will be a part of this group that is judged by you, and by me. There are people who have been done to death by the activity of Satan. But they will see him again, standing in judgment before them. We will be a part of that tribunal that makes right everything that is wrong in the world.

As a part of the army of Jesus Christ we will return to conquer. We will inherit the universe. The Bible says:

Whether Paul, or Apollos, or Cephas, or the world, or life, or death, or things present, or things to come; all are yours, And ye are Christ's, and Christ is God's (1 Corinthians 3:22, 23).

It's no small thing to be a Christian. It is to be an inheritor of the universe. But I'm sure that you get the picture. A mighty invasion, the saints come back, and the saints do away with those armies that are in the process of conquering the nation of Israel. Israel is delivered by the Church, it is the Christians who will deliver the nation of Israel.

Then, of course, finally, we must mention that the Tribulation ends. Remember Jesus said, "And except those days be shortened, there should no flesh be saved…" (Matthew 24:22).

Well, the days were ended. How? By this invasion from heaven, in which Christ comes again. We are the ones who shorten the dreadful days of the Great Tribulation.

We are the ones who relieve the siege of the city of Jerusalem. And we are the ones who say to the world, "Here is the Lord; now you are free."

During the Tribulation, there will have been many who have accepted the Lord, and believe the Gospel of the Kingdom. And what will happen as a result of that faith for them? When the Tribulation ends by the return of Christ, He will come, and not only deliver the nation of Israel, but He will set up His Kingdom. Where will the capital of that Kingdom be? Jerusalem, the Holy City, called the "city of the great King" (Psalm 48:2) in the Old Testament. He will establish His throne there, and He will reign over the world for 1000 amazing and remarkable years.[120]

Second-Coming Readiness

Most all people in Western culture and society who are mature, so far as age is concerned, have heard of the term "the Second Coming." Few, however, understand it. An even smaller number of those who think they understand have it right. The accuracy of what they think they know depends upon adhering to what the Bible says on the awe-inspiring topic. Interpretation must be undertaken from the viewpoint that God is speaking to His creation—mankind—in a literal sense. That is, His foretelling must be taken as literal, not as being spiritualized, symbolic, allegorical, or as things that have already occurred in any way, shape, or form.

The Second Coming, also called the Second Advent, is a literal future event that will take place at a literal moment in literal time, by the literal King of all kings and Lord of all lords. It is Jesus Christ's return to earth to put down all rebellion, restore the planet, and rule and reign from His throne atop Zion for, literally, a thousand years.

With that as an admittedly simplistic frame of reference, we'll move more deeply into the subject through a stupendous body of prophecies yet to unfold that will profoundly affect every human being that has ever been conceived within the long history of this now fallen sphere. We'll look particularly at the prospect of Christ's return as it affects each person presently alive. To us, being "Second-Coming ready" is the most important preparation any individual can make, because it means a person's soul—one's eternal being—is in God's family forever.

Dissecting the Second Coming

Comprehending the Second Coming of Jesus Christ to restore all things to conformity with God's will requires understanding that God deals with mankind in "dispensations" through covenants throughout human history.

The study of dispensationalism becomes quite involved; we don't have space here for an in-depth examination. We'll simply look at the dispensation we live in today—the Age of Grace, also called the Church Age—and the dispensation that will follow this one—the Tribulation. We've looked closely at these things before, so will delve only briefly into these as they reflect on our topic.

One Second Coming, Two Phases

The return of Christ makes no sense if viewed only as a one-phased event. This is because the Scriptures present conflict and confusion if we try to make the Second Coming simply about the Lord breaking through the black clouds of Revelation 19:11, then defeating all rebels and moving to Jerusalem to set up His millennial kingdom.

Some passages reveal that no one can know the exact day or hour of Christ's return. Others say that the number of days to His return to earth can be precisely calculated. Matthew 25:13 says Jesus will return at an unknown time, while Revelation 12:6 indicates that the Jews will have to wait on the Lord 1,260 days, starting when the Antichrist stands in the temple of God and declares himself to be God. This takes place, as we've discussed, three and a half years into the Tribulation period.

Which is it? Can Christ's time of return be known for sure? God isn't the author of confusion (see 1 Corinthians 14:33); His Word is orderly and always makes sense when proper context is applied and the reader is faithful to seek out what it really says. It is vital, therefore, to study Bible prophecy, as with the Word of God in general, thoroughly, and in total context. It can be hard work, but blesses the soul every time it's done.

So, we see that the area dealing with knowing or not knowing the time of Christ's return to earth presents what might be construed as contradiction. Bible prophecy seems to say different things about earth dwellers being aware of exactly when He is coming again. In-depth study on the matter, however, reveals that Christ will return to the planet in two distinct phases. Additionally, it is essential to understand that God is working within two prophetic programs, one involving the Church of the Lord Jesus Christ, and one involving His chosen people, the nation Israel. The two dovetail into the playing-out of the most glorious event in human history to occur since Christ's First Coming.

Phase 1: The Rapture

This event involves the Church—all born-again believers in Jesus Christ for salvation. As we've emphasized throughout this book, a person is "born again" (John 3: 3) into the family of God by accepting that Jesus is the Christ, the Son of the Living God. This is the "rock" upon which Jesus said He would build His Church (Matthew 16:18).

All people who have been born since the Church began have lived in the Church Age or Age of Grace. That is, during this period, this dispensation, all who accept Christ's blood as atonement for sin are under the grace of God and receive reconciliation with Him, their sins forever removed from receiving His judgment.

Rapture of the Church, as foretold by the apostle Paul in 1 Thessalonians 4:13–18 and 1 Corinthians 15:51–55, will be the one *atomos* of time (faster than the eye can blink) when Jesus will call all believers of the Church Age to be with Him forever. This is the "mystery" Paul showed believers, fully revealing what Jesus meant when He said the following:

Let not your heart be troubled: ye believe in God, believe also in me.

In my Father's house are many mansions: if it were not so, I would have told you. I go to prepare a place for you.

And if I go and prepare a place for you, I will come again, and receive you unto myself; that where I am, there ye may be also. (John 14:1–3)

The prerequisite, then, for being Rapture ready is to accept Christ as Savior. Paul tells us that ALL will be changed in that "twinkling of an eye." Who is the "ALL" he wrote about? It's every individual during the Church Age who will accept Christ for personal salvation.

The Rapture is the first phase of the two-phase Second Coming. Thus, those who are Rapture ready are also Second-Coming ready. *All*, not some, will go to be with the Lord when He calls, as He did to John in Revelation 4:1. Each believer is Rapture ready in the sense that each will go to be with Jesus in that stupendous event. No one will be left behind.

However, not every Christian will be "ready" in another important sense. Those who have lived carnal lives—not walking in the will of God as instructed in His Word—will lose rewards at the bema or judgment seat of Christ. More about that a bit later. As believers, we must do our best to live the way God expects of His children while still in this mortal flesh. Those who don't won't be kicked out of God's family or left behind to suffer His wrath (for we're not to endure the wrath of God; see 1 Thessalonians 5:9). But, those who choose to live apart from the Father's instructions will have disappointed their Lord, and at the bema judgment will see their carnal works burned in the holy fire that purges unrighteousness. Sinful acts, through commission or omission, cannot enter God's eternal kingdom.

Children of God should take this truth very seriously. How we attempt to walk righteously here on earth will determine our eternal service status when we look into the Lord's omniscient eyes.

Phase 2: Second Advent

The physical touchdown of the Lord Jesus atop the Mount of Olives will take place at least seven years after the Rapture of the Church. This will be the second phase of His Second Coming. It will come at the end of the Tribulation.

The Tribulation era will begin with God dealing with Israel supernaturally. He will, during this horrific time, purge, through the fiery crucible of Antichrist's genocidal rage, a special remnant of the Jewish people. They will be His nation as head of all nations during the millennium, the earlier-mentioned thousand-year era that will follow the Tribulation. However, before those Jews will enjoy the millennial earth, the time will be worse for the Jewish people than at any other during the many anti-Semite persecutions and diasporas (scatterings) through the ages.

Jeremiah, the Old Testament prophet, said the following about that horrendous time:

> Alas! for that day is great, so that none is like it: it is even the time of Jacob's trouble; but he shall be saved out of it. (Jeremiah 30:7)

Hell on Earth

The Tribulation will produce an increasingly hell-like planet, God's direct judgments falling upon Antichrist and the rebellious earth-dwellers the closer the time of Christ's return to earth comes. Still, rather than repent of their horrendous sin against the Almighty, they will hide themselves in the caves and crannies of the mountains and shake their fists in blasphemy against Him.

Jesus said about this time:

> For then shall be great tribulation, such as was not since the beginning of the world to this time, no, nor ever shall be. (Matthew 24:21)

Only the great mercy of God will keep some flesh from succumbing to the twenty-one judgments that will pour upon and smash into the planet.

While all armies of earth gather in the Middle East at Armageddon, Christ will return to put an end to all war (Revelation 19:11). He will rule in righteousness upon a planet made pristine again by the Creator of all things. Israel will be the host nation to the Lord's throne atop Mount Zion (Mount Moriah remade and raised above the terrain). King David, in his resurrection body, will be Christ's coregent for Israel, while Christ reigns as king over the earthly kingdom. Thus, all promises God made to Abraham, Isaac, and Jacob will be fulfilled.

Getting Ready Now Is Crucial

Nothing is more critical than being Second-Coming ready.

We must be ready for the moment when Jesus will say "Come up here," as He did to John in Revelation 4:1. The only way we can prepare is to be dedicated to the reason we've been placed on earth: to carry out the will of God. We can do this through prayer and Bible study, then translating that prayer and study into living every minute of every day with the thought of abiding in God's will. We're to be royal ambassadors in a foreign land.

Christians are to be outward-turning, not inward-focused—i.e., we're supposed to think more of others than of ourselves while we go about our daily lives. This doesn't mean assuming a pious, head-in-the-clouds attitude. It means we should be like Christ, meeting and interacting with people the way Jesus did. We should be about helping others in material ways—but always secondarily to informing them that Jesus, alone, is the way to God the Father for eternity (John 14: 6). This is how to be Rapture ready, in the sense of being worthy to hear Jesus say, "Well done, good and faithful servant."

Judgment Seat of Christ

There will most likely be a brief interlude between the Rapture of the Church and the Antichrist-to-be confirming the covenant of Daniel 9:26. While that's going on in earth time, magnificent things beyond imagination will be taking place in the heavenly dimension.

Then, as the Tribulation begins to rumble with tornado-like violence on the earth, those who have been lifted from this fallen sphere by their Bridegroom, Jesus Christ, will come before the bema—the judgment seat of Christ. Believers of the Church Age will stand before Him to receive rewards for the race they've run as royal ambassadors while back on earth.

This judgment will not be for determining whether they will enter heaven or go to the lake of fire. They're all in God's holy family. They are, in heavenly symbolism, the very Bride of Jesus, and they're before the bema to receive rewards for their faithfulness to the service of God. They've run the race (Hebrews 12:1–3) for the high calling of Christ. Now they're about to receive unfathomable riches as joint heirs with God's Son, the Lord Jesus Christ.

All things they did while in the flesh on earth will be reviewed. All things they did out of a motive other than to honor Christ will be burned in the holy fire of God's omniscient purification. All things they did to honor the Lord will get glorious recognition, with the recipients being bestowed various crowns. This judgment will determine the positions each person will hold in administering Christ's rule throughout His thousand-year reign and all of eternity.

Won't Regret Obedience

Our obedience will be worth the troubles we endured in this life. And, that's a real understatement. Our rewards for living as our Lord wants us to while under such persecution will be beyond our wildest imaginations. Crowns of victory will be given at the bema that will make everything we might have endured in life fade to nothingness.

Paul, expounding upon Isaiah 64:4, wrote:

But as it is written, Eye hath not seen, nor ear heard, neither have entered into the heart of man, the things which God hath prepared for them that love him. (1 Corinthians 2:9)

Let's look at those crowns under examination of Scripture.

Great Rewards Await!

The Bible mentions at least five crowns/rewards.

1. **The incorruptible crown, given to those who master the old nature.**

And every man that striveth for the mastery is temperate in all things. Now they do it to obtain a corruptible crown; but we an incorruptible.

I therefore so run, not as uncertainly; so fight I, not as one that beateth the air: But I keep under my body, and bring it into subjection: lest that by any means, when I have preached to others, I myself should be a castaway. (1 Corinthians 9 25–27)

2. **The crown of rejoicing given to soul winners.**

For what is our hope, or joy, or crown of rejoicing? Are not even ye in the presence of our Lord Jesus Christ at his coming? For ye are our glory and joy. (1 Thessalonians 2:19–20)

The fruit of the righteous is a tree of life; and he that winneth souls is wise. (Proverbs 11:30; see also Daniel 12:31)

3. **The crown of life, given to those who successfully endure temptation.**

My brethren, count it all joy when ye fall into divers temptations; Knowing this, that the trying of your faith worketh patience. (James 1:2–3)

Fear none of those things which thou shalt suffer: behold, the devil shall cast some of you into prison, that ye may be tried; and ye shall have tribulation ten days: be thou faithful unto death, and I will give thee a crown of life. (Revelation 2:10)

4. **The crown of righteousness for those who especially love the doctrine of the Rapture.**

Henceforth there is laid up for me a crown of righteousness, which the Lord, the righteous judge, shall give me at that day: and not to me only, but unto all them also that love his appearing. (2 Timothy 4:8)

5. **The crown of glory, given to faithful preachers and teachers.**

Feed the flock of God which is among you, taking the oversight thereof, not by constraint, but willingly; not for filthy lucre, but of a ready mind; Neither as being lords over God's heritage, but being ensamples to the flock. And when the chief Shepherd shall appear, ye shall receive a crown of glory that fadeth not away. (1 Peter 5:2–4; see also Acts 20:26–28; 2 Timothy 4:1–2)

Keeping in mind that we strive for crowns with which to honor our Lord, let us be empowered by the promise of God's prophetic Word!

Tribulation Saints Must Be Ready

Being Second-Coming ready for the person who will enter the Tribulation following the Rapture of the Church is another matter. But, getting ready to go through that terrible time is essential. If you have been left behind when millions vanish, to be less than ready will mean enduring torment forever, apart from the God who moved heaven and hell to bring you into His eternal family.

Faithful to the End

Getting Second-Coming ready during the Tribulation will mean turning one's life over to Christ and trusting Him for salvation. It will mean standing for Christ no matter the challenges. It will mean refusing the mark of the Antichrist, thus being targeted for death. But, standing for Christ will bring eternal blessings, as promised to the martyrs of the Tribulation era.

> And it was given unto him to make war with the saints, and to overcome them: and power was given him over all kindreds, and tongues, and nations.
>
> And all that dwell upon the earth shall worship him, whose names are not written in the book of life of the Lamb slain from the foundation of the world.
>
> If any man have an ear, let him hear. He that leadeth into captivity shall go into captivity: he that killeth with the sword must be killed with the sword. Here is the patience and the faith of the saints. (Revelation 13:7–10)

Why Being Rapture Ready Is Essential

If you're reading this before the Rapture, it is essential, in the view of many prophecy scholars, that you get ready now for the Second Coming of Christ, rather than await the Tribulation era. There is significant evidence that those who are given, but refuse, the Holy Spirit's call to accept Jesus Christ as Savior might not hear such a call during that last seven years.

The Scripture passage in question indicates that God's offer during the Tribulation might not extend to those who, before the Tribulation, clearly knew they should accept Christ, but didn't.

> And for this cause God shall send them strong delusion, that they should believe a lie. That they all might be damned who believed not the truth, but had pleasure in unrighteousness. (2 Thessalonians 2:11–12)

The Time to Get Ready Is Now

There are no prophecies that precede the Rapture of the Church. Yet most every signal given by Jesus and the Old and New Testament prophets for the end of the age is on history's horizon.

The hour is late; the Rapture is imminent—it could literally take place at any moment. There are no guarantees of future opportunities for salvation. The apostle Paul gives God's Word about the urgency of the hour:

> We then, as workers together with him, beseech you also that ye receive not the grace of God in vain.
>
> (For he saith, I have heard thee in a time accepted, and in the day of salvation have I succoured thee: behold, now is the accepted time; behold, now is the day of salvation.) (2 Corinthians 6:1–2)

20

The Millennial Reign

The most horrendous time of human history still lurks just over the prophetic horizon, as we have seen. That period will consummate with the triumphant return of Jesus Christ. There will be unprecedented bloodshed at Armageddon, where the armies of the world will instantly be destroyed by the multiple millions.

This is foreboding to consider. But, as is said, it is darkest just before dawn. The final rays of sunlight will have been totally quenched. But, then, the world brightens and soon the glorious dawn brings spectacular scenes of the bursting forth of a brand-new day.

This is the time of Armageddon versus the dawning of Christ's millennial reign.

The coming of the King of kings will move with brilliant light as the clouds of apocalypse part like a scroll. The earth will soon experience the full glory of the Lord of lords as He brings His thousand-year era of the kingdom of God to a pristine earth as it was before the Fall in Eden's garden.

So there is a magnificent future ahead that will erase all vestiges of a fallen planet. It is one we can look to with excitement. Doing so will brighten these days while the darkness is gathering for the windup of this troubled age.

Fantastic Changes!

Jesus will restore the earth to perfect glory. He will assume the throne that belongs to Him alone—the throne of David. David, apparently, will—in his supernatural state—also rule over the nation Israel during the millennial era.

> When the Son of man shall come in his glory, and all the holy angels with him, then shall he sit upon the throne of his glory. (Matthew 25:30)

The terrain of Jerusalem and the whole world will supernaturally change in accordance with a masterful sweep of King Jesus' majestic hand. We're given a glimpse of those astonishing topographical and environmental changes prophesied to take place in that day (see Zechariah 14:4–9).

Like Eden

Jesus will make the earth like it was at the time of the Garden of Eden. It will be a crime-free world, for the most part; anyone who does commit a crime will be dealt with immediately, and from a righteous justice system that has perfect knowledge of all things involved. Many prophecy students believe Church Age saints will be officers of the Supreme's Court of Justice in the administration of King Jesus. As supernatural officers of the Court, they will certainly be equipped to handle such a duty.

But, crime will be almost nonexistent compared to that in our present hour. Christ's saints, both flesh and blood and supernatural, will doubtless have wonderfully creative things to do for all those years. Anticipating that time of glorious service should empower us for our service here on earth.

Jesus Christ will reign in His glorious kingdom following the Rapture, the Tribulation, and the Second Coming. It is fascinating to think on what the kingdom will be like. Let's explore some of its basic characteristics.

The Duration of the Kingdom

We find a description of the kingdom in Revelation, following the account of Christ's Second coming in chapter 19 and before the foretelling of the great white throne judgment in Revelation 20:11–15 and the eternal kingdom in chapters 21 and 22.

> And I saw an angel come down from heaven, having the key of the bottomless pit and a great chain in his hand.
>
> And he laid hold on the dragon, that old serpent, which is the Devil, and Satan, and bound him a thousand years, And cast him into the bottomless pit, and shut him up, and set a seal upon him, that he should deceive the nations no more, till the thousand years should be fulfilled: and after that he must be loosed a little season.
>
> And I saw thrones, and they sat upon them, and judgment was given unto them: and I saw the souls of them that were beheaded for the witness of Jesus, and for the word of God, and which had not worshipped the beast, neither his image, neither had received his mark upon their foreheads, or in their hands; and they lived and reigned with Christ a thousand years.

But the rest of the dead lived not again until the thousand years were finished. This is the first resurrection. Blessed and holy is he that hath part in the first resurrection: on such the second death hath no power, but they shall be priests of God and of Christ, and shall reign with him a thousand years.

And when the thousand years are expired, Satan shall be loosed out of his prison, And shall go out to deceive the nations which are in the four quarters of the earth, Gog and Magog, to gather them together to battle: the number of whom is as the sand of the sea.

And they went up on the breadth of the earth, and compassed the camp of the saints about, and the beloved city: and fire came down from God out of heaven, and devoured them.

And the devil that deceived them was cast into the lake of fire and brimstone, where the beast and the false prophet are, and shall be tormented day and night for ever and ever. (Revelation 20:1–10)

This passage states clearly several important things. Satan will be bound. He will be prohibited from influencing mankind in any way.

The first resurrection, the resurrection of the Old Testament saints (Daniel 12:2–3 and 12:13) and Tribulation saints, will take place at the establishment of the kingdom. This resurrection is not to be confused with that of the Christians at the Rapture, which, again, will happen seven years before the Tribulation.

Paul was the first to receive information about the mystery of the Rapture. That great event wasn't presented in the Old Testament or by Jesus in His earthly ministry (except, in our view, in His reference to returning and receiving believers to Himself and taking them back to the Father's house where He was preparing mansions for believers [John 14:1–3]).

As we've said, Christ's kingdom will be in place for a thousand years. This passage makes it very clear by telling us not just once but six times that it will last that long. Satan will be released for a brief period after that time.

Some might be confused by this kingdom, as opposed to the eternal kingdom. Read Revelation chapters 21 and 22 for a description of the eternal kingdom that will follow this one.

Changed Animal World

The book of Isaiah is full of prophecies regarding the characteristics of the millennial kingdom. Isaiah 11:6–9 states the following:

> The wolf also shall dwell with the lamb, and the leopard shall lie down with the kid; and the calf and the young lion and the fatling together; and a little child shall lead them.
>
> And the cow and the bear shall feed; their young ones shall lie down together: and the lion shall eat straw like the ox. And the sucking child shall play on the hole of the asp, and the weaned child shall put his hand on the cockatrice' den.
>
> They shall not hurt nor destroy in all my holy mountain: for the earth shall be full of the knowledge of the LORD, as the waters cover the sea.

We see that animals that are currently carnivorous will begin to feed only on vegetation. Therefore, they won't fear one another, and they won't be dangerous to people.

Some who look at this prophecy spiritualize it (interpret it allegorically), but in doing so, they skirt the truth. The passage plainly states that all animals will literally be herbivores in the future kingdom. It also says that all animals once were herbivores, since neither man nor beast ate animal flesh prior to the Great Flood.

Genesis 1:29–30:

And God said, Behold, I have given you every herb bearing seed, which is upon the face of all the earth, and every tree, in the which is the fruit of a tree yielding seed; to you it shall be for meat.

And to every beast of the earth, and to every fowl of the air, and to every thing that creepeth upon the earth, wherein there is life, I have given every green herb for meat: and it was so.

The Hebrew word *oklah,* translated "meat" by the King James Version of the Bible, simply means "food" or "that which is devoured." Notice that the beasts aren't given for Adam's food or one another's food. Both Adam and the beasts are given herbs and fruits to eat. So man and beast were all vegetarian. However, God changed things after the Flood. In Genesis 9:2–3 God says to Noah:

And the fear of you and the dread of you shall be upon every beast of the earth, and upon every fowl of the air, upon all that moveth upon the earth, and upon all the fishes of the sea; into your hand are they delivered.

Every moving thing that liveth shall be meat for you; even as the green herb have I given you all things.

The Fall in the Garden of Eden changed everything. Death came into the world. The animals began to fear man, because man was, following the Fall, allowed to eat the animals. Many animals became carnivorous at that time.

The world we live in today is filled with people who deny the deity of Jesus Christ, including many who even reject the existence of God. But that won't be the case in the kingdom. Isaiah 11:9, quoted above, states that "the earth shall be full of the knowledge of the LORD, as the waters cover the sea."

Longer Life Spans

There is great news for the future of the world during the millennium:

There shall be no more thence an infant of days, nor an old man that hath not filled his days: for the child shall die an hundred years old; but the sinner being an hundred years old shall be accursed.

And they shall build houses, and inhabit them; and they shall plant vineyards, and eat the fruit of them. They shall not build, and another inhabit; they shall not plant, and another eat: for as the days of a tree are the days of my people, and mine elect shall long enjoy the work of their hands.

They shall not labour in vain, nor bring forth for trouble; for they are the seed of the blessed of the LORD, and their offspring with them. And it shall come to pass, that before they call, I will answer; and while they are yet speaking, I will hear.

The wolf and the lamb shall feed together, and the lion shall eat straw like the bullock: and dust shall be the serpent's meat. They shall not hurt nor destroy in all my holy mountain, saith the LORD. (Isaiah 65:20–25)

There is a tremendous promise in this prophecy. Great increase in life spans will mark this marvelous age. Like the Isaiah 11 passage we've looked at previously, some have taken what this passage says about increased life span and spiritualized it. They say it is only to be thought of as some nebulous reference to life on an ethereal plane. They say it's not literal. Bible truth, however, says that life spans will greatly increase. It will be much like things were before the Flood of Noah's day.

The genealogy from Adam to Noah, given in Genesis 5 and 9:29, shows there are extremely long life spans. When we exclude Enoch, who was taken by God (Genesis 5:24) at the age of 365 years, and Lamech, who died at the age of 777 years, we find that all of the other eight lived between 895 and 969 years. After the Great Flood, there was a rapid drop in length of life to a little over 400 years. Around the time of the tower of Babel, the number dropped to a little over 200 years. Then they began to slowly decrease to more modern life spans over a period of hundreds of years.

Like all skeptics of biblical truth, the naysayers inevitably say that to think people lived 900 years is ludicrous. Factors of profound influence, however, explain the great changes in man's environment and/or lifestyle.

Regardless of whether these influences on life spans were positive or negative, some of them are:

1) Prior to the Flood, it didn't rain on the earth; rather, the earth was watered by mist that came up from the ground (Genesis 2:5–6).
2) As previously mentioned, it was after the Great Flood that man began to eat meat for the first time (Genesis 9:3).
3) The removal of the vast layer of waters above the firmament (Genesis 1:7 and 7:11) may have affected the sun's rays, the earth's magnetic field, or the air pressure.
4) After the Flood, the human race was replenished through only eight people (Genesis 6:18), which required the marriage of some near relatives.

These and other factors might also have had profound influence and a tremendous effect on human life. Suffice it to say that we mortals are incapable of knowing what the Creator-God knows, thus we're wise to simply believe His Word regarding the tremendous effects of the Fall and what the restored, immaculate, millennial earth will be like when Jesus reigns for that future thousand years.

God said man lived nine hundred years in that pre-Flood time. We will live a thousand years, we're told in the descriptions of the millennium. There is sometimes misconception that the millennium will be akin to being in heaven. Some think of people sitting on clouds, strumming harps, etc. This is a misconception of heaven, and it's definitely a misconception of the era that will be the millennial kingdom of Christ.

These descriptions give us pictures of normal activities such as building houses, living in them, planting vineyards, eating fruit, bearing children, and sometimes even dying. This prophecy also provides further evidence of carnivorous animals becoming herbivores, which we've previously seen.

One common misunderstanding is to think that only those who are resurrected or changed into immortal bodies will enter the kingdom. If that were the case, no one there could possibly sin or die. But Matthew 25:31–46 describes Jesus Christ dividing the sheep from the goats at the end of the Great Tribulation. This is the judgment of the Gentile nations (verse 32). All the people gathered on the Lord's right hand are survivors of the Great Tribulation and will pass into the kingdom in their mortal bodies. They will bear children who are human as well. The same is true for the many Israelites who will survive the Great Tribulation and will bear children in the kingdom. Ezekiel 37:25–26 says:

> And they shall dwell in the land that I have given unto Jacob my servant, wherein your fathers have dwelt; and they shall dwell therein, even **they, and their children, and their children's children** for ever: and my servant David shall be their prince forever.
>
> Moreover I will make a covenant of peace with them; it shall be an everlasting covenant with them: and I will place them, and **multiply them,** and will set my sanctuary in the midst of them for evermore. (Emphasis added)

All of these people and their descendants will be capable of both sin and death in the millennial kingdom, even though Satan will be in chains and unable to influence them.

No More War

The millennial reign of Jesus Christ will assure that there is no more war on the planet. This will be true until the very end of the thousand years. At that time, Satan will be released from his holding cell in the bottomless pit (Revelation 20:7–9) for a short period at the end. In reference to Jesus Christ, Micah 4:3 says:

> And he shall judge among many people, and rebuke strong nations afar off; and they shall beat their swords into plowshares, and their spears into pruninghooks: nation shall not lift up a sword against nation, neither shall they learn war any more.

Isaiah 2:4 is similar. Not only will there no longer be any war, but the weapons will be dismantled and battle strategies will no longer be taught.

Israel will be at peace and dwell safely in the kingdom.

> Behold, the days come, saith the LORD, that I will raise unto David a righteous Branch, and a King shall reign and prosper, and shall **execute judgment and justice in the earth.**
>
> In his days Judah shall be saved, and **Israel shall dwell safely:** and this is his name whereby he shall be called, THE LORD OUR RIGHTEOUSNESS. (Jeremiah 23:5–6, emphasis added)

Today, this is far from the case. Israel is surrounded on all sides with enemies who are blood-vowed to wipe it off the map. The call by hate-filled Islamic leaders to destroy the Jewish state is certainly in contrast to the promise of millennial peace. There will be no threat to Israel when the Prince of Peace sits on the throne in Jerusalem.

Jesus Christ's Judgment and the Restored Judges

The Micah and Jeremiah verses we just looked at also refer to Jesus Christ judging the nations of the earth. He'll do so in all wisdom and perfect justice, with a rod of iron:

> And out of his mouth goeth a sharp sword, that with it he should smite the nations: and **he shall rule them with a rod of iron**: and he treadeth the winepress of the fierceness and wrath of Almighty God. (Revelation 19:15, emphasis added)

He will reign as a literal king on a throne, dwelling in Jerusalem, and will also restore the judges to Israel:

> And I will **restore thy judges** as at the first, and thy counsellors as at the beginning: afterward thou shalt be called, The city of righteousness, the faithful city. (Isaiah 1:26, emphasis added)

Who will the judges of the twelve tribes of Israel be? Jesus Christ told His disciples:

> Verily I say unto you, That ye which have followed me, in the regeneration when the Son of man shall sit in the throne of his glory, ye also shall sit upon twelve thrones, judging the twelve tribes of Israel. (Matthew 19:28)

Israel: A Kingdom of Priests

Thus saith the LORD of hosts; It shall yet come to pass, that there shall come people, and the inhabitants of many cities: And the inhabitants of one city shall go to another, saying, Let us go speedily to pray before the LORD, and to seek the LORD of hosts: I will go also.

Yea, many people and strong nations shall come to seek the LORD of hosts in Jerusalem, and to pray before the LORD.

Thus saith the LORD of hosts; In those days it shall come to pass, that ten men shall take hold out of all languages of the nations, even shall take hold of the skirt of him that is a Jew, saying,

We will go with you: for we have heard that God is with you. (Zechariah 8:20–23)

Now therefore, if ye will obey my voice indeed, and keep my covenant, then ye shall be a peculiar treasure unto me above all people: for all the earth is mine:

And ye shall be unto me a **kingdom of priests**, and an holy nation. These are the words which thou shalt speak unto the children of Israel. (Exodus 19:5–6, emphasis added).

The Feast of Tabernacles

One interesting prophecy in Zechariah 14:16–19 concerns the Gentile nations keeping the Feast of Tabernacles in the millennial kingdom:

And it shall come to pass, that every one that is left of all the nations which came against Jerusalem shall even go up from year to year to worship the King, the Lord of hosts, and to keep the **feast of tabernacles**.

And it shall be, that whoso will not come up of all the families of the earth unto Jerusalem to worship the King, the Lord of hosts, even upon them shall be no rain.

And if the family of Egypt go not up, and come not, that have no rain; there shall be the plague, wherewith the LORD will smite the heathen that come not up to keep the **feast of tabernacles.**

This shall be the punishment of Egypt, and the punishment of all nations that come not up to keep the **feast of tabernacles.**

Here we see that in the kingdom, the Gentiles must keep the Feast of Tabernacles which was formerly a feast just for Israel. To do so, they must travel to Jerusalem once each year in the autumn to "worship the King," Jesus Christ. He will reign on His throne in Jerusalem like Ezekiel 43:7 says:

And he said unto me, Son of man, the place of my throne, and the place of the soles of my feet, where I will dwell in the midst of the children of Israel for ever, and my holy name, shall the house of Israel no more defile.

Church-Age Saints

What will believers of the Church Age do during this time? Jesus is on the throne and Bible prophecy promises that we will always be with Him.

For the Lord himself shall descend from heaven with a shout, with the voice of the archangel, and with the trump of God: and the dead in Christ shall rise first:

Then we which are alive and remain shall be caught up together with them in the clouds, to meet the Lord in the air: and so shall we ever be with the Lord. (1 Thessalonians 4:16–17)

We've looked at what people who are flesh-and-blood survivors of the Tribulation will do in the millennial kingdom. But what will be the activities and duties of those who were raptured before the Tribulation and who will always be with their Bridegroom, the Lord Jesus Christ?

Daymond Duck, one of today's best-known prophecy writers and speakers, has presented an excellent outline of what believers in their supernatural bodies will do during the thousand-year reign of King Jesus.

A one-thousand year period of time is mentioned six times in the Book of Revelation (Rev. 20:1–7).

1) Satan will be bound for one thousand years.
2) The nations won't be deceived for a thousand years.
3) Saints will reign with Jesus for a thousand years.
4) The lost won't be raised until the thousand years end.
5) The saints will be priests of God and Jesus for a thousand years.
6) Satan will be loosed at the end of the thousand years.

Those who believe this will be a literal thousand years call it the "Millennium." The word "Millennium" comes from two Latin words "milli" which means one thousand and "annum" which means years.

Many people know that Jesus will sit on the throne of David and rule the world (Jer. 23:5–6; Zech. 14:9; Luke 1:31–33), that the Temple will be rebuilt (Ezek. 40–48), that the Word of the Lord will go forth from Jerusalem (Isa. 2:3), that there will be peace and justice on earth (Isa. 9:6-7) and more. But some ask, "What will we do during the Millennium?"

Below are seven things that the saved will do:

1) Worship (Revelation 4:9–10).
2) Keep the Feast of Tabernacles (Zech. 14:16–19).

3) Visit Jerusalem to learn (Isa. 2:2-3; I Corinthians 13:11–12).

4) Fellowship (Revelation 19:9).

5) Serve Jesus (Ps. 72:11; Revelation 22:3).

6) Judge fallen angels (1 Corinthians 6:3).

7) Reign on the earth (Luke 19:11–27; Rev. 5:10; 2 Tim. 2:12).

These things will be more than enough to keep us busy.[121]

Destiny of Millennial Mankind

Saints of the Tribulation who make it through the seven years alive will, individually, go into the nations that have treated Israel kindly. However, it must be recognized that the children who will be born during the millennium will have to make the same decision their parents made to accept or reject Christ for salvation. Millions won't, and will be as rebellious as the rebels before this time of Christ's glorious reign on earth for a thousand years. These unsaved will join Satan in the final rebellion when he is released for a brief time from the bottomless pit. All will be destroyed, and will spend eternity in hell apart from God.

Millions of others who are the children of the saints who go into the millennium will accept Christ, and will ultimately live eternally with God. These offspring of the Tribulation saints who go into the millennium will continue to repopulate the earth for the thousand years. They will be saved for eternity.

21

Great White Throne/Heaven and Hell

We've looked at what it means to stand before a throne upon which the Lord Jesus Christ will sit. The bema, or judgment seat of Christ, was, in earth time, one thousand or more years earlier. It was experienced by all believers of the Church Age, or Age of Grace.

This judgment took place immediately upon all believers—those who lived and died during the Age of Grace—going to Christ when He called (Revelation 4:1). Rapture removed all who accepted Christ as Savior so they wouldn't have to endure the Tribulation, which would put on trial or test the whole world of rebels (Revelation 3:10).

Their Lord, symbolically called their "Bridegroom," then whisked them to His Father's house, heaven, where He had been preparing "dwelling places" for them. As a matter of fact, they will sit down to a huge marriage supper—the marriage supper of the Lamb. It will be for Jesus and His Bride, the Church, for which He died to redeem from sin. This will be their eternal homes, where they will forever be with the Savior and, symbolically, their Bridegroom.

Upon entering heaven, at some point, these believers will individu-ally stand before the bema. The heavenly dimension is outside of time. It has no beginning and no end. So, it is not tied to a specific date as an event is in earth time. We believe the Tribulation will be taking place on earth during this great event in heaven.

The bema will be for bestowing rewards on all Church-Age saints. There is no punishment whatsoever meted out at this judgment. Any sin is forgotten, because, for those who have repented of sin and accepted Christ as Savior, Jesus paid all sin debt when He died on the cross at Calvary. God no longer remembers their sin since the moment when Jesus said while suspended between heaven and earth, "It is finished!"

Now, however, we look at a judgment that is 180 degrees opposite of the bema. This is the most terrible fate that could befall any living being. It is final in every respect. There is no avoiding it once one stands before this great white throne.

Jesus will be the Judge in this judgment seat, too. But, this time, He won't be the loving Savior, Advocate, and Bridegroom. He will at this eternal moment be both judge and jury. He is prosecutor, and the one who will hand out the punishment to those who are already con-demned. They wouldn't stand before this judgment bar if they were not guilty as charged. Each will have his or her life examined by the piercing, omniscient eyes of God the Son. His all-knowing gaze will look into the very soul of every person. All will stand before Christ in resurrected bod-ies that are made for eternal destruction. The fires of their destination will not consume these indestructible bodies. At the same time, in some way the infinite mind can't grasp, their bodies will be in a constant state of dying. And this state will last *FOREVER*.

To us, the authors, this is the least desirable part of all of God's pro-phetic Word to have to examine and relay to you the reader. But it is absolutely essential that we do so. Your very fate hangs in the balance.

How you respond to the truth found in God's Holy Word about this matter will determine whether you on one eternal day will stand, condemned, before the great white throne. We see this most terrible event for the unrepented-of sins of mankind in the following verses:

> And I saw a great white throne, and him that sat on it, from whose face the earth and the heaven fled away; and there was found no place for them.
>
> And I saw the dead, small and great, stand before God; and the books were opened: and another book was opened, which is the book of life: and the dead were judged out of those things which were written in the books, according to their works.
>
> And the sea gave up the dead which were in it; and death and hell delivered up the dead which were in them: and they were judged every man according to their works.
>
> And death and hell were cast into the lake of fire. This is the second death. And whosoever was not found written in the book of life was cast into the lake of fire. (Revelation 20:11–15)

We have looked at Adolf Hitler's attempt to carry out his Final Solution. This volume has examined Antichrist's coming genocidal Fourth Reich that will be even more intensive. God has his own Final Solution in mind—the Final Solution for the rebellious evil of Satan and God-rejecting mankind.

Dr. Dwight J. Pentecost writes about the place of eternal torment for the lost souls of human history:

> Before the great white throne appear all "the dead" (Rev. 20:12). Those resurrected unto life have all been called out of the grave a thousand years earlier (Rev. 20:3–6). Those resurrected here are to be judged to be appointed unto the "second death" (Rev. 20:14), that is, eternal separation from the kingdom of God. This is the final act in the program that was enacted "that God may be all in all" (1 Cor. 15:28). Since this program has been

developed previously it need not be repeated here. The summary of Kelly suffices:

The dead were judged, but not out of the book of life which has nothing to do with judgment. "The dead were judged out of those things which were written in the books according to their works." Why then is the book of life mentioned? Not because any of their names were written therein, but in proof that they were not. The book of life will confirm what is gathered from the books. If the books proclaim the evil works of the dead that stand before the throne, the book of life offers no defense on the score of God's grace. Scripture records no name whatever as written there among those judged. There was the sad register of undeniable sins on the one side; there was no writing of the name on the other side. Thus, whether the books or the book be examined, all conspire to declare the justice, the solemn but most affecting righteousness, of God's final irrevocable sentence. They were judged, each one, according to their works. "And if any one was not found written in the book of life, he was cast into the lake of fire." Thus the only use that seems made of the book is negative and exclusive. Not that any of those judged (and the scene described is solely a resurrection of judgment) are said to be written there: we are shown rather that they were not found in the book.

Neither the sea nor the unseen world could longer hide their prisoners. "And the sea gave up the dead that [were] in it, and death and hades gave up the dead that [were] in them: and they were judged, each one, according to their works."

Again, Death and Hades are said to come to their end, personified as enemies. "And death and hades were cast into the lake of fire. This is the second death, the lake of fire." Thus was concluded all dealing on the Lord's part with soul and body, and all that pertains to either. The race was now in the resurrection state either for good or for ill; and thus it must be forever. Death and Hades, which had so long been executioners in a world where sin reigned, and still did their occasional office when righteousness reigned, themselves disappear where all traces of sin are consigned for ever. God is "all in all."

God's purpose in the judgments prior to the millennium was to "gather out of his kingdom all things that offend, and them which do iniquity; And shall cast them into a furnace of fire: there shall be wailing and gnashing of teeth" (Matt. 13:41–42). God's purpose in the judgments at the end of the millennium is to remove from the eternal kingdom "all things that offend, and them which do iniquity." By this judgment God's absolute sovereignty has now been manifested....

The destiny of the lost is a place in the lake of fire (Rev. 19:20; 20:10, 14–15; 21:8). This lake of fire is described as everlasting fire (Matt. 25:41; 18:8) and as unquenchable fire (Mark 9:43–44, 46, 48), emphasizing the eternal character of the retribution of the lost. In this connection Chafer well observes:

In attempting to write a comprehensive statement of the most solemn doctrine of the Bible, the term retribution is chosen in place of the more familiar word punishment since the latter implies discipline and amendment, which idea is wholly absent from the body of truth which discloses the final divine dealing with those who are eternally lost. It is recognized that, in its earlier and broader meaning, the term retribute was used for any reward, good or evil. The word is used...of the doctrine of hell only as reference is made to the eternal perdition of the lost.

Concerning the retribution of the lost, it is important to observe that the lake of fire is a place, not just a state, although a state is involved.

As heaven is a place and not a mere state of mind, in like manner those reprobated go to a place. This truth is indicated by the words *hades* (Matt. 11:23; 16:18; Luke 10:15; 16:23; Rev. 1.18; 20:13–14) and *gehenna* (Matt. 5:22, 29–30; 10:28; James 3:6) a place of "torment" (Luke 16:28). That it is a condition of unspeakable misery is indicated by the figurative terms used to describe its sufferings—"everlasting fire" (Matt. 25:41); "Where their worm dieth not, and the fire is not quenched" (Mark 9:44); "the lake which burneth with fire and brimstone" (Rev. 21:8); "bottomless pit" (Rev. 9:2); "outer darkness," a place of "weeping and gnashing of teeth" (Matt. 8:12); "fire unquench-able" (Luke 3:17); "furnace of fire" (Matt. 13:42); "blackness of darkness" (Jude 1:13), and "the smoke of their torment ascen-deth up for ever and ever: and they have no rest day nor night" (Rev. 14:11). In these instances a figure of speech is not a license to modify the thought which the figure expresses; it is rather to be recognized that a figure of speech, in these passages, is a feeble attempt to declare in language that which is beyond the power of words to describe.... It is well to observe, also, that nearly every one of these expressions fell from the lips of Christ. He alone has disclosed almost all that is revealed of this place of retribution. It is as though no human author could be depended upon to speak forth all of this terrible truth.

The student will find that "THE grave," taken literally as well as figuratively, will meet all the requirements of the Hebrew *Sheol*: not that *Sheol* means so much specifically A grave, as generically THE grave. Holy Scripture is all-sufficient to explain the word *Sheol* to us. (v.) If we enquire of it in the above list of occurrences of the word *Sheol*, it will teach (a) That as to *direc-tion* it is down. (b) That as to *place* it is in the earth. (c) That as to *nature* it is put for the *state of death*. Not the *act* of dying, for which we have no English word, but the *state* or duration of death. The Germans are more fortunate, having the word *ster-*

bend for the act of dying. *Sheol* therefore means *the state of death*; or *the state of the dead*, of which *the grave* is a tangible evidence. It has to do only with the dead. It may sometimes be personified and represented by a coined word, "Grave-dom," as meaning the dominion or power of *the grave*. (d) As to *relation* it stands in contrast with the state of the living, see Deut. 30:15, 19, and I Sam. 2:6–8. It is never once connected with the living, except by contrast. (e) As to *association*, it is used in connection with mourning (Gen. 37:34–35), sorrow (Gen. 42:38; 2 Sam. 22:6; Ps. 18:5; 116:3), fright and terror (Num. 16:27–34); weeping (Isa. 38:3, 10, 15, 20), silence (Ps. 31:17; 6:5; Eccles. 9:10), no knowledge (Eccles. 9:5–6, 10), punishment (Num. 16:27–34; I Kings 2:6, 9; Job 24:19; Ps. 9:17, R. V., RE-turned, as before their resurrection). (f) And, finally, as to *duration*, the dominion of *Sheol* or the grave will continue until, and end only with, *resurrection*, which is the only exit from it (see Hos. 13:14, etc., and compare Ps. 16:10 with Acts 2:27, 31; 13:35).

2. The second word to describe the place of the dead is Hades. In the New Testament this word is practically equivalent to Sheol, translated "hell" in every instance but one (1 Cor. 15:55, where it is translated "grave"). Generally this word has in view the unsaved dead, who are in misery, awaiting the resurrection unto the great white throne. On Hades it is observed:

If now the *eleven* occurrences of Hades in the New Testament be carefully examined, the following conclusions will be reached: (a) *Hades* is invariably connected with *death*; but *never with life*: always with *dead* people; but never with the *living*. All in *Hades* will "NOT LIVE AGAIN," until they are raised from the dead (Rev. 20:5). If they do not "live again" until after they are raised, it is perfectly clear that they cannot be *alive* now. Otherwise we do away with the doctrine of resurrection altogether. (b) That the English word "hell" by no means represents the Greek *Hades*; as we have seen that it does not give a correct idea of its Hebrew equivalent. *Sheol.* (c) That *Hades* can mean only and exactly what *Sheol* means, viz., the place where "corruption" is seen (Acts 2:31; compare 13:34-37); and from which, *resurrection* is the only exit."

Scofield is representative of many who distinguish between the abode of departed saved individuals before and after Christ's resurrection. He says:

(1) *Hades before the ascension of Christ.* The passage in which the word occurs make it clear that hades was formerly in two divisions, the abodes respectively of the saved and of the lost. The former was called "paradise" and "Abraham's bosom." Both designations were Talmudic, but adopted by Christ in Lk. 16:22; 23:43. The blessed dead were with Abraham, they were conscious and were "comforted" (Lk. 16:25). The believing malefactor was to be, that day, with Christ in "paradise." The lost were separated from the saved by a "great gulf fixed" (Lk. 16:26). The representative man of the lost who are now in hades is the rich man of Lk. 16:19-31. He was alive, conscious, in the full exercise of his faculties, memory, etc., and in torment.

(2) *Hades since the ascension of Christ.* So far as the unsaved dead are concerned, no change of their place or condition is revealed in Scripture. At the judgment of the great white throne, hades will give them up, they will be judged, and will pass into the lake of fire (Rev. 20:13–14).[122]

New Heaven and New Earth

Following the millennium, the heavens and the earth will be dissolved. God will then create new heavens and a new earth (Isaiah 65:17, 66:22; 2 Peter 3:13; Revelation 21:1). The new earth will be to fulfill promises to Israel. God will by a specific act of creation call into being a new heaven and a new earth.

This creation will be the scene of His eternal theocratic kingdom of God.

His promise to Israel guaranteeing He will keep His covenants that the people will forever inherit the land will thus come to fruition. He has promised a national existence, a kingdom, a king, and spiritual blessings in perpetuity. He will create an eternal earth to fulfill these promises.

That Israel will be brought into the new earth out of the old earth is the promise:

> Behold, the tabernacle of God is with men, and he will dwell with them, and they shall be his people, and God himself shall be with them, and be their God. (Revelation 21:3)

The creation of the new heavens and new earth is the final preparatory act anticipating the eternal kingdom of God. It is now true that God has a kingdom "wherein dwelleth righteousness" (2 Peter 3:13).

Whereas the Church is assured of an eternal place in relation to a person—the Lord Jesus Christ, the Bridegroom—the nation Israel is pledged an eternal, recreated, pristine earth. The promise of a place is a fantastic thing to contemplate (John 14:3); that promise is overshadowed, however, by the Person into whose presence the Church Age believer is taken.

> And if I go and prepare a place for you, I will come again, and receive you unto myself, that where I am, there ye may be also. (John 14:3)

> When Christ, who is our life, shall appear, then shall ye also appear with him in glory. (Colossians 3:4)

> For the Lord himself shall descend from heaven with a shout, with the voice of the archangel, and with the trump of God; and the dead in Christ shall rise first:

Then we which are alive and remain shall be caught up together with them in the clouds, to meet the Lord in the air: and so shall we ever be with the Lord. (1 Thessalonians 4:16–17)

Beloved, now are we the sons of God, and it doth not yet appear what we shall be: but we know that, when he shall appear, we shall be like him; we shall see him as he is. (1 John 3:2)

The Person of the Lord Jesus is the great promise the Bride of Christ longs for. The place is thus secondary in consideration of the glorious future we look toward.

Dwight J. Pentecost writes further:

It has already been demonstrated from passages such as Revelation 21:3 that the Lord Jesus Christ will be dwelling with men on the new earth in the eternal kingdom. Since Scripture reveals that the church will be with Christ, it is concluded that the eternal abode of the church will likewise be in the new earth, in that heavenly city, New Jerusalem, that has been especially prepared by God for the saints. Such a relationship would be the answer to the Lord's prayer for those God had given Him: "Father, I will that they also, whom thou hast given me, be with me where I am; that they may behold my glory, which thou hast given me" (John 17:24). Since the eternal glory of Christ will be manifested in the eternal kingdom, in his eternal rule, it is natural that the church should be there to behold that glorification of Christ forever.[123]

Heaven is the magnificent place all believers long to one day live. All Christians want to enjoy the fantastic things the Lord has promised we will inherit for eternity. One day we will be given entrance into that place of incomprehensible beauty where every tear will be wiped away forever, where we will be reunited with those we've been apart from because of death, where all evil and temptation will be thrown into the abyss of forgetfulness.

Our mortal eyesight and earthly cognitive abilities and imaginations will never in the slightest grasp heaven's infinite glory. But one day, we will know this beauty, where all pain, suffering, and tears will be absent! Revelation 21:4 tells us:

> And God shall wipe away all tears from their eyes; and there shall be no more death, neither sorrow, nor crying, neither shall there be any more pain: for the former things are passed away.

There, we will hear a constant, increasingly euphoric praise by a chorus of angels continually proclaiming "Holy! Holy! Holy!" in exaltation of the One who sits on the throne. Angels surround the glorious, heavenly seat of power and authority as God reigns over all that is. Some of the angelic creatures are described as beasts, full of eyes, with six wings who don't rest day or night in proclaiming God's holiness (see Revelation 4:8–11).

Although from an earthly perspective, we can't know what heaven is like, God has put it in our spiritual senses to trust that He tells the truth about that glory we'll one day experience:

> Eye has not seen, nor ear heard, nor have entered into the heart of man the things which God has prepared for those who love Him. (1 Corinthians 2:9)

That we will forever be in the presence of our God and Savior will doubtless outweigh every other consideration in the matter of the glorious future that awaits us. Heaven will be a place of perpetual light. God, Himself, will negate the need for any artificial lighting. The same, dynamic light that exploded from His omnipotence at the Creation and at the resurrection of His Son will provide illumination throughout the streets and structures of pure, translucent gold.

The river of life will flow from the throne throughout all of His creation in perpetual purity.

Today, we might, from our earthly thoughts and understanding, think our Lord will be just a holy figure in heaven that we see from a distance—like one of our pastors. Nothing will be farther from the truth. We'll talk with Him, ask Him questions…be close to Him at all times.

How will that be possible with the millions and millions of saints and heavenly creatures that will no doubt inhabit that realm? It will be limitless in terms of space available. And, if our God can create all that is out of nothing, with only a Word from His mouth, will He have any difficulty being able to talk and be personal with each of us at all times? Will a God who knows every hair on our heads and how many grains of sand are on every beach have any problem at all being up close and personal in that eternal sphere?

When the heavens and earth are dissolved and remade, the Holy City, New Jerusalem, will descend and be situated on the earth, which, we have heard it said, will be greatly increased in size. Why? Because the New Jerusalem will be so massive that if it sat upon the present earth, its base would extend out over the earth's curvature.

That city will be 1,500 miles, in, most likely, a cubed configuration—i.e., it will be 1,500 miles wide at its squared base and 1,500 miles high its squared top. Revelation 21:1–2 describes this magnificent city:

> And I saw a new heaven and a new earth: for the first heaven and the first earth were passed away; and there was no more sea.
>
> And I John saw the holy city, new Jerusalem, coming down from God out of heaven, prepared as a bride adorned for her husband.

John's comprehensive description of the city that gives a look into the glory of heaven should cause thrilling anticipation for the child of God.

And he carried me away in the spirit to a great and high mountain, and shewed me that great city, the holy Jerusalem, descending out of heaven from God, Having the glory of God: and her light was like unto a stone most precious, even like a jasper stone, clear as crystal;

And had a wall great and high, and had twelve gates, and at the gates twelve angels, and names written thereon, which are the names of the twelve tribes of the children of Israel: On the east three gates; on the north three gates; on the south three gates; and on the west three gates.

And the wall of the city had twelve foundations, and in them the names of the twelve apostles of the Lamb.

And he that talked with me had a golden reed to measure the city, and the gates thereof, and the wall thereof.

And the city lieth foursquare, and the length is as large as the breadth: and he measured the city with the reed, twelve thousand furlongs.

The length and the breadth and the height of it are equal. And he measured the wall thereof, an hundred and forty and four cubits, according to the measure of a man, that is, of the angel.

And the building of the wall of it was of jasper: and the city was pure gold, like unto clear glass.

And the foundations of the wall of the city were garnished with all manner of precious stones. The first foundation was jasper; the second, sapphire; the third, a chalcedony; the fourth, an emerald; The fifth, sardonyx; the sixth, sardius; the seventh, chrysolyte; the eighth, beryl; the ninth, a topaz; the tenth, a chrysoprasus; the eleventh, a jacinth; the twelfth, an amethyst.

And the twelve gates were twelve pearls: every several gate was of one pearl: and the street of the city was pure gold, as it were transparent glass.

And I saw no temple therein: for the Lord God Almighty and the Lamb are the temple of it.

And the city had no need of the sun, neither of the moon, to shine in it: for the glory of God did lighten it, and the Lamb is the light thereof. And the nations of them which are saved shall walk in the light of it: and the kings of the earth do bring their glory and honour into it. And the gates of it shall not be shut at all by day: for there shall be no night there.

And they shall bring the glory and honour of the nations into it. And there shall in no wise enter into it any thing that defileth, neither whatsoever worketh abomination, or maketh a lie: but they which are written in the Lamb's book of life. (Revelation 21:10–27)

The very tabernacle of God will dwell among men at that time. Heaven is any place where God is.

And I heard a great voice out of heaven saying, Behold, the tabernacle of God is with men, and he will dwell with them, and they shall be his people, and God himself shall be with them, and be their God. (Revelation 21:3)

Revelation 21 offers the most complete description of heaven in God's Word. Its glory can't be encompassed by human words or understanding. Yet God has given us what He wants us to know about the place those who know Him as Heavenly Father will spend eternity.

Eternity, itself, is something that can't be fathomed by the mortal mind. The instant we see Jesus Christ at the Rapture, or the moment we open our eyes following death, we will begin to at last comprehend what it means to have our names written in the Lamb's book of life.

The world of religionists and philosophers tell Satan's lies when they say there are many ways to God. This growing blasphemy is leading men, women, and children to the place prepared for the devil and his angels. Sadly—tragically—hell will be these victims' eternal place of torment if they refuse to accept God's great grace gift of salvation.

That gift is found only in Jesus the Christ, who said:

I am the way, the truth and the life; no man comes to the Father except by me. (John 14:6)

Jesus, who willingly hung on the cross and died so that people can be redeemed from sin that otherwise forever separates human beings from God, also said:

I Jesus have sent mine angel to testify unto you these things in the churches.

I am the root and the offspring of David, and the bright and morning star.

And the Spirit and the bride say, Come. And let him that heareth say, Come.

And let him that is athirst come. And whosoever will, let him take the water of life freely.

For I testify unto every man that heareth the words of the prophecy of this book, If any man shall add unto these things, God shall add unto him the plagues that are written in this book:

And if any man shall take away from the words of the book of this prophecy, God shall take away his part out of the book of life, and out of the holy city, and from the things which are written in this book.

He which testifieth these things saith, Surely I come quickly. Amen. Even so, come, Lord Jesus. (Revelation 22:16–20)

Notes

1. William L. Shier, *Rise and Fall of the Third Reich*, xii.
2. Gregory Myers, July 17, 2016, https://www.britannica.com/biography/Genghis-Khan.
3. Ephesians 6:12.
4. Erin Kelly, "Lebensborn, The Nazi Breeding Program to Create a Master Race," November 22, 2017, https://allthatsinteresting.com/lebensborn.
5. "Final Solution": Overview | The Holocaust Encyclopedia, https://encyclopedia.ushmm.org/content/en/article/final-solution-overview.
6. Daymond R. Duck, "Forewarning the Future Führer," in *Piercing the Future: Prophecy and the New Millennium*, Terry James, Gen. Ed. (CKN Christian Publishing, 2018), 310.
7. Dr. Thomas Ice, Pre-Trib Study Group, "The Ethnicity of the Antichrist."
8. Dave Breese, "The Roman Empire's Greatest Caesar," in *Raging into Apocalypse*, William T. James, Gen. Ed. (Green Forest, Arkansas: New Leaf Press, 1996), chapter 4.
9. Henry M. Morris, "The False Prophet," *The Revelation Record* (Chicago: Tyndale, 1983), 246.
10. Ibid.
11. Ibid.
12. Dr. John F. Walvoord, *Every Prophecy in the Bible* (Colorado Springs, Colorado: Chariot Victor Publishing, 1999), 604–607.

13. Dave Hunt, "Flashes of Falling Away," in *Forewarning* (Eugene, OR: Harvest House, 1998), chapter 1.

14. Terry James, *Rapture Ready…Or Not* (Green Forest, AR: New Leaf, 2016), chapter 12.

15. Dwight J. Pentecost, *Things to Come*, (Grand Rapids, Michigan: Zondervan, 1958).

16. For an in-depth look at this topic, see Robert L. Maginnis, *Collision Course: The Fight to Reclaim Our Moral Compass Before It Is Too Late* (Crane, Missouri: Defender Publishing, 2020).

17. Britt Gillette, "Unhindered March Toward Globalism," https://www.raptureready.com/2019/06/20/ unhindered-march-toward-globalism-britt-gil.

18. https://www.interdependence.org/about/overview-mission/ declaration-of-interdependence/.

19. https://billofrightsinstitute.org/founding-documents/ primary-source-documents/washingtons-farewell-address/.

20. https://www.brainyquote.com/quotes/john_adams_391045.

21. David Reagan, "Third Temple/Jews," Lamb and Lion Ministries, christinprophecy.org/articles/the-third-temple/.

22. It reportedly took eleven years and more than a hundred thousand dollars to complete the outfits for worship.

23. https://www.hollandsentinel.com/article/20130731/NEWS/307319931.

24. Daymond Duck, "Satan's Plan to Steal Jerusalem," raptureready.com.

25. Dr. Thomas Ice, "Is It Time for the Temple?" raptureready.com.

26. Hal Lindsey, "Russia-Syrian-Iranian Axis," Magog Update, first published in September 2006 *Personal Update News Journal*.

27. Dr. Jack Van Impe, "A Message of Hope, The Coming War with Russia," Jack Van Impe Ministries.

28. http://www.charismamag.com/video/42954-pat-robertson-denounces-trump-s-decision-to-withdraw-from-syria-saying-christians-will-be-massacred.

29. Michael Hile, "Who and What Are the Beasts of the Bible?, raptureready.com.

30. Dr. John Walvoord, "Beast and the False Prophet," https://walvoord.com/article/271.

31. Professor John McCarthy, "The Father of AI. What is AI?" http://jmc. stanford.edu/artificial-in- telligence/what-is-ai/index.html http://jmc. stanford.edu/artificial-intelligence/what-is-ai/in- dex.html (accessed: 17 April 2018).

32. Vincent James, "Google's AI Is Warming Up for World Domination by Killing Inbox Spam," *The Verge,* 10 July 2015. https://www.theverge. com/2015/7/10/8927573/google-ai-gmail-spam, (accessed: 23 April 2018).

33. https://www.statista.com/statistics/420391/spam-email-tra c-share/.

34. Ray Kurzweil, *The Age of Spiritual Machines: When Computers Exceed Human Intelligence*, (New York: Penguin Books, 1998), https://archive. nytimes.com/www.nytimes.com/books/first/ k/kurzweil-machines.html (accessed: 22 April 2018).

35. Arthur Samuel: quoted in Calum McCleeland, "The Di erence Between Artificial Intelligence, Machine Learning, and Deep Learning," *Medium,* 4 December 2017, https://medium.com/iot- forall/the-di erence-between-artificial-intelligence-machine-learning-and-deep- learning-3aa67b 5991 (accessed: 22 April 2018).

36. Machine Learning Concepts. *Amazon.* https://docs.aws.amazon.com/machine-learning/lat- est/dg/machine-learning-concepts.html.

37. Ben Dickson, "The Darker Side of Machine Learning," *Tech Crunch,* October 26, 2016, https:// techcrunch.com/2016/10/26/the-darker-side-of-machine-learning/ (accessed: 22 April 2018).

38. http://grammarist.com/idiom/ghost-in-the-machine/ (accessed: 18 April 2018).

39. Dave Hunt, Interview in *The Last Religion,* Jeremiah Films, 2018.

40. Ray Kurzweil. *The Singularity Is Near: When Humans Transcend Biology,* (New York: Viking, 2005).

41. Elon Musk, quoted in *Maureen Dowd,* "Elon Musk's Billion-dollar Crusade to Stop the AI Apocalypse," *Vanity Fair,* March 26, 2017, https://www. vanityfair.com/news/ 2017/03/elon-musk-billion-dollar-crusade-to-stop-ai-space-x (accessed April 21, 2018).

42. Ibid.

43. Ibid.

44. Catherine Clifford, "Hundreds of A.I. Experts Echo Elon Musk, Stephen Hawking in Call for a Ban on Killer Robots," CNBC, November 8, 2017. https://www.cnbc.com/2017/11/08/ai-experts- join-elon-musk-stephen-hawking-call-for-killer-robot-ban.html, (accessed April 23, 2018).

45. Chuck Missler, Interview in *The Last Religion,* Jeremiah Films, 2018.

46. Jolene Creighton. "The 'Father of Artificial Intelligence' Says Singularity Is 30 Years Away," *Futurism,* February 14, 2018, https://futurism.com/father-artificial-intelligence-singularity-decades-away/ (accessed April 18, 2018).

47. Paul Maguire, Interview in *The Last Religion,* Jeremiah Films, 2018.

48. Creighton.

49. Aaron Franz, "The Coming Hive Mind: The Jesuit Priest Who Influenced Transhumanism," *Truth Stream Media,* 1 May 2009, http://truthstreammedia.com/2016/01/26/the-coming-hive- mind-manmachine-merger-and-the-global-transhuman-society/ (accessed April 18, 2018).

50. Ibid.

51. Creighton.

52. Frank Peretti, Interview in *The Last Religion,* Jeremiah Films, 2018.

53. Rozina Sabur, "Cambridge Analytica Accused of Breaking US Election Law," *The Telegraph,* March 26, 2018, https://www.telegraph.co.uk/news/2018/03/26/cambridge-analytica-accused-breaking-us-election-law/ (accessed: April 22, 2018).

54. James Vlahos. "Surveillance Society: New High-Tech Cameras Are Watching You," *Popular Mechanics,* September 30, 2009, https://www.popularmechanics.com/military/a2398/4236865/, (accessed: April 24, 2018).

55. Ibid.

56. Louis Rosenberg. "Super-Intelligence and the Virtues of a Hive Mind," Singularity Weblog, February 10, 2016, https://www.singularityweblog.com/super-intelligence-and-hive-mind/, (accessed 18 April 2018).

57. George Orwell, *1984,* (London: Secker and Warburg, 1949). Print.

58. Chuck Missler, Interview in *The Last Religion,* Jeremiah Films, 2018.

59. Hugo de Garis (1996), "CAM-BRAIN: The Evolutionary Engineering of a Billion Neuron Artificial Brain by 2001 Which Grows Evolves at Electronic Speeds Inside a Cellular Automata Ma chine (CAM)," *Towards Evolvable Hardware; the Evolutionary Engineering Approach*: 76–98.

60. 30 Hugo de Garis (2005), *The Artilect War: Cosmists vs. Terrans: A Bitter Controversy Concerning Whether Humanity Should Build Godlike Massively Intelligent Machines*. (Palm Springs, CA: ETC Publications).

61. Britt Gillette, "Transhumanism and the Great Rebellion," *End Times Bible Prophecy*, http:// www.end-times-bible-prophecy.com/transhumanism-and-the-great-rebellion.html (accessed April 19, 2018)

62. Ray Kurzweil. *Ray Kurzweil on Bringing Back the Dead*. PBS interview. 12 July 2012. https:// www.youtube.com/watch?v=ZlhYY3z5Hv8.

63. Jessica Roy, "The Rapture of the Nerds," April 7, 2014 , *Time*, https://time.com/66536/terasem-trascendence-religion-technology/.

64. Tom Horn, Interview in *The Last Religion*, Jeremiah Films, 2018.

65. R. U. Sirius and Jay Cornell, *Transcendance, The Disinformation Encyclopedia of Transhumanism and Singularity* (San Francisco: Disinformation Books, 2015), 214.

66. Schuyler English, "The Two Witnesses," *Our Hope*, Pentecost note 53, English note 47, p. 665, April, 1941; Pentecost note 55, English, Ibid., p. 671.

67. Bill Salus, *The LAST Prophecies: The Prophecies in the First 3 ½ Years of the Tribulation* (Prophecy Depot Publishers, 2019).

68. Pentecost, *Things to Come*.

69. Dr. David Jeremiah, "144,000 in the Book of Revelation," David Jeremiah Blog, https://davidjeremiah.blog/The-144000-in-the-book-of-revelation.

70. Dr. David Reagan, "Mysterious 144,000," Revelation, Lamb and Lion Ministries, https://christinprophecy.org/Articles/The-mysterious-144000.

71. Gary Stearman, "The Extraterrestrial Question," *Prophecy in the News*, March 2010, 10.

72. Thomas Horn, *Zenith 2016* (Crane, MO: Defender, 2013).

73. Jane Picken, "Medical Marvels," *Evening Chronicle* (April 13, 2007).

74. Joseph Infranco, "President Barack Obama Warped and Twisted Science

with Embryonic Stem Cell Order," LifeNews, April 13, 2009, http://www. LifeNews.com.

75. Wikipedia contributors, "Transhumanism," Wikipedia http://en.wikipedia. org/w/index.php?title=Transhumanism&oldid=346807522.

76. William Grassie, "What Does It Mean to Be Human?" John Templeton Foundation Research Lecture Query (2006).

77. Doug Wolens, "Singularity 101 with Vernor Vinge," *H+ Magazine*, http:// hplusmagazine.com/articles/ai/singularity-101-vernor-vinge.

78. Nick Bostrom, "Transhumanist Values," Nick Bostrom, http://www. nickbostrom.com/ethics/values.html.

79. "Facing the Challenges of Transhumanism: Religion, Science, Technology," http://transhumanism.asu.edu/.

80. The University of Arizona, "The Sophia Project," http://lach.web.arizona. edu/Sophia/.

81. Leon R. Kass, *Life, Liberty, and the Defense of Dignity: The Challenge for Bioethics* (New York: Encounter, 2002).

82. Rick Weiss, "Of Mice, Men, and In-Between," MSNBC (November 20, 2004) http://www.msnbc.msn.com/id/6534243/.

83. Mark Stencel, "Futurist: Genes Without Borders," *Congressional Quarterly* (March 15, 2009), http://news.yahoo.com/s/cq/20090315/pl_cq_politics/ politics3075228.

84. George Annas, Lori Andrews, and Rosario Isasi, "Protecting the Endangered Human: Toward an International Treaty Prohibiting Cloning and Inheritable Alterations," *American Journal of Law and Medicine*, 28, nos. 2 and 3 (2002) 162.

85. Hendrik Poinar, "Recipe for a Resurrection," *National Geographic*, May 2009, http://ngm.nationalgeographic.com/2009/05/cloned-species/ Mueller-text.

86. Chuck Missler and Mark Eastman, *Alien Encounters* (Coeur d'Alene, ID: Koinonia House, 1997), 275.

87. Thomas R. Horn, *Shadowland* (Crane, Missouri: Defender, 2019).

88. Dr. Tim LaHaye, "Rising Sun Nations on the Move," *Foreshadows of Wrath and Redemption* (Eugene, Oregon: Harvest House, 1999) chapter 8.

89. Ibid.

90. Ibid.

91. Ibid.

92. Chuck Missler, "Kings of the East Lust Westward," *Foreshocks of Antichrist*, Gen. Ed. William T. James (Eugene, Oregon: Harvest House, 1997), chapter 7.

93. LaHaye, "Rising Sun Nations," chapter 8.

94. Dr. Arnold Fruchtenbaum, *The Footsteps of the Messiah* (Tustin, CA: Ariel Ministries Press, 1983), p. 161.

95. Dr. Mark Hitchcock, *Babylon Second Coming*, note on Robert Thomas 26, (Multnomah Press, 2003).

96. Dr. John Walvoord, "Destruction of Ecclesiastical Babylon," https:// walvoord.com/article/275.

97. M. J. O'Brien, *An Historical and Critical Account of the So-Called Prophecy of St. Malachy Regarding the Succession of Popes* (Dublin: M. H. Gill & Son, 1880), 82.

98. Thomas Horn and Chris Putnam, *Petrus Romanus: The Final Pope Is Here* (Crane, Missouri: Defender Publishing, 2012).

99. John Walvoord, "Antichrist, Armageddon and the Second Coming of Christ," *Forewarning: Approaching the Final Battle Between Heaven and Hell* (Eugene, OR: Harvest House) chapter 14.

100. https://www.jcpa.org/phas/phas-jones-f04htm.

101. https://www.thejc.com/news/israel/israel-arrests-malka-leifer-woman-wanted-on-child-sex-abuse-charges-at-australian-jewish-school-1.458662.

102. https://www.thejc.com/news/world/australian-jewish-leader-condemn-senator-fraser-anning-speech-calling-for-final-solution-1.468332.

103. https://www.google.com/amp/s/www.foxnews.com/world/anti-semitic-bullying-australia.amp.

104. https://www.thejc.com/news/world/australian-teenager-charged-for-making-jewish-boy-kiss-another-student-s-shoes-1.490685.

105. https://www.cis.org.au/commentary/articles/we-cannot-let-anti-semitism-spread-here/.

106. https://10daily.com.au/news/australia/a191124hsgly/report-shows-anti-semitism-on-the-rise-following-outrage-over-party-nazis-20191125?&utm_medium=paid-search&utm_source=10daily&utm_campaign=digital:na&utm_term=google&utm_content=dsa&gclid=EAIaIQobChMI0IzskZOa5wIVi5yzCh2paw FPEAMYASAAEgLDbPD_BwE.

107. https://www.thejc.com/news/world/antisemitic-assaults-and-threats-up-by-30-per-cent-in-australia-new-report-finds-1.493612.

108. https://wwwgoogle.com/amp/s/www.jta.org/quick-reads/australia-sees-30-percent-increase-in-anti-semitic-incidents/amp.

109. http://www.israelnationalnews.com/Articles/Article.aspx/24901.

110. https://www.adl.org/resources/reports/global-anti-semitism-select-incidents-in-2019.

111. https://www.thejc.com/news/world/australian-jewish-survivors-recount-how-the-fire-swept-into-their-home-in-45-minutes-1.495182.

112. https://www.thejc.com/news/world/holocaust-survivor-suffering-flashbacks-after-nazi-flag-flown-metres-away-beulah-australian-home-1.495548.

113. https://www.thejc.com/comment/comment/the-bbc-has-shamed-itself-with-orla-guerin-s-holocaust-report-1.495792.

114. Walvoord, "Antichrist, Armageddon," chapter 14.

115. Adam Eliyahu Berkowitz, "Australia Slammed with Hail, Pestilence, Darkness Plagues in One Week," Breaking Israel News, Latest News. Biblical Perspective, January 22, 2020.

116. See https://t.co/0jmjbKmRnz.

117. Arnold Fruchtenbaum, *Second Coming of Jesus the Messiah* (Tustin, California: Ariel Ministries).

118. Ibid.

119. John Walvoord, "From Armageddon to the Millennium," *Foreshadows of Wrath and Redemption*, William T. James, Gen. Ed. (Eugene, Oregon: Harvest House, 1999), chapter 17.

120. David Breese, "Cyclone of Apocalypse," *Forewarning: Approaching the Final Battle Between Heaven and Hell*, William T. James, Gen. Ed. (Eugene, Oregeon: Harvest House, 1998) chapter 13.

121. Daymond Duck, "What Will We Do During the Millennium?" Prophecy Plus Ministries.

122. Pentecost, *Things to Come*.

123. Ibid.